A New Physiognomy of Jewish Thinking

Bloomsbury Studies in Jewish Thought

Bloomsbury Studies in Jewish Thought presents scholarly monographs offering traditional and contemporary reflection on Jewish intellectual history, philosophy, and thought. Books in the series will seek to address a range of concepts central to Jewish modern thought, evaluate the contributions of Jewish thinkers, and demonstrate a critical understanding of the relationship between Jewish thought and history.

A New Physiognomy of Jewish Thinking

Critical Theory After Adorno as Applied
to Jewish Thought

Aubrey L. Glazer

B L O O M S B U R Y
LONDON · NEW DELHI · NEW YORK · SYDNEY

Bloomsbury Academic
An imprint of Bloomsbury Publishing Plc

50 Bedford Square   175 Fifth Avenue
London   New York
WC1B 3DP   NY 10010
UK   USA

www.bloomsbury.com

First published by Continuum International Publishing Group 2011
Paperback edition first published 2012

© Aubrey L. Glazer, 2011

British Library Cataloguing-in-Publication Data
A catalogue record for this book is available from the British Library.

ISBN: HB: 978-1-4411-3398-4
PB: 978-1-4411-4612-0

Library of Congress Cataloging-in-Publication Data
Glazer, Aubrey L.
A new physiognomy of Jewish thinking : critical theory after Adorno as applied to
Jewish thought / Aubrey L. Glazer.
p. cm.
Includes bibliographical references.
ISBN: 978-1-4411-3398-4
1. Critical thinking. 2. Jewish philosophy. 3. Philosophy, Modern–21st century.
4. Adorno, Theodor W., 1903–1969–Criticism and interpretation. I. Title.
B809.2.G53 2011
181'.06–dc22 2010041957

Typeset by Newgen Imaging Systems Pvt Ltd, Chennai, India

To Elliot R. Wolfson
in gratitude and friendship

Gedichtzu, Gedichtauf:	poem-to, poem-fro:
hier fahren die farben	here come colors
zum schutzfremden	to another foxholed
freistirnigen	free-headed
Juden . . .	Jew . . .
Niemand knetet uns wieder aus Erde	No One again kneads us of earth
und Lehm,	and soil,
niemand bespricht unsern Staub.	No One invokes our pollen.
Niemand.	No One.
Gelobst seist du, Niemand.	Blessed are You, No One
Dir zulieb wollen	In Your sight
wir bluhn	we'd flower.
dir	In spite of
entegen.	You.
Ein Nichts	A No Thing
waren wir, sind wir, werden	we were, are, becoming
wir bleiben, bluhen:	to be, flowering:
die Nichts-, die,	the No Thing, the
Niemandsrose.	No-One-Rose.
Mit	With
dem Griffel seelenhell,	soulpure pistil,
dem Staubfaden himmelswust,	wildsky stamen,
der Krone rot	red corona
vom Purpurwort, das wir sangen	we sang from the purpleword
uber, o uber	over, O over
dem Dorn.	to the thorn.

—"Psalm", Paul Celan

Contents

Abbreviations

Adorno's Primary Sources

AR
2000   *The Adorno Reader*, ed. Brian O'Connor, Blackwell Publishers, Oxford.

AT
1997   *Aesthetic Theory* [1970], trans. R. Hullot-Kentor, University of Minnesota, Minnesota.

BTPM
1998   *Beethoven: The Philosophy of Music*, ed. R. Tiedemann, trans. E. Jephcott, Stanford University Press, Stanford.

EM
2002   *Essays on Music*: Theodor W. Adorno, trans. S. H. Gillespie, comm. R. Leppert, University of California Press, Berkeley.

ISW
1981   *In Search of Wagner*, trans. R. Livingstone, NLB, Great Britain.

JA
1973   *Jargon of Authenticity*, trans. K. Tarnowski and F. Will, Northwestern University Press, Chicago.

MAMP
1992   *Mahler: A Musical Physiognomy*, trans. E. Jephcott, University of Chicago Press, Chicago.

MM
1951   *Minima Moralia: Reflexionen aus dem beschädigten Leben*, Suhrkamp, Frankfurt.
1974   *Minima Moralia: Reflections from Damaged Life*, trans. E. F. N. Jephcott, Verso, London.

ND
1966   *Negative Dialektik*, Suhrkamp, Frankfurt.

1973   *Negative Dialectics*, trans. E. B. Ashton, Continuum, New York.
2001   *Negative Dialectics*, trans. Dennis Redmond, http://www.efn.org/
         ~dredmond/ndtrans.html.

NL
1991   Notes to Literature, vol. 1, trans. S. W. Nicholson, Columbia
         University Press, New York 1991.

NM
2009   *Night Music: Essays on Music 1928–1962*, trans. W. Hoban, ed.
         R. Tiedemann, Seagull Books, London.

QUF
1963   *Quasi Una Fantasia: Essays on Modern Music*, trans. R. Livingstone,
         Verso, London.

SF
1999   *Sound Figures*, trans. R. Livingstone, Stanford University Press, California.

Where relevant, in the notes I will refer to Adorno's original German text
as follows: German original/translation.

   *The only deviation from this format will be when referring to *Negative
Dialectics*.

   Given the problems with Ashton's 1973 English translation of *Negative
Dialectics*, I am making primary use of the Redmond's 2001 translation. In
those situations, the formatting will be as follows: German/Redmond trans./
[Ashton trans.].

Wittgenstein's Primary Sources

The following bilingual editions of Ludwig Wittgenstein have been consulted
and unless otherwise noted, the translations follow these editions.

PI
1953   *Philosophical Investigations* (1945), trans. G. E. M. Anscombe, Basil
         Blackwell, Oxford.

TL-P
1967   *Tractatus Logico-Philosophicus* (1922), ed. G. E. M. Anscombe and
         G. H. von Wright, Basil Blackwell, Oxford.

Z
1967   *Zettel*, ed. G. E. M. Anscombe and G. H. von Wright, Basil Blackwell,
         Oxford.

Preface:
Adorno's "Dialectic of Enlightenment"—
a Theological Exploration

In this remarkable and seminal work, Rabbi Dr. Aubrey L. Glazer seeks to demarcate novel constellations for Jewish Thinking in our time. Glazer seeks to offer us a novel theology, one which is attuned to the exigencies of the zeitgeist, as well as the normative and epistemological predicates of our epoch. This he achieves, inter alia, via the instrumentality of Adorno's ruminations on the essence of music.

Glazer cogently and creatively demonstrates the manner in which Adorno's quasi mystical musings about the essence of music can indeed facilitate a "new song," a *Shira Hadasha*—a theological melody harmonious with the metaphysical desire of our generation, a theology which recognizes the imperative of scientific excellence, yet does not fall prey to dogmatic epistemological presuppositions.

In a word, Glazer takes it upon himself to demonstrate the manner in which Adorno's illuminations pertaining to music can play a role in the formulation of a mature, sophisticated theology for our time. A theology which is enriched by critical scholarship, yet at the same time does not shy away in its vigorous intellectualism and critical scholarship from the Eros of faith.

Tacitly echoing Max Weber's celebrated notion of the "iron cage," Glazer ruminates about the disenchanting nature of contemporary Jewish theological discourse, particularly for those who remain steadfast in their relentless commitment to traditional Judaism on the one hand, and the humanistic and political ideals of the Enlightenment ethos on the other hand.

Ours is the epoch of Jewish bipolarism: dogmatic fundamentalism on the one hand, and utter metaphysical impoverishment on the other hand. This metaphysical impoverishment, intimates Glazer, is the direct result of a pervasive failure of an intellectual and spiritual elite to successfully and compellingly translate modern cultural discourses into the language of a viable and contemporary rejuvenated Jewish Theology.

This chronic lack of a sophisticated contemporary theological discourse in traditional Judaism devalues prospects for an authentic spirituality by positivistically reducing the transcendent dimension of existence in a twofold manner.

Primarily, it diminishes the metaphysical longing to achieve *Unio Mystica,* which the Jewish mystical tradition depicts as *Devekut* (cleaving), a phenomenological orientation aimed at cosmic consciousness. This deflation of devotional life ends up sucking the very lifeblood of the religious experience, thereby positivistically reducing Jewish spirituality into mere folklore.

Secondly, this metaphysical impoverishment is a direct derivative of a pervasive methodological failure. By this I am alluding to the inability of critical scholarship to appreciate the salience of a metahermeneutical layer present in scripture and other foundational Jewish texts, a hermeneutical layer which dehistoricizes the text and revitalizes it as an ontological fable, a cosmic drama occurring within the deepest realms of the human soul (the psychologization of Lurianic Kabbalism in Hasidism being a clear case in point).

Increasingly, there is a growing sentiment in some traditional Jewish milieus that we are in the midst of a theological crisis, that there is a highly pervasive and chronic deficit in our religious life. As traditional Jews, many of us are embracing both modern values and the enduring existential assets of Jewish spirituality.

In the eyes of many, traditional Judaism today fails to live up to its full potential and offer a real alternative to the modern subject who all too often exists as an isolated Leibnizian monad. Religious life is in some places banalized and vulgarized into mere folklore, accompanied by an exclusively critical engagement with foundational texts. Transcending this reductionist lens, implies Glazer, constitutes the chief intellectual and spiritual endeavor for traditional Judaism in our time.

If Judaism is to be reinvigorated for our generation, in the commencement of the twenty-first century, if Judaism is to be enhanced, celebrated, and perpetuated as "something more than [mere] nostalgia" as Glazer writes, then it is indeed incumbent upon us to do away with these crude dichotomies of fundamentalist Judaism versus folkloric Judaism.

Enlightenment values and a scientific outlook need not necessarily entail an *adieu* to spiritual Eros and a metaphysical temperament, Glazer asserts. We need to revitalize our Jewish lives as infused with monotheism as faith and not mere folklore. Glazer's contribution in this present volume to the awesome endeavor of formulating the guidelines for a New Jewish Thinking may well be regarded as neo-Heschelian. Its rigorous scholarly nature, combined with its in-depth analysis of some of the greatest thinkers and artists of modernity, is complemented by a passion for the transcendent horizon. In a manner comparable to Heschel's *chef d'oeuvre, God in Search of Man,* Glazer urges us to realize that Judaism, after Emmanuel Lévinas, is "a religion for adults."

Traditional Judaism today is an overt call for a mature and courageous theology, a theology which is "beyond fundamentalism and beyond positivism"— the two nemeses of modern metaphysics. The former is an epistemological wasteland, turning its back on the scientific and normative achievements of modernity. The latter is utterly blind to the metaphysical yearnings to achieve self-transcendence inherent in the human condition, which Lévinas depicts as "the metaphysical desire."

Positivism, if taken too far and inferred to all domains of life, can precariously dissuade us from recognizing and appreciating modernity's inherent compatibility with a profound ontological attitude toward that which is "otherwise than being or beyond essence." Returning to Adorno in order "to point the way through the thickets obscuring [contemporary] Jewish thinking," Glazer offers us an audacious and invigorating novel "dialectic of re-enlightenment," a dialectic in which historicism is commensurate with the deeper layers of Judaic ontology, with Lévinas' understanding of Judaism as a "comprehension of being."

Alluding to Adorno's celebrated dialectic of the general and the particular, Glazer evokes the existential outlook envisaged by Yirmiyahu Yovel in his seminal work on the Marranos.[1] For both Yovel and Glazer are well attuned to the dialectical interplay of the external and internal inherent in the identity of the modern subject, a subject typified by multifaceted modes of being, a subject at once part of a particular ethos and community, and at the same time an integral part of humanity at large. Yovel sees this existential dialectic as "a basic human freedom"; Glazer recognizes it also as a primary theological challenge.

Tacitly echoing Husserl's phenomenology, Glazer encourages us to return to the things themselves, without forfeiting our modern sensibilities. Modern Jews who wish to be spiritually literate need to learn the Husserlian art of phenomenologically bracketing, or in Heschel's terms—to distinguish between the conceptual (which is an intellectual category) and the experiential (which is existential and metarational).

This is what Glazer wants us to revitalize as a form of re-enlightenment. He achieves this not only in a veritable tour de force, with dazzling expositions of composers of stature, including Wagner and Mahler, but also by scrutinizing critical junctures in modern intellectual history, with Heidegger and Celan in addition to other leading great minds of the modern epoch whose *oeuvres* constitute the basic cultural furniture of the modern condition.

Glazer demonstrates in this book the manner in which the loftiest raîson d'être of the aesthetic—art as immanent sublimation of the quotidian—is at least in potentiality infused with a cosmic vocation to enhance the straits of being and usher in a novel appreciation of the transcendent horizon.

One of Glazer's chief religious concerns is correlated to the ontology of alterity. Glazer rightfully and acutely recognizes the imperative need for what he calls "a contemporary theology and theosophy of the gentile," thereby transcending the manner in which historically, different religions ontologized xenophobia, at times to the point of virtual dehumanization, Judeo-Christianity being no exception to this sordid mode of fundamental/ist ontology.

Glazer shares with his readers the underlying agenda of his scholarly and theological journey, his own *Lech Lecha*. His own "earnest search for authenticity that combines critical thinking with a yearning for a heartfelt poetics," because, he writes, many of us still insist upon coming back to our roots—"returning to religion with the hope of achieving or at least glimpsing at some kind of redemption."

The Hebrew term for Judaism as a basic ontological attitude toward being, *Yahadut*, etymologically intimates its ultimate vocation as *Hodaya*—the art of cosmic gratitude. Immanuel Kant famously thanked David Hume for having epistemologically awakened him from his "dogmatic slumbers." In this book Rabbi Aubrey L. Glazer seeks to contribute his share to the awakening of traditional Judaism from its own dogmatic slumbers. We need a new paradigm. Glazer points phenomenologically toward music as one vital key to unlock the gates of heaven in an age of *Hester Panim*, of paramount metaphysical darkness.

There are gates in heaven which only music can open, our sages tell us. Jews commence every day of their existence singing *Psukey De-Zimra*, poetic verses of praise and gratitude. This is in order to nurture and cherish a cultivated state of existential awareness, one which looks at the world with a profound sense of longing for the beyond, with awe and bewilderment. As Jews we are summoned to tune in to the poetics of existence.

En route to receiving the Torah at Sinai, the ancient Israelites sang at the splitting of the sea. This song is also an integral part of the morning liturgy in Judaism. The Torah also ends with poetics, with *Shira*, with music. Glazer urges us to return to this immortal melody, this music which has been accompanying the Jewish odyssey for several millennia by now. To reattune ourselves, in conjunction with our modern sensibilities, to its everlasting relevancy, resilience, and pertinence. For music, like love, is part of our ongoing attempt to articulate the mystery of being. Music, like love, is a glorious and formidable abstraction, always thrusting itself ahead, further, well beyond the confinements of the human cognitive horizon, to Infinity.

Dr. Tal Sessler
New York, New York
Erev Rosh Hodesh Elul, 5769

Acknowledgments

Sincere thinking requires time for true friendship and inspiration. I am grateful to many teachers, guides, and inspirations throughout this decade-long period of incubation. How remarkable that so many of these relationships that were seeded as teacher-student relationships have blossomed into friendships among colleagues.

For the generosity of spirit and daring to think beyond conventional boundaries, I will forever be grateful to those listed below, across time, space, and circumstance.

Chapter 1: I am forever grateful to Dr. Elliot R. Wolfson (New York University) for sharing in our ongoing *Sprachdenken* over the years, especially for igniting the spark of this entire investigation by guiding me through a passage of Adorno's journals on musical thinking, *Beethoven: The Philosophy of Music*, as correlated to Scholem's reading of Jewish mysticism during a fire drill in Washington Square in the dead of winter during his Zohar seminar at NYU. I am also deeply grateful to Rabbi Dr. Shaul Magid (Jewish Theological Seminary of America, Indiana University) and Rabbi Moshe Aaron Krassen (Rain of Blessings, Arizona, Colorado) for their ongoing dialogue and reflection on what Jewish Thinking and its praxis should mean in light of our current paradigm. Magid in particular revealed many concealed paths on Fire Island for which I am grateful.

Chapter 2: I am grateful to Dr. Robert Gibbs and Dr. Graeme Nicholson (University of Toronto) for their inspiration, guidance, and friendship. Nicholson was especially patient and generous with his time and also generously shared his preliminary translations of some early (as of yet untranslated) Heidegger lectures.

Chapter 3: I am grateful to Dr. Rebecca Comay (University of Toronto) for her guidance in this discourse. Her passion and insight for close readings of Adorno, and specifically his relationship to Walter Benjamin, in many ways served as the spark that lit the fire for a good part of this entire investigation.

Chapter 4: I am grateful to Peter Cole (Jerusalem), Rabbi Tamar Eldad-Apelbaum (Jerusalem and New York), and Rabbi Dr. Shaul Magid for their willingness to challenge and critique from a place of deep love and yearning for Zion that allowed this discourse to evolve.

Chapter 5: While grappling with this issue of authenticity remains a daily practice for me, I know that recent conversations with my *Atidat Ami Rabbinic-Resnick Intern*, Tal Sessler (Jewish Theological Seminary) and Rabbi Moshe

Aaron Krassen have renewed my concern for articulating a bypath. I am grateful to Rabbi Dr. Norton Shargel (JCC of Harrison) for his time in reviewing together in Yiddish much of Heschel's work on *Emesdikeyt.*

Chapter 6: A preliminary version of this chapter was presented as a paper titled, "*Des juifs radicaux au radicalisme juif: La vérité du témoignage, modèle fondateur de la Communauté,*" at the inaugural International Conference: "Readings of Difficult Freedom," (July 5–9, 2010, Toulouse, France). I am grateful to the Société internationale de recherches Emmanuel Lévinas (SIREL, Paris) and North American Levinas Society (NALS, USA) for their invitation to participate in this discursive project of such expansive depth and reconsideration. Working through Lévinas' relationship to the post-1968 revolutionaries and its effect on community allowed me to rethink how Critical Theory could still transform conscious community. The post-1968 thinkers pose a unique challenge in their integration into normative French Jewish communal structure, in contrast to the alienation of the Frankfurt School from the German (or American) Jewish community structure. Special thanks to Joseph H. Bravo in finalizing the French version of this paper.

Chapter 7: I am grateful to Bob Schack (JCC of Harrison), a philosopher of the first order, for our near five years of conversation and reflection on the place of religion and science today, an issue that is very close to his heart.

Chapter 8: I am grateful to Rabbi Dr. Magid's masterful sketches on *halakhah* as art early on in his research which inspired this correlation into Adorno's *Aesthetic Theory* in relation to *halakhah.* My years of praxis in painting through the auspices of the studios of the Art Gallery of Ontario as well as Claude Watson School for the Arts and the private studio of Mary T. Carmichael added a unique texture to these reflections on aesthetics and art, as theory and praxis.

Chapter 9: A preliminary version of this chapter was presented as "Poetics of Jewish Mystical Texts: Methodological Considerations," at the Association for Jewish Studies 37th Annual Conference (Washington, D.C., December 18, 2005). I am grateful to Rabbi Dr. Shaul Magid and Rabbi Dr. Gordon Tucker (Temple Israel Center, White Plains, New York) for their years of conversation and reflection on this issue. Tucker's approach to *meta*-halakhah remains an important model for expanding the system. Harold Bloom also shared many insights into his discussions with Scholem over the years with me and took interest in the trajectory of this study, especially when it challenged his notion of canon.

Chapter 10: I am grateful to Dr. Joseph Bryant (University of Toronto) for guiding and sharing in this investigation into the sociological aspects of Adorno's thinking and their relevance today. While discussing a difficult passage in Adorno on Stravinsky with Jonathan Osser (JCC of Harrison) I was led to the reflections of Bernstein on Adorno.

giving established scholars grades?

Prelude:
Criterion for Attuning to a New
Physiognomy of Jewish Thinking

What is true of intervals holds good as well for other elements of composition. This objective loss of tension has its equivalent in the human subjects, who inevitably find themselves handing down something that cannot be handed down and diluting to a jargon something that has never aspired to the status of a language. Their manner reminds us of *people who write a book in order to write a book, in contrast to those who have something to say.*

> —Theodor Adorno[1]

Silence arose and stood.
In the end, the matter *will be known.*

> —Yonadav Kaploun[2]

. . . for in music both *memory* and *anticipation* are *integral* elements in the *present reality.*

> —Theodor Adorno[3]

In his remarkable way of being *in the world* he was thinking through but *not of it*—at once piano player and philosopher, insider and outsider, half-Jew and half-German exile, subjective and objective thinker—Theodor W. Adorno's remarks on aesthetics can serve to demarcate a great lacuna of Critical Theory's influence upon Jewish Thinking today. In his "Criteria for New Music," Adorno sought to respond to the question of criteria by which one could judge new music, noting that such judgment called for reflection not merely "on the criteria themselves, but on the methods needed to discover them."[4] By way of prelude to *A New Physiognomy of Jewish Thinking: Critical Theory after Adorno as Applied to Jewish Thought*, I hope to reflect on why new methods are needed to rediscover the elusive spirit of Jewish Thinking today. In time, each component of the title will be further elucidated to set out the project at large. But at the outset, it is important to appreciate how unique Critical Theory is in its insistence upon "a mediation of theory and history in a concept of socially effective rationality."[5] The challenge, however, in "[d]esignating the legacy of Critical Theory for the new century necessarily involves recovering from the idea of a social pathology of reason as an explosive charge that can still be touched off today."[6] Part of the present challenge then is to clarify the present context in which "social criticism stands side by side with the demands of a historically evolved reason."[7] While taking much of our methodological inspiration from a third generation critical theorist, Axel Honneth, who also serves as current director of the Institute for Social Research at Goethe University, the present investigation intends to not only find a new language that can make clear in present terms what Critical Theory intended in the past,[8] but to also map out the contours of a New Jewish Thinking that needs to emerge from this correlation for the future.

Rather than write a book simply for the sake of writing a book, I have chosen to remain silent for over a decade entangled in these reflections. But the further I reflect—as scholar and as rabbi—on what indeed can be handed down to the next generation of critical thinkers and seekers, the more disenchanting things appear. Authenticity cannot be diluted into some jargon—truth must be sought. Yet too many seekers today seem bereft of the tools and criterion for such a seeking of truth. As statisticians like to point to the rising numbers of those engaged in Jewish life as either situated within the categories of Orthodoxy or Interfaith, the once profound critical thinking typical of centrism is being eclipsed. Bookshelves are overflowing with weak apologia or diluted introductions that never penetrate the veils toward truth. For without some kind of sustained reflection within the present reality of Jewish Thinking, memory fades into nostalgia and anticipation resonates as titillation. Judaism can be something more than nostalgia and titillation only if it is propelled into its deeper orbit by new constellations of Jewish Thinking.

The challenge before such a study that dares to be titled *A New Physiognomy of Jewish Thinking* is precisely to what degree something new and of value to the evolution of Jewish thought is being articulated? Is there something innovative about thinking through Judaism with the tools of Critical Theory? Why Critical Theory and why now? What is entailed in attunement to such thinking? Why the need for a new physiognomy of Jewish Thinking? Moreover, is it possible to fulfill this challenge of *Critical Theory after Adorno as Applied to Jewish Thought* considering the thorny Jewish question? After all, Adorno was asked to "drop the Wiesengrund from his name, because there were too many Jewish-sounding names on the *Institut*'s roster."[9] As to the prominence of Jewish lineage in most of the apparently assimilated Frankfurt School and *Institut* thinkers, third generation critical theorist Jurgen Habermas has already speculated that Jewish identity is linked to thinking patterns. Crucial to any understanding of Critical Theory, claims Habermas, is the recurrent trope of aniconicism or what Adorno calls the *Bilderverbot* and its relation to Kabbalistic thinking. It is the distance between the ideal and the real, between the sacred language of Hebrew and the profane languages of the Diaspora, according to Habermas, that elicits that same distrust of the current universe of discourse, linking Critical Theory to Kabbalah.[10] Moreover, the Frankfurt School's "reluctance to flesh out its notions of utopia was very similar to the [k]ab[b]alistic stress on words rather than on images."[11]

But why Critical Theory, and *why now?* After all, as Axel Honneth rightly remarks, "with the turn of the century, Critical Theory appears to have become an intellectual artifact."[12] Seeing that authenticity is a concern of our present project, one must admit that the grand historical and philosophical ideas undergirding Critical Theory appear outdated, antiquated, or irretrievably lost. Going beyond appearances, as third generation critical theorists like Honneth argue, there is "no doubt that the basic historical-philosophical and sociological assumptions of the Frankfurt School can no longer be defended,"[13] still I remain convinced that there is something of great value waiting to be rediscovered in this application of what I am calling *Critical Theory after Adorno,* specifically in its applications to Jewish Thinking. The guiding question after Adorno and the legacy of Critical Theory as envisioned through his disciples like Honneth, "is the question of whether the central idea behind the whole project [of Critical Theory] can still be defended today."[14] If the high standard of Critical Theory is to remain a viable form of social criticism in our day, then its challenge must be addressed. Honneth is instructive in outlining the program of Critical Theory in the following way that influences the very structure of this present investigation:

1. The *constructive justification* of a critical standpoint is to provide a conception of rationality that establishes a systematic connection between social rationality and moral validity.
2. It is then to be *reconstructively shown* that this potential rationality determines social reality in the form of moral ideals.
3. And these moral ideals, in turn, are to be seen under the *genealogical proviso* that their original meaning may have become socially unrecognizable.[15]

Once seen anew through this constellation of *Construction-Reconstruction-Genealogical Proviso,* Critical Theory then really comes down to the idea that "the turn to a liberating practice of cooperation should not result from affective bonds or feelings of membership or agreement but from rational insight."[16] There is a need, however, to modify and expand Honneth's take on Critical Theory in its current application to Jewish Thinking, namely that it is not only rational but also *supra*-rational insight that must be used to establish a sense of belonging to some collective form. Even if that collectivity exists on the margin, there is a need to link the discovered insight to others in some kind of community. For without that link, there is less likelihood of the necessary persistence and durability of the very approach to thinking called Critical Theory. To reiterate, even though our focus within the Frankfurt School of Critical Theory remains as seen through the lens of Adorno's thinking, the present search is to "reconstruct the ideal form of this kind of criticism, not its execution in individual writings by the Frankfurt Circle."[17] Adorno then really represents a rigorous and creative way of thinking critically that can inspire Jewish Thinking onwards in its evolution.

What is entailed in "attunement" to such thinking? To access the imagination, a cornerstone of original thinking, Adorno saw no substitute for a "speculative ear" and its ability to attune to the nuances of new music. In a landmark late essay from 1966, aptly titled, "Difficulties," Adorno laments the atrophying of the imagination and our growing inability to cultivate the "capacity to combine divergent things, to create unity, in tandem with the music, in true variety."[18] The new music he returns to time and again is a symptom of a larger cultural malaise that afflicts thinking in general. In a prophetic remark by Adorno in 1938 as the music of National Socialism is already in ascent, he relates how the inability of society to listen with depth and intention is a sign of rapid dehumanization.[19] This abiding concern never left Adorno. Even after Auschwitz, in exile, he admitted that the depth of listening demanded of the listener by new music is paradoxical. It must at once encompass the intention to be understood and the hesitancy to completely capture the entirety of what is being conveyed. Of this dialectical tension, Adorno remarks, "[o]ne cannot escape this contradiction by thinking about it. The only thing one can do is to elevate it to the level of consciousness, to speak it; at best there remains the hope of a music whose power compels the understanding of those who now feel indifference or animosity."[20]

Musical understanding is possible through a certain kind of cultivated listening. Adorno referred to such a cultivation in a 1965 essay, aptly titled, "Little Heresy."[21] While differing modes of listening may be in tension, heresy for Adorno is that only one such mode necessarily leads to "musical cultivation with human dignity."[22] In opposition to atomistic listening, "which loses itself weakly, passively in the charm of the moment, the pleasant single sound, the easily graspable and recollectable memory," Adorno juxtaposes structural listening, which remains critical despite all temptations to be otherwise. That critical posture of structural listening, especially in listening to music, is foundational to critical thinking, as Adorno alludes, "[s]ince music, after all, lacks concepts, the person who listens atomistically is not capable of perceiving it sensually as something intellectual and spiritual [*Geistiges*]."[23] The clarion call for musical understanding as an exemplar of critical thinking is to cultivate the sensual perception that brings together an experience of the *Geistiges*, which overflows the boundaries of the intellectual as separate from the spiritual. The difficulty dissolves in understanding Adorno's dialectical thinking to be explored further on once it is seen in light of musical thinking. The correlation between musicality and thinking is clarified further by Adorno in the same essay, when he remarks: "If the true musical whole does not impose a blind dominance of so-called form, but is rather result and process in one—very closely related, by the way, to the metaphysical conceptions of great philosophy—then it makes sense that the way to understand the whole would have to lead up from the individual part as well as down from the whole."[24]

Indeed, there remains the hope of attunement within a few voices in Jewish Studies. According to Fishbane's recent theological ruminations and his call for "attunement" to the sacred within textual existence,[25] the term is evolving and returning to Jewish Thinking. Attunement [*Befindlichkeit*] now expands into a textual component of relationality built upon its original existential usage as defined by Heidegger as follows: "What we indicate ontologically with the term attunement is ontically what is most familiar and an everyday kind of thing: mood, being in a mood."[26] While deeper engagement toward authenticity can indeed begin in a mood, there is a shift in Fishbane that implies a praxis that ontically grounds any ontological theory. Unifying realms of theory and praxis, so central to Critical Theory, echoes through this expansion of attunement. This critical transformation of the existential basis of authenticity will become more apparent in our fifth chapter, Returning to Authenticity: From Jargon to Praxis of Critical Judaism.

What then is a physiognomy of Jewish Thinking and why the need for a new one? While physiognomy literally refers to a person's facial features or expression, especially indicative of character,[27] a physiognomy of thinking means to address the figure of a life lived where theory and praxis are meant to be unified. Already from his 1931 Frankfurt inaugural lecture, Adorno was prescient in his social-theoretical analysis of capitalism not to limit himself with explanatory theory, rather he provided "a hermeneutic of a failed form of life."[28] The real purpose of this social critique for Adorno was to contribute a physiognomy of social reality, that is, in "determining figures of action such that they can be understood as bodily or gestural expressions of the capitalist form of life."[29]

The far-reaching meaning of physiognomy in Adorno's thinking is his conviction that "mental abilities are reflected in the corporeal nature of human beings."[30] Adorno was calling for a much bolder "expansion of social analysis beyond its traditional object domain," to include "gestures, mimicry, modes of practical intercourse in and with the world."[31] This call demands moving beyond linguistic utterances or written texts (the delimited domain of Fishbane's aforementioned "attunement") to include the "physical form of a way of life as a whole" to "become the object of an ideal-typical interpretation that seeks to break through the surface appearances to signs of a deformation of our reason."[32] What remains then is the "difficult task of holding open the possibility of transforming the frozen, reified reality: "Out of the construction of a configuration of reality," as he already put it in his inaugural lecture, "the demand for its real change always follows promptly."[33] What Adorno accomplishes with a physiognomy of a "failed form of life" is the redemptive possibility of internal forms of reflection. Every bodily impulse possesses such an internal form of reflection, as Adorno remarks: "The corporeal moment registers the cognition that suffering ought not to be, that things should be different."[34] It is this desire, albeit concealed, to be liberated from this felt deformation of thinking that resides within every human being.

The final step in unpacking Adorno's "physiognomy" of thinking is its relationship to childhood. The working assumption for Adorno is that "human reason develops by way of a childlike imitation of loved ones; only the mimetic imitation of the other's perspective affords the young child the opportunity to decenter his own perspective to the point that it outweighs his own, and he can thus forge ahead to rational judgments on states of affairs."[35] It is only by way of this thorough physiognomy of thinking that Adorno is thus able to show how "these early childhood experiences, in which our thinking develops through love, have a continued existence as trace memories through the socially compelled instrumentalization of our minds."[36] No matter the degree of concealment, disconnection, and depravity, seeing the origins of thinking as nascent in "early moments of empathy and care"[37] holds out a redemptive hope for thinking. Despite our delusions, through this childhood residue, there is always, according to Adorno's defiant confidence, the possibility of liberation through our reason. It is precisely from this crucial insight and its gap that our present study takes one further step back into that childhood residue so as to move forward into a more expansive Jewish Thinking. That very childhood residue of empathy and caring flows forth from the larger font of the *supra*-rational to be explored in the first chapter, namely, the imaginal realm. That interworld between imagination and reality, which Wolfson has been so deft at correlating to his reading of Jewish mysticism,[38] is accessed more readily when there is a reunited correlation between adulthood and childhood, between theory and praxis, between reality and the imagination. After Adorno, who was unyielding in his search for the means to such experience as "exact imagination [*exakte Phantasie*],"[39] this search must continue in exacting attunement to the imaginal within thinking.

* * *

The present study really incubated over the course of a decade, beginning while I was only a few blocks away from one of the main homes of the *Institut* in exile. Since 1936 the exilic home of the *Institut* was in Morningside Heights, New York, across from Columbia University. While a student from 1994–2000 at the Jewish Theological Seminary, the bastion of *Wissenschaft des Judentums*, I yearned for a more critical way of integrating theory and praxis of Judaism that I was becoming immersed in. It seemed to me, for all intents and purposes, that the renowned scholarship of *Wissenschaft des Judentums* that opened Judaism to critical inquiry was methodologically frozen in an early stage of positive-historical Hegelianism. What remained to be seen was how to translate the fruits of *Wissenschaft* scholarship into practice, while the commitment espoused by Critical Theory to do just that remained neglected and continued to beckon me. While I immersed myself in *Wissenschaft des Judentums* hailing from the late 1800s at its bastion in the Jewish Theological Seminary of America at West 122nd Street, only a few blocks away at the Extension Division at Columbia in Morningside Heights dwelt the home away from home of Critical Theory in America through the *Institut*. While only separated physically by a few blocks, these worlds remained worlds apart from one another.

Of the entire Frankfurt School, why focus on Adorno? Surely Horkheimer, Marcuse, or others would have appeared to have been a better fit? After all, Adorno's Judaism was the most marginal of the group. By taking seriously the *Institut*'s preference for words over images, Adorno's turn to music explores "the most non-representational of aesthetic modes, as the primary medium"[40] providing a profound discursive basis for his negative dialectics and critique of the culture industry. Combined with Adorno's deep philosophical acumen, as well as his profound insight into aesthetics, his thinking remains as vibrant and influential today as the day it was written.[41]

Despite the draw of Critical Theory espoused by Adorno and the Frankfurt School, the closest contact made with this rigorous form of contemporary thinking during my years of study in the bastion of *Wissenschaft des Judentums* was through the thinking of Franz Rosenzweig. While a certain excitement and hope surround the new translation of Rosenzweig's *The Star of Redemption* into English, for example,[42] few remain willing to persevere and penetrate the remarkable steps in the New Thinking offered by Rosenzweig. The general tendency, as Wolfson and Hughes rightly note, is to "defang" the intellectual rigor of a living Jewish philosophy.[43] The unwillingness and inability of most current approaches to Jewish philosophy to engage in it as a "way of life" or see it as a "living and engaged practice,"[44] is precisely the malaise that beckons for the present study.

The notable exception is found in a cluster of thinkers willing to engage in Jewish philosophy as a "moving beyond the traditional *Wissenschaft* model."[45] That shift requires a willingness to relinquish obsessions about reading the past on its own terms, rather moving to "expand the contours of Jewish philosophy—redefining its canon, articulating a new set of questions, showing its counterpoints with other disciplines—as a way to demonstrate the vitality and originality of the topic."[46] Amidst the hopes compelling this much needed *New Directions in Jewish Philosophy*, there is a yearning to establish "new conceptual models, modes of analysis, and theoretical paradigms to apply to the study of Jewish philosophy . . . seek[ing] new and dynamic ways to engage the material both to specialists in the field and to those in cognate disciplines with an interest in Jewish philosophy and critical theory."[47] Amidst these hopes, however, the most penetrating thinking and concrete possibility of correlating Jewish philosophy and Critical Theory comes from Elliot R. Wolfson,[48] who thinks along the lines of German Jewish thinker, Franz Rosenzweig. Traversing subversively through these footsteps, Wolfson dares confront the implications of the Rosenzweigian "apophatic turn [that] challenges the theistic faith," whereby "[w]hat is lost is the personal God of the Jewish tradition."[49] Revelation becomes the "unfathomable ground where mysticism and atheism insidiously shake hands"[50] which necessitates a complete reorientation to the nature of Jewish Thinking. Not only must the concept of "God" be rethought but so too the nature of Torah,[51] as well as boundaries of alterity to be traversed if thinking must forever be negotiated from the standpoint of preserving the identity of difference in the difference of identity."[52] Exploring how philosophy and Judaism change in relationship to each other[53] also means that one must question indeed whether "a non-Jew cannot produce Jewish philosophy?"[54]

At one critical juncture in my own journey through Jewish Thinking, I recall how my teacher, Professor Seymour Feldman, discouraged me from entering into studying medieval Jewish philosophy as a vocation. In a sober moment of studying this teacher's rigorous annotated translations of Gersonides' sustained supercommentary on Maimonides,[55] Feldman lamented over the paucity of publications, institutions, and overall support for the pursuit of real Jewish Thinking today. What was once the pursuit of the ideal was now becoming a question of survival in a world that gave little thought to thinking. Upon completion of a private curriculum of classic medieval texts, from Maimonides to Gersonides, Professor Feldman agreed I was now ready to enter the modern period under his guidance. However, our entry into the modern period of philosophy began and ended with Kant's *Critique of Pure Reason* (along with the requisite commentary by Norman Kemp Smith).[56] Our focus was primarily upon the difference between sense and understanding and the role of imagination in acting as a mediator for thinking. The further we delved into Kant, the more it became clear that the creative quality of thinking I sought to deepen had to be relegated to the *noumenal* side of the imagination, whereas what really could be counted upon for true and reliable thinking was understanding that came from the *phenomenal* side.[57] This reticence to delve further into the noumenal side of New Thinking (even on the part of a giant in medieval Jewish Thinking like Feldman) is what led me to continue onwards, past mere passions for truth,[58] but toward the abyss where the spirit might still rise from the ashes as present in the thinking of the Frankfurt School.

It is precisely through the lens of Adorno's keen philosophical eye that we turn to the *noumenal* side of thinking as present in music. Returning to Adorno to point the way through the thicket obscuring Jewish Thinking could not be more urgent:

> Of course, it is no objection to new music to point out that in the dialectic of the general and the particular it is always bumping up against the limits of the particular. Only, it must have the power to carry this dialectic through to its end. All of this revolves around the concept of internal musical tension and its enfeeblement, a phenomenon that forces itself on our attention today and yet obstinately resists identification. The process is objectively determined. The concretization of musical idiom whose whole impulse rebels against concretization is enforced by its language-like nature, even though it is in conflict with its own underlying ideal.[59]

That very musical tension and enfeeblement in thinking is what allows for the resistance of identification with and closure from the concept to override New Jewish Thinking. By remaining "in conflict with its own underlying ideal," the texture of that internal tension within Jewish Thinking remains brilliant and inspiring. Without that internal tension that Adorno, time and again, refers to as the Negative Dialectic, there is no possibility of encountering the sparks of the imagination nesting in the noumenal realm. Moreover, through the ages when Jewish Thinking has slipped into complete identification with either universalism or particularity, it de facto loosens that internal tension, desecrating any of its musical depth or what will be referred to as musicality.

I have intentionally excluded the work of accomplished Jewish philosopher David Novak and his prolific ruminations on Natural Law as well as his reflections on chosenness[60] simply because they remain mired in the realm of theological apologia, doing little to further the project of a New Jewish Thinking. This kind of atavistic thinking submits to the concretization of the particular enforced by a given idiom or a priori thought and so resists any conflict with its own underlying ideal. Unfortunately, studies of this kind do more to bury the possibility of a New Jewish Thinking than to allow its truth to be uncovered and carried forward. What this kind of apologetic thinking suffers from, taking our cue from Adorno, is a profound inability to "carry this dialectic through to its end" and as a result remains merely a reactionary enfeeblement of thought rather than a celebration of that very internal dialectic that makes thinking overflow with musicality.

Notwithstanding the aforementioned challenges, there have been some valiant, albeit unrealized attempts to allow a New Thinking in Judaism to take place. In particular, consider a few recent experiments in this vein: *Integral Halachah,*[61] *Radical Judaism: Hasidism for a New Era,*[62] and *Jewish Theology in Our Time.*[63] As will become evident through the course of this investigation, these aforementioned works, while valiant, do not quite make the commitment for speculative listening that musical thinking demands. *Jewish Theology in Our Time* is ab initio a lost project of a bygone era as discussed further on regarding theology and metaphysical atheism in our first two chapters. *Radical Judaism* on the other hand rehearses classic theological tropes that are apparently revisioned radically for this age, *yet just how radical this theology really can be remains an open question.* By contrast to these two works of theology, *Integral Halachah* requires much deeper attunement as discussed in Chapters 8 and 9. This is the more daring (*albeit* unrealized) ongoing experiment by Rabbi Zalman Schachter-Shalomi to correlate the evolution of spiritual consciousness espoused by philosophers of religion, like Ken Wilber, into the fold of Jewish discourse.

Of these works, it is *Integral Halachah*[64] where the most challenging correlations do not fade but shine brighter with the passage of time. For critical thinkers like Magid, who are ready to engage more deeply and systematically in the discourse of a burgeoning American Jewish postmonotheism, both Schachter-Shalomi and Green proffer something uniquely American.[65] Magid astutely notes that both theologians are offering the "first non-elective Jewish metaphysics"[66] in the American postmonotheism. What is of great interest to our present investigation is the degree to which these theologians seek possible pathways out of the *huis-clos* posed by Adorno's metaphysical atheism. What Magid makes clear in his latest study, *Jews and Judaism in Post-Ethnic America*,[67] is the degree to which a negative dialectical thinking is still influencing these theologians.

Despite the limitations of these radical theologies manifest in Schachter-Shalomi and Green, Magid's critical thinking mines a metaphysical kernel that must be confronted— a nonelective Jewish metaphysics. Although Magid is more interested in the "theo-political realm in an attempt to understand how Jews, and Judaism, in the contemporary American Diaspora can thrive without the exclusivist doctrines that arguably contributed to their survival,"[68] the question of negative dialectical thinking looms large. Namely, is negative dialectical thinking still possible when the tension between exclusivity and inclusivity collapses? In other words, once the universal and the particular are conflated to the point where the particular is no longer necessary for the survival of a given way of thinking, is that thinking still critical? Is it still engaged in the dynamics of a negative dialectics? Even amidst a nonelective Jewish metaphysics, critical thinking would challenge whether such a metaphysics is still possible and necessary. Finally, what Magid's critical thinking redresses is the lack of rigor and systemization that remain a *desideratum* once one re-enters the broken realm of theology (no matter how radical). Still in need of revision is the question of how to critically think through the evolution of spiritual consciousness. In order to make that step in thinking that does not destroy the negative dialectical turn, there remains a need to revise the lens of correlation within *Integral Halachah* from the derivative thinking of Ken Wilber (b. 1949) back to the original genius lost in neglecting the thinking of Jean Gebser (1905–1973). How telling then that it is only Gebser's neglected critical thinking on music that is capable of addressing and critiquing Adorno's musical thinking like no other to date.

This brings us to a more pressing issue relating back to authenticity. With a loss of the will to truly think anymore, and then for those who are thinking to be enfeebled by an inability to resist identification with the particularity of concepts, the least constructive elements continue to be drudged forward. While the real need remains for a contemporary theosophy of the Gentile[69] that allows for more integral thinking to emerge within Jewish Law or *halakhah*, the fear and anxiety blocking such thinking from emerging is disheartening. Turning back to Adorno to see forward once again, thinking can take its cue from music:

> By negating both the general and the particular, new music presses forward to absolute identity, and in so doing, it aspires to the voice of the non-identical—of everything that refuses to be submerged.[70]

In the true search for authenticity that combines critical thinking with a yearning for heartfelt poetics, many continue returning to religion with the hope of achieving, or at least glimpsing redemption. Yet too often it remains either a re-enchantment devoid of thinking or a disenchantment devoid of poetics. What the following study attempts is to work through the thicket of *Construction-Reconstruction-Genealogical Proviso*:

1. How negative dialectics can restore the imaginal power of Jewish Thinking;
2. How a poetics of alterity can guide the search for God;
3. How a metaphysics of musical temporality can redeem thinking;
4. How Reification of Israel needs to overcome forgetting to re-member Zion;
5. How authenticity informs an integrated praxis of Critical Judaism;
6. How community can be transformative through the truth of testimony;
7. How awareness of infinity can be cultivated in correlating physics and metaphysics;
8. How a Poet*h*ics of Theory and Praxis that enhance existence can be experienced as *halakhah*;
9. How ethics needs incompleteness within Jewish Law;
10. How musical thinking can redeem religion without succumbing to the pitfalls of Utopia.

The desire, albeit concealed, to be liberated from our contemporary deformation of thinking still resides within every human being. It is high time we heeded the words of the poet, by way of re-turn [*heim-kehren*] to what Celan called more "creaturely by-paths" [*kreatürliche Um-wege*][71] and redoubled our efforts to seek that truth and keep it from being swallowed in apathy's darkness:

Tongue extending to hand
thrown into *darkness*

On my beloved's face
imploring language,
upon the lip of the abyss shall I indicate for us

Disappearing god
his visage *shining*[72]

Dr. Aubrey L. Glazer
Harrison, New York
Elul, 5770

Part I

Construction

Chapter 1

New Imaginal Thinking: Origin and Future of *Machshevet Yisrael* after Negative Dialectics

To those who have had the undeserved good fortune to *not be completely adjusted in their inner intellectual composition to the prevailing norms*—a stroke of luck, which they often enough have to pay for in terms of their relationship to the immediate environment—it is incumbent to make the moralistic and, as it were, representative effort to express what the majority, for whom they say it, are not capable of *seeing* or, to do justice to reality, will not allow themselves to see. *The criterion of truth is not its immediate communicability to everyone.*

—Theodor Adorno[1]

The cognition which wishes for content, wishes for utopia. This, the consciousness of the possibility, clings to the concrete as what is undistorted. It is what is possible, never the immediately realized, which obstructs utopia; that is why in the middle of the existent it appears abstract. *The inextinguishable color comes from the not-existent. Thinking* serves it as a piece of *existence*, as that which, as always negatively, reaches out to the not-existent. Solely the most *extreme distance* would be the *nearness*; philosophy is the prism, in which its colors are caught.

—Theodor Adorno[2]

On the Possibility of Jewish Thinking within *Machshevet Yisrael*

In the search for truth, proximity is paradoxically distance. Is it still possible to claim that the prism of philosophy is sufficient to convey the search for truth in Judaism? If realizing limits delimits an openness to the limitless nature of thinking, then what are the parameters of Jewish Thinking and what influences the expansion and contraction of such thought? *Machshevet Yisrael* is the term originally used to denote the project of Jewish philosophy or Jewish Thinking. Before we can embark on our task of seeking out a New Thinking for Judaism informed by Critical Theory, it is crucial to understand the path already trodden. To get beyond the apogee of twentieth-century Jewish Thinking as embodied in Adorno's music-like composition[3] of *Negative Dialektik*, one must go back a few centuries in order to clear that path to move forward. Even the term Jewish Philosophy as a form of *Machshevet Yisrael*, brought into the English speaking world as Jewish Thinking as recently as 1961 by Eliezer Berkovits, delimits the very discourse it attempts to describe.[4] This chapter then attempts to outline the origins of the term and its problematic assumptions, and then to suggest contemporary modes of redeeming a new physiognomy of thinking about Judaism once freed from reified concepts.

If one harkens back to the first glimmers of *Wissenschaft des Judentums* revisioning the project of its thinking, its most influential definitions were provided by Julius Guttman: "[s]ince the days of antiquity, Jewish philosophy was essentially a philosophy of Judaism."[5] What Guttman contributes to this perennial quest is the perspective that through the ages philosophies of Judaism have captured the scope of the project rather than a philosophy that is Jewish per se. This remains so even if the shift in terminology denotes a stance outside looking in, whereby a philosophical justification of Judaism becomes the main focus.[6]

There remains, however, a trace of that embarrassment that continues to delimit the contours of New Thinking in Judaism and what constitutes authentic thought. For instance, should the source and measuring stick for New Thinking hail from rationalism or supra-rationalism? Even in the question itself we already confront a delimitation in bifurcating how we know what we know. Release from the bifurcating hold of Maimonideanism over Jewish Thinking is an ongoing challenge. That brilliant medieval mind still influences contemporary Jewish thinkers into places of severely limited thinking. Why is the nature of mind and experience still considered to be bifurcated between the rational and the supra-rational? What are the boundaries between philosophy and theology and when should such boundaries be crossed? What role and primacy is played by the imagination within thinking? The vestiges of a clear hierarchy of the rational above all else remain a strong influence of Maimonides. Even so, there are always thinkers who dare to think outside accepted forms and their reifications.

Shifting into the contemporary period, there are distinct streams into which Jewish Thinking tends to be divided. The essentialist approach, championed by Emil Fackenheim[7] (1916–2003), suggests Jewish philosophy combines an essential Jewish message with a general philosophical method. That message is an ethical teaching of the prophets of ancient Israel, while the method remains that of Socrates, Plato, and Aristotle. This marginal definition encounters problems when it comes to philosophizing something other than ethics. Such essentialism presumed by Fackenheim, which claims there is an objectively identifiable and definable essence, can be seen to run even deeper through the scholarship of Julius Guttmann (1845–1919) and Alexander Altmann (1906–1987).[8] Jewish philosophy then is the mode of philosophical inquiry into the religious essence of Judaism.[9] By entitling his investigation into Jewish Thinking as *Die Philosophie des Judentums* (deliberately mistranslated into English as *Philosophies of Judaism*), Guttman is functioning as a philosopher of religion, whereby "Judaism is something given, a datum, something that is there before the philosophers begin to philosophize about it."[10] If such notions of essentialist objectivity no longer hold, then Jewish Thinking needs a different direction at this contemporary moment.

When one considers why there has not yet been an organic development of a Jewish philosophy in the way that French or German philosophy has evolved, it seems perplexing. Yet it is the very prospect of Jewish Thinking in the Diaspora, at least according to the essentialist view, that prevented any fuller sense of development. The futility of trying to present Judaism as a philosophic system, according to Altmann, stems from Judaism being a religion, wherein "the truths it teaches are religious truths. They spring from the source of religious experience, not from pure reason."[11] How then is such experience to be conveyed in thinking itself?

In an attempt to expand the discourse beyond the essentialist approach influencing much thinking in Jewish philosophy, Arthur Hyman, as editor of the Jewish philosophy division of the *Encyclopaedia Judaica* (1971), described Jewish philosophy as "the explication of Jewish beliefs and practices by means of general philosophic concepts and norms. Hence it must be seen as an outgrowth of the biblical and rabbinic traditions on which Judaism rests as well as part of the history of philosophy at large." Hyman then modifies this essentialist position to be more expansive, whereby the subject matter of Jewish philosophy appears in a threefold division, namely (1) as interpretation of unique aspects of Jewish tradition; (2) as philosophy of religion; (3) as philosophy proper, it studies topics of general philosophic interest.

Approaching the precipice of a dialectic, a much-needed modification of essentialism becomes evident with French scholar of medieval philosophy, Colette Sirat. She maintains both essentialist conditions, contending that "only the combination of philosophy and Jewish tradition forms Jewish philosophy" makes the harmonizing of particular systems of thought possible with Jewish sources.[12] Harmonizing still presupposes a Jewish essence, or at least a definitive Jewish tradition, all the while avoiding a definition of that essence and tradition.

Understanding of Jewish philosophy from the perspective of the history of ideas has been deeply influenced by the brilliant contributions of Harry Austryn Wolfson (1887–1974) who viewed Philo as the originator of Jewish Thinking amidst Hellenized culture. Philo's lasting influence is a function of interpreting Greek philosophy in terms of Hebrew Scripture. Wolfson points to the lasting influence of Philo's ideas until Baruch Spinoza (1632–1677). With the arrival of Spinoza, rational questioning of Jewish faith now becomes possible. Jewish philosophy for Wolfson then begins with Philo and, for all intents and purposes of the historian, ends with Spinoza. Beyond those bookends, there is nothing new, especially in the Diaspora in terms of Jewish philosophy, let alone any significant steps toward a New Thinking in Judaism.

The influence of these and other essentialisms upon Jewish philosophy has greatly limited the evolution of New Thinking in Judaism. Once everything is limited to explication or verification of given truths, namely that Judaism has its datum and as a religion has its essence, this then undermines the basic openness to the philosophical method. It also erases any distinction between philosophy and theology. Such erasure of these very boundaries brings us back full circle to Maimonides' prescient distinction between philosophy and theology, thus informing his critique of the Kalam theologians. When reality is made to conform to hypotheses rather than adapting it to reality,[13] truth is obfuscated if not altogether lost.

Finally, any introduction to *Machshevet Yisrael* in the Diaspora would be incomplete without taking into account the contributions of Eliezer Berkovits. It is precisely Berkovits' attempt to define the *Machshavah* intrinsic to *Yisrael* that gives rise to his classic article, "What is Jewish Philosophy?"[14] Despite Berkovits' clear delineation of the boundaries within which Jewish philosophy must necessarily conform in order to authentically contemplate its thought as *Machshevet Yisrael*, these concepts risk reification, potentially creating an orthodox thinking. By narrowing down the focus of any philosophical investigation to three foundational concepts, as in Berkovits' case of God-Torah-Israel, the essence of Judaism is a priori defined and delimited to suit his aims as an orthodox thinker. Any thinking that takes place outside these concepts, especially from the noumenal side, is not considered to be part of Jewish Thinking that is philosophically viable. In the quest for truth that a new Jewish Thinking seeks, such concepts endanger the inner dialectic to remain a reactionary enfeeblement of thought rather than a celebration of that very internal dialectic that makes thinking overflow with musicality.

The assumption of these essentialists is that there is a continuous and uniform thing that we may call "Judaism" or "the Jewish tradition," only then to be harmonized with a given foreign philosophy. The problem with this presumption is that it does not provide an adequate paradigm or method for dealing with the prior encounters of that "Judaism" or "tradition" with foreign cultures and its adaptations back into Judaism. Ideas perceived as heterodoxical in one period become orthodoxy in later periods. The integral part of what is perceived to be Jewish tradition is in constant motion within its cultural context and zeitgeist. "Instead of thinking of Jewish philosophy as providing a Jewish context for philosophy," as Hughes and Wolfson suggest, there is an urgent need to shift into "a philosophical reasoning that is shaped by the singularity of a specific cultural matrix, and it is from the standpoint of this particularity that the universal is to be thought."[15] Such a heterodoxical flow cannot be overlooked if a new physiognomy of Jewish Thinking is to authentically emerge.

Ever since the overwhelming embrace of universalism that came with the Enlightenment and its consequent introduction of the critical study of Judaism, or *Wissenschaft des Judentums*, a certain embarrassment over the supra-rational as a way to truth has been noticeable.[16] This is especially evident after the *Shoah*, where the embarrassment over the intersection of esoteric and critical knowledge has only increased. It is a twofold embarrassment: on the one hand, the mystic is embarrassed by the scholar's utter disconnection from the experience undergirding the subject under investigation; on the other hand, the scholar is embarrassed by the mystic's immersion in an experience beyond the scope of rational investigation.[17]

The possibility of Jewish Thinking as authentic philosophy resurfaces in the epilogue to philosopher Robert Gibbs' critical work on Emmanuel Lévinas and Franz Rosenzweig. Gibbs is inspired to delimit what he calls "Seven Rubrics for Jewish Philosophy,"[18] by offering "a regulative ideal for what Jewish philosophy should struggle to approach."

1. *Universal Accessibility:*
   (a messianic universalism that is theocentric);
2. *Primacy of Ethics:*
   (encountering truth through praxis);
3. *Sociality not Individuality:*
   (responsibility in community and public society);
4. *Prophecy and Messianic Politics:*
   (a messianic vision of contemporary cultural critique);
5. *Resurrection and the Material World:*
   (the materialism of sociality);
6. *The Suspension of the State:*
   (shift of radical responsibility for the other);
7. *Halakhah and Social Institutions:*
   (pursuit of radical ethics in an association of autonomous individuals).

In these rubrics, Gibbs expands the normative triad of God-Torah-Israel into a more subtle yet thoroughly modernist universe of discourse. That discourse begins in a theotropic mode whereby God is a compass for the ensuing rubrics (1); Torah is a lens insofar as it relates to praxis and communal action (2, 7); while Israel is read most expansively to include all aspects of a redemptive community and sociality (3–6). It is evident that the stress in these rubrics is on the way that diverse aspects of sociality support ethics. While this model explores the limits of community through expanding Israel, there remains a reticence to engage in sustained reflections of God and Torah as well as expanding the rubrics, as Braiterman duly notes, beyond modern to postmodern topoi.[19] Any future rubric for Jewish Thinking needs to expand into a renewed dialectical process, not limited by modernist discourse, but transcending and including it.

A further attempt at bringing the concepts within this normative triad of God-Torah-Israel to bear on Jewish Theology has recently been explored by Neil Gillman.[20] In rehearsing the arguments for the timelessness of concepts like God, Torah, and Israel within modern Judaism and its theology there resurfaces a familiar limiting of its capacity to think beyond itself. Yet one must question the strength of Gillman's argument for such timeless categories, especially after J. Z. Smith's admission that there is no hard datum for religion, rather the study of religion remains an interpretive venture, and the creation of the scholar.[21] If the primary purpose of "*Machshevet Yisrael* is the never-ending attempt on the part of Jews to make some rational sense of the primary religious events that define their existence as Jews,"[22] then the nature of those facts are presumed to be immutable and prone to objectivity and standardization. Here then is where the problem arises, and no educational theory, no matter how integrative in intention, can succeed at bridging the "significant gap between *Machshevet Yisrael* instruction and the students' world view."[23] As we shall see later on, the gap is precisely where, for Adorno, the sparks of insight from dialectical thinking reveal themselves. It is the delusion of utter objectivity, a hold over from *Wissenschaft des Judentums*, which no longer suffices in "returning the study of *Machshevet Yisrael* back to its natural location, as an outgrowth of the study of the facts of Judaism."[24]

Two noble and creative attempts have been made to expand the concepts that traditionally delimit *Machshevet Yisrael*, each one with its own contribution to the possibility of furthering Jewish Thinking into New Thinking. The first work has been proffered by Arthur Green. In *Radical Judaism*,[25] Green seemingly pushes the envelope of the inherited concepts, *God-Torah-Israel*. One must wonder, as does Magid, whether Green indeed pushes these concepts far enough into the realm of the truly "radical."[26] Regardless of how reified this conceptual triad of *God-Torah-Israel*[27] has been throughout its history, Green attempts to salvage them through his creative re-readings. Still one much question how radical such Jewish Thinking can really be if it is ultimately unable to transcend the stranglehold of the reified concept? It remains to be seen whether Green's important project will glean new insight from the gaps within and between these concepts to inspire the next generation of radical Jews who are thinkers or whether the resultant thinking remains locked in the grip of reification.

A different approach altogether, one that is uniquely phenomenological and highly poetic without being in any way bound to this particular conceptual triad, is proffered by Elliot R. Wolfson in his brilliant monograph entitled *Alef, Mem, Tau: Kabbalistic Musings on Time, Truth, and Death*.[28] Rather than adhering to "familiar methodology adopted by scholars of Jewish mysticism, focusing on a particular historical period or individual personality," Wolfson underscores the deeply philosophic turn in his work, which is organized around "the three points of the curvature of the timeline."[29] His intention to "articulate an ontology of time that is a grammar of becoming"[30] must be lauded for its original thinking. Wolfson unites form and substance in this project by writing about temporality (before, between, and beyond) from the markers of truth itself

(*EMe"T = Alef-Mem-Tau*). "By heeding the letters of *emet* we have come to discern something of the truth of time manifestly concealed in the time of truth, the beginning that cannot begin if it is to be the beginning, the middle that re/ marks the place of origin and destiny, and the end that is the figuration of the impossible disclosing the impossibility of figuration, the finitude of death that facilitates the possibility of (re)birth, the closure that opens the opening that closes."[31] What is remarkable about this work is the ability of Wolfson to proclaim a noble intention and realize it in the form and substance of the investigation proper. This returning to the hermeneutics of experience in illuming the nexus of Time, Truth, and Death is all the while guided by the rabbinic "semiotic signposts" of *emet* or "truth" comprising the first, middle, and last letters of the Hebrew alphabet, which again reveals a unitive moment of language and experience.[32]

That aforementioned grammar of becoming opens a new by-path, whereby "[t]he correlation of truth and divinity underscores that truth."[33] This opens up a highly phenomenological approach to textuality that also pushes Jewish Thinking forward into the realm of New Thinking. By specifically addressing Rosenzweig at the conclusion of *Alef-Mem-Tau*, Wolfson is attempting to reveal the concealed temporality of thinking that is normally enveloped in before, between, and beyond moments. Wolfson remains a singular voice of one such radical Jew that dares to truly think.

The lingering question, however, is whether or not, from Berkovits to Green, there indeed remains a reification of the concepts God, Torah, and Israel. Is there a way out of this *huis-clos* that Adorno's *Negative Dialectics* might enhance in this search for authenticity without reifying the concepts? Is it possible to discover a by-path to New Thinking through "a language into which the symbol is translated is itself a symbolic language?"[34] Is Wolfson's adept suggestion of "a hermeneutical criterion of objectivity that avoids the extremes of absolute relativism, on the one hand, and relative absolutism, on the other"[35] really possible? Is there a path that balances the particular within the universal and the universal within the particular? Is it possible to open the horizon of textuality as the measure of incommensurability?[36] What remains an open question within Wolfson's project, however, is whether enough critical space is possible for a hermeneutical criterion of objectivity by dint of the predominance of "the particular cultural ambiance of medieval kabbalah."[37] Each of these critical questions continues to guide the prospects of a new physiognomy of Jewish Thinking. How far can this new physiognomy morph in challenging the present reified paradigm of *Machshevet Yisrael*, and still be so called? If the desire to embark unto the true authenticity of experience escapes any recognizable physiognomy of inherited forms, at what point will it cease to be Jewish Thinking? At what point does yearning for true authenticity of experience move beyond Mosaic shattering into Abrahamic leave-taking altogether?

Negative Dialectics: A Sketch

Having spent significant effort in searching out and critiquing those thinkers nearing this critical horizon of theory and praxis, it is fitting to close with a reflection on the methodology that contributes most to the lacuna in Jewish Thinking. It is that very quest for a new physiognomy, namely, a new way of thinking critically through life's forms that brings us to Adorno's masterpiece of methodology for Critical Theory, aptly titled, *Negative Dialectics*. To appreciate the leitmotif of that inner musical tension that Adorno seeks to restore within thinking, it is necessary to read his dialectics in a nuanced way. What follows is a sketch of the contours of the methodology nascent within negative dialectics. These contours are intended to reveal what Adorno is practicing in his Critical Theory by way of negative dialectics.

There are three discernable theses operative in Adorno's "Introduction" to *Negative Dialectics*.[38] First, there is the move from positive to negative dialectics, a bold step mapping out the territory that distinguishes the Frankfurt School from Hegelianism at large. Secondly, this necessary form of negative dialectics seeks to rebalance the correlation and does justice to both the "object" as well as the "subject of knowledge." Thirdly, the method of contemporary philosophical thinking can only serve in the capacity of self-critique.[39] Each of these theses needs to be further elucidated to clarify this methodology for Critical Theory.

(1) When Adorno decries the project of "[p]hilosophy, which once seemed outmoded to remain alive because the moment of its realization was missed,"[40] there still hovers a hopeless hopefulness for redemption. The missed realization of redemption comes by way of Idealism whether in Hegel or Marx. For dialectics to be redemptive it must be *negative* rather than *positive*. Of course, this may seem insignificant, but upon this difference turns an entire way of seeing, thinking, and living in the world. To discover and apply this negative dialectics, one must first appreciate the dangers of positive dialectics and its stranglehold on Idealism. If dialectics is "the proof of the insufficiency of a conceptual determination with regard to the object to be grasped," then to practice the positive dialectical method requires a commitment to demonstrating that "the whole of reality is rationally constituted."[41] Yet such a totalizing demonstration then compels one "to exclude everything qualitatively divergent" thus becoming "a closed system."[42] In opposing such positive dialectics, Adorno is against any process that closes the system of thinking, which limits its content through synthesis. The legacy of Hegel is the common dialectical model which sees the limiting possibility of resolution coming from the synthesis of thesis-antithesis. Remaining vigilant against any such synthesis or closure in thinking is critical for Adorno's method, as this very process avoids the pitfalls of Utopia and opens the hope of redemption amidst a failed life. Therein lies the first reason why Jewish Thinking needs negative dialectics, namely, to "bring to light the preintellectual, drivelike, or practical roots of all spiritual phenomena."[43] Although this intention of negative dialectics in Adorno's

thinking is vastly overlooked it can still be recovered to further nuance the way that the critical theorist of Judaism must approach the correlation of realms both rational and supra-rational, phenomenal and noumenal, real and imaginary, material and spiritual. To read Adorno merely as a hyper-rationalist, proto-Hegelian philosopher is to miss his contribution to thinking through a vital dialectics, albeit negative, of the spiritual within the material world.

(2) The necessary form of negative dialectics seeks to rebalance the correlation to both the object as well as the subject of knowledge. While there is nothing more important to Adorno's philosophical project than "the resonance of the object in subjective experience,"[44] the affective response elicited cannot degenerate into merely bearing a point of view. There is a need for a synthesis of "expression and stringency"[45] in this model of thinking. What then does this kind of self-criticism of philosophy look like in the form of negative dialectics? Conceptual inefficiency continues to be the guide insofar as there remains no possibility of total conceptual mediation, rather each phenomenon grasped is disclosed uniquely. Insofar as identity-thinking has damaged the pristine object of knowledge at hand, negative dialectics is an attempt to restore what was lost. Such restitutional justice happens by exploring thinking's roots in the preintellectual realm as well as by allowing "qualitative properties [to] start to emerge in the resonances of subjective experience."[46]

(3) The method of contemporary philosophical thinking can only serve in the capacity of self-critique. The project of trying to "grasp reality as a rational whole" is what leads Adorno to embrace this proposed version of neo-Hegelian dialectics.[47] The self-critical turn in dialectics, which he calls negative, is in response to philosophy's failure in directly accessing reality.[48] But negative should be understood as reaching into the chasm of nonbeing that might spawn new colors of illumination. In light of philosophy's failure to provide that illumination on both the practical and theoretical levels, its project must be restricted to self-criticism—for how else could philosophy remain faithful to its own concept?[49] The purpose of philosophy, Adorno reaffirms, is to align concept and actuality, spirit and reality,[50] such that any hope of revolution needs to be mitigated into the more gradual transformation that may arise through the path of thinking. This is the hopeless hopefulness for redemption, "the prism in which its color is caught,"[51] that still hovers on the horizon of Critical Theory.

Notwithstanding Adorno's critique of the reliance on intuition as a source of knowledge,[52] some of his most important writing and thinking were inspired by his own dream life. While in his exile of New York and Santa Monica, where he produced *Minima Moralia*, Adorno "claimed that he always noted down his dreams immediately after waking" and then "later selected a certain number of them for publication."[53] This willingness to draw on the imaginal as a deeper doorway into subjective desire allows the search for objective truth to be more clarified. I argue there remains uncharted territory of the imaginal that Adorno necessarily draws upon once negative dialectics is operative in thinking. It is possible to voyage into such uncharted territory to expand thinking if the shift from the rational to the supra-rational happens through the rigorous process of negative dialectics. What the negative turn in dialectics allows for is a necessary "decentering" of the knowing subject.[54] The tension in decentering implies that the subject no longer grasps itself as the center of reality regarding its conceptual constitution while at the same time this very loss allows for a new self-understanding from the outside. Seeing the world this way means there is a new clarity no longer obscured by the closed systematization mired in the mediation of concepts.[55] What is crucial in this negative turn in dialectics is a decentering of the subject to no longer be capable of rationally penetrating all of reality, thus allowing for a liberation from the compulsion of unifying all its knowledge. What emerges is a subject with access to a different kind of knowing. This knowing, which I refer to as supra-rational, stems from "all the stirrings of its senses triggered by the uncontrollable world of objects and events in an open and undifferentiated way."[56] In what follows, I explore some contours of that "uncharted" territory, that interworld between imagination and reality, known as the *imaginal.* Such an anchor in the rational is what allows the insight of the supra-rational to shine forth and illumine the preintellectual making possible thinking to undergo its necessary *in*volution.[57]

Opening to the Imaginal through the Negative in Adorno's Dialectics

Just as within the aniconic surface of Judaism[58] there remains a highly culti-vated formless iconic embodiment within its mystical layers, so too within the rationalism undergirding Adorno's neo-Hegelian dialectical process, there are other colors shining forth from the chasm of nonbeing. The formless embodiment is referred to as the *interworld* between imagination and reality or *imaginality.* In order to see how this imaginal realm emerges from the nega-tive turn in Adorno's dialectics, it is necessary to turn the imagination more generally. This is accomplished then by momentarily turning to the writings of Cornelius Castoriadis (1922–1997). By nuancing the distinction between first and second imagination,[59] the role and application of this emerging imaginality within Critical Thinking becomes possible.[60]

This same commitment to resisting thematization and ontologization con-verges with Adorno's negative turn in dialectics. What remains unexplored for Adorno in the depth of that turn is here referred to in Castoriadis as the "scandal of the imagination."

Whereas the radical imaginary is constantly catalyzing and transforming, the transcendental imagination lacks dynamism. Calling into question an indi-vidual's situatedness, there is an inevitable collapse as the transcendental imagination attempts imagining anything. The radical imaginary is battling against the Kantian legacy of an inert creative imagination. This stagnation leads to ontological limitation, unless thinking cultivates new by-paths that can arouse once again the first imagination. Continuing along the same path of these schema leads to reductionism and sublimation.[61] It is through the transformative ontological creativity that society gives birth to institutions as a real psychic desire.[62]

Harnessing the radical imaginary is crucial for the dialectical process to achieve its aims. Recall Adorno's demand for *second reflection* that continues the mediations of thinking to *second immediacy* and ultimately constructs a *second language*.[63] Once Critical Theory has taken this deeper dialectical turn through the negative, its resurfacing through the imaginal allows for a more immediate reflection in thinking that gives rise to a more vibrant language.

transition. ?

Liberating Poetic Desire: Hebrew Thinking after Adorno

If indeed for Adorno "metaphysics stands convicted of the crime of trans-figuration, which can no more be atoned and made amends for than the misery and suffering of the past,"[64] then how is it possible for a language of the first imagination itself as well as its enacted works to remain ineffable and inexplicable? Hovering beyond all ontologization and identity-thinking is what leaves the door open for that very "scandal of the imagination" that nourishes the radical imaginary.[65] There remains a nuanced interrelation between the twofold order of both the Greek imagination already explored in Castoriadis as well as the already explored Hebrew imagination.[66] To remain true to his calling as a critical thinker, Adorno is committed to rediscovering that very instant when rationality transcends its existent discourse from within.[67]

That possibility of self-transcendence, which avoids ontologization and identity-thinking is possible when the twofold nature of the Greek imagination is released and opened to that of the Hebrew imagination. Within the Hebrew imagination is a liberation from the dualism of the Greek imagination. Within the Hebrew language there is an indication of a deeper difference at play which then affects thinking. The Hebrew imagination is integrally embodied in the doubling of language, expressed by *hoshev mahashavot*. That doubling of the same upon itself leads to the very self-transcendence Adorno needs in thinking. Hebrew thinking is intrinsically imaginal as expressed in its root verb, *hsv*. What the Hebrew imagination then facilitates is an integral relationship between the inceptual roots of the imagination that spread forth into its conceptual branches. From the path of these inceptual roots there is the experience of a deeper poetics: the musicality of imagination.[68]

Musicality is embodied in song. The word *shir* in Hebrew is a wondrously diaphanous moment—at once both song and poem. Yet the song in its begin-ning [*bereishith*] is always a song of desire [*shir ta'av*].[69] This desire dwelling within the song emanates from the world of creatures yearning to reunite with their Creator through the singing of poems. Through an awareness of this diaphanous word, *shir*, recurrent motifs and archetypes can further reveal this imaginal realm within the designatory word itself.[70]

Words, however, may not be enough to convey the power of this experience of the interworld that nourishes the radical imaginary. Rather an image or a sound oftentimes contains a more direct experience of the supra-rational within this imaginal realm. The archetype of the imaginal is the angel. Angels vacillate between poetry and song. This most lucid recounting of the musicality of the imagination happens in Adorno's fragmentary journals on Beethoven. Like notes and musical phrases, angels are constantly fluttering *to and fro* but their only recognizable form is their temporal guise. It is instructive that the critical theorists draw from Adorno's willingness to engage that radical imaginary, as modeled in his reflections upon these unsaid angels. By delving into this realm as part and parcel of the negative dialectical process, what emerges is a powerful temporality of music, or what Adorno recovers as the metaphysics of musical time.[71]

The challenge in recovering the metaphysics of musical time remains accessing the imaginal realm. The perception in the philosophic world too often remains that the imagination cannot be trusted. Such a "scandal of the imagination" suggests a lingering perception of childhood which is immature and thus irrational. The act of recovering the imaginal then is that necessary recovery of a sublimated imaginality of childhood, a kind of "second naïveté,"[72] back into the realm of the thinking subject. Adorno reflects on this loss of the "extremely tender and subtle layer of inner subjectivity, of the spontaneous, and of the instinctive"[73] and his thinking displays a yearning to engage in its recovery and application to thinking. Continuing to cultivate this lost tenderness, as embodied in epistemic concerns, then allows for music to evince an abiding conviction that such remnants of the imaginality "can become 'a centre of power that stands against' its own societal and historical conditions of possibility."[74] This missed note needs to be recovered if such a metaphysics of musical temporality is to be heard once again. Recalling again Adorno's most prescient comment on the task of philosophy as "the prism in which its color is caught,"[75] in contrast to the previous "interworlds," there remains much work to be done on the revelatory colors of mystical imaginalities within Jewish Thinking. The correlation of angels, sounds, and colors all point to that fleeting instance of self-transcendence. This timeless instance reveals a deeper texture in its cycle of creation, dissolution, and resuscitation all taking place within a redemptive temporality that needs to be listened to so as to be seen.[76]

Chapter 2

From Thinking the Last God of Thought to the Limitless Poetic: Metaphysical Atheism between Thinking Poetry and Poetics of Alterity

God is dead! God remains dead!

—Nietzsche[1]

Whoever *believes* in God, therefore *cannot believe* in God. The possibility, for which the *divine name stands*, is held fast by those who do *not believe*.

—Adorno[2]

Imagining God after God: The Necessity of Metaphysical Atheism

Is it still possible to imagine God after God, from within such violent concatenations in thinking and experience? Does thinking need to undergo any transformation for a rapprochement with God, or god? Moreover, how is thinking to be thought and poetry envisioned in the time, place, and circumstance of such overwhelming demise? Is it possible to escape the paradox of a critique of thinking by thinking itself?[3] What about the reality of metaphysical atheism, in the wake of thinkers like Nietzsche and Adorno, might affect a thinking poetry and a poetics of alterity? These stand as our guiding questions.

To simply go on thinking as usual, in denial of the urgent metaphysical reality of the hour is a betrayal of the first order. There is no longer a place for categorical expositions in the form of pat theology if that form denies the reality of lived experience. Too often weak thinking and supernatural grace are masked beneath discussions of faith and belief rather than convictions, even if that faith is quest-driven.[4] Indeed there is a need for alternative narratives that expand the horizon of a given religion beyond its own borders,[5] but theology no longer seems capable of such a task.

Rather than articulate a "theology of our time," sincere theologians prefer a "theology for today in which the echoes and resonances of the tradition can be heard as fresh and powerful voice, able to help us live better when facing challenges and opportunities of the current age."[6] Sincere theology is nearly never critical enough. The problem is twofold: first, after Auschwitz, lived experience grounded in history cannot be denied its effect on thinking; secondly, invoking tradition in a post-traditional world does not necessarily inspire critical thinking. Regarding the latter claim on tradition, Adorno remarks: "Only that which inexorably denies tradition may once again retrieve it."[7] Namely, in order to move beyond its own entrenchment, naturalization, and nonreflexivity, a "critical approach to tradition"[8] requires a way of seeing and listening to the forgotten, to the dismissed—the "scars" of where preceding works misfired.[9] Regarding the former claim, ironically it is the Sages of the Talmud who already dared to understand just how much lived experience grounded in history needed to influence their theology, a lesson somehow forgotten by theologies for today.[10]

To rise again from the ashes of such deicide is to return to confront the razed limits of the limitless. But along the path of such a return, one must question whether it is possible for language, de facto delimited, to contain such a pronouncement over the Limitless?[11] Moreover, is it possible for those endowed with language to delimit spatial and temporal origins of the Limitless? What form of thinking, poetry or prayer might act as such a container to that which resists containment, to the Limitless delimited by the limiting of theism? Seeing that any strategy of immanent critique, after Adorno, cannot escape a transcendent demand,[12] the path becomes ever more treacherous. All the more so, considering references to religious categories like "the absolute," "God," and "meaning [*Sinn*]," Adorno necessarily swerves from pathways already traversed by Nietzsche.[13]

Such grounding questions will hover over the guiding questions of our *problèmatique*. This is a crossing of the boundaries of thought and poetry: a passing over and through boundaries wherein thought and poetry once reigned over a ground of origins [*ab-grund*] now derived from "being adrift" [*être en dérive*].[14] Our intention is to unveil comparative aspects of each origin, even with when its absence stands as presence, that provide the foundation for thought and poetry as well as the time, place, and circumstance of such a rapprochement with metaphysical atheism.

Correlating Religion and Philosophy: The Worlds of Bands and Restoration

However, to ground this *problèmatique*, a preliminary reflection on the correlation of Religion and Philosophy is in order. One index that always points to a wellspring of boundary crossing possibilities is Jewish Mystical Thinking. Already nascent within sixteenth-century Lurianic Kabbalah, there is a preliminary response to deicide. It is intimately linked to this grounding question of the container and what is contained vis-à-vis language as a delimitation of the Limitless. The creative consciousness that gives rise to both thinking and poetry dwells within the archetypal creativity that creates the worlds we inhabit. Two such worlds of consciousness stand in shining opposition: the World of Bands [*Olam ha-Akudim*] and the World of Restoration [*Olam ha-Tikkun*].[15] The former is the realm wherein the sparseness of words is able to contain a fecundity of expression, whereas the latter is the realm wherein a plethora of words is able to express a sparseness of ideas. Poetry is represented by the *Olam ha-Akudim*, akin to naïveté, whereas the Law is represented by the *Olam ha-Tikkun*, akin to a maturation whereby there is a loss of naïveté. The dialectic of these two realms echoes the earlier dialectic. It hovers beneath a grounding of the ground [*ab-grund*] while deriving existence from "being adrift" [*être en dérive*].[16] Allowing this dialectical tension to remain unsynthesized is a pathmark in Jewish Thinking, especially within its mystical branches, that will recur throughout the present investigation.

Adrift in Bands and Restoration: *Halakhah* and *Aggadah* Reconsidered

Regarding this tension between World of Bands [*Olam ha-Akudim*] and World of Restoration [*Olam ha-Tikkun*], much insight is to be gleaned from a tangential remark of French Jewish thinker Emmanuel Lévinas (1906–1995). Granted Lévinas rallies against the dangers of mysticism and *extasis* in his ongoing critique of German philosopher, Martin Heidegger (1889–1976), we draw on the following general remark and extrapolate it for the purposes of correlating Philosophy and Religion in general. In relation to this dialectical tension between worlds which parallels the dichotomy of *Halakhah* (way of the Law) and *Aggadah* (way of the Lore), Lévinas explains how this tension is endemic to Philosophy (akin to *Aggadah*) in its correlation to Religion (akin to *Halakhah*). Remarking on this seeming tangential correlation within a Talmudic elucidation, Lévinas remarks:

> I do not regret having brought together philosophy and religion in my preceding sentence. Philosophy for me derives [*dérive*] from religion. It is called into being by a religion adrift, and probably religion is always adrift [*est en dérive*].[17]

Let us listen further to what it means to be adrift. If something is adrift, like a boat, for instance, it is not anchored at bay or stabilized at shore. Any attempt to anchor or steer its path is counterproductive to the directionality of its over-whelming flow. Yet, only when Religion unmoored meanders along its path can it provide Philosophy with the factical material from which its inquiry might begin. The brilliant play on the word *dériver*—which literally means to alter a path upon the riverbed's course—stems from a realization that Philosophy exists only insofar as it derives from [*dériver de*] Religion's stream, which itself is intrinsically adrift [*est en dérive*].[18] Our extrapolation of Lévinas' comment then sets the stage for this negative dialectic, as well as for further reflection upon wandering and exile.

The dialectal tension that Adorno resuscitates in his metaphysical atheism is both alarming and reassuring. Alarming, because it leaves us seemingly unmoored, but reassuring because it dares to speak the truth. When Adorno decries that "Whoever *believes* in God, therefore *cannot believe* in God," the thinker is confronting the reality that after Auschwitz, any pretense at continuing the same metaphysical speculations removed from experience is inauthentic. Yet an authentic yearning still breaths through the embers of that "possibility, for which the divine name stands, is held fast by those who *do not believe*."[19] By daring to proffer a metaphysical atheism after such deicide, Adorno is opening a negative dialectic *par excellence* to explore anew the possibility of thinking, saying, and even praying after Auschwitz. Just as negative dialectics demands a deeper self-reflection through a thinking *against thought*, so too must there be a praying *against prayer*. The implications of making space for such a "minimal theology" amidst a necessary metaphysical atheism will be addressed within the course of this altered stream.

Thinking Poetics and Poetic En-Thinking:
Heidegger and Célan Reconsidered

Such a dialect invites a further tension to be explored between a thinking poetics of the *Denker* and a poetic en-thinking of the *Dichter*. Both the thinker, or *Denker*, Martin Heidegger (1889–1976), and the poet, or *Dichter*, Paul Célan (1920–1970), each carve out a unique path to address and redress this dialectic. What is remarkable about the seeming disparity between Heidegger and Célan is the degree to which the thinker cannot restrain from entering into the poetic realm while the poet straddles the precipice of thinking. Withdrawal and refusal as well as exile become key gestures that both the thinker and the poet will draw upon to redress the tension and envision anew from within the dialectical poles of Philosophy and Religion.

The task of Heidegger as *Denker* in *Contributions to Philosophy* is to recover the thread of the guiding question that shapes Western philosophy.[20] This is a recovery from Platonic and Cartesian identity-thinking whereby "identity becomes the essential determination of a being as such."[21] When "thinking becomes *I*-Think"[22] insofar as it remains "fore-grasping and unifying, thinking then posits the unity of what it encounters. Thus thinking lets what it encounters be encountered as a being."[23] This is precisely how a being becomes an object and ontology is flattened into identity-thinking. The cloud of identity-thinking that obscures the guiding question of Western philosophy further obstructs the light of its guiding thread. This clouding occurs when knowing as self-knowing is the utmost identity. As such, it is possible for a being at the same time to condition every other objectness in its manner of knowing. What is other to the "I" then is itself determined as manifest spirit. Ultimately identity is lifted up into the absoluteness of indifference, as opposed to mere emptiness.[24] However, that emptiness sought to be restored by the thinker is first and foremost vis-à-vis divine absence.

The guiding thread of this pathmark to inceptual thinking is clarified by way of the Hölderlin-Kierkegaard-Nietzsche triad proffered by Heidegger. It is no coincidence that "these three, who each in his own way, in the end suffered profoundly the uprooting to which Western History is being driven and who at the same time intimated their gods most intimately—that these three had to depart from the brilliance of their days prematurely."[25] In intimating their god most intimately, these two thinkers and one poet take leave of their living luminescence before their time. What is remarkable here is how Heidegger first of all effectively sees no distinction between thinker and poet—each is of equal influence within the given triad. To be a thinker of truth, one must enter this triad by way of the turn [*kehre*] away from philosophical thought toward poetry. Moreover, the existences of each of those who "intimate their gods most intimately"[26] are all profoundly marked by withdrawal, refusal, and exile. Such a thinking poetics can only take place in exile. Just as such a thinking poetics takes place in exile, so in turn is this reflective of an intimated withdrawal of their personal, immanent god.

The investigation at hand draws upon this spatial, temporal, and circumstantial insight that exile reveals and its effect on thought and poetry. As *Denker*, Heidegger goes one step further. Although we began our remarks with the call "to rise again from the ashes of deicide"—Nietzsche's death toll for the god of Western Civilization—this thinker was the last one of the Hölderlin-Kierkegaard-Nietzsche triad. There is an obscured guiding thread intrinsic to Heidegger's own thinking amidst the ashes by way of his triad. This thread of the guiding question is recovered by "the one who poeticized the furthest ahead."[27] Only by returning to the first, the one who intimated God most intimately—whereby "Holy names are lacking" [*es fehlen hielige Namen*][28]—is it possible to come to terms with the ashen thought of the last. It is this one, "the last which not only needs the longest forerunning but also itself is not the ceasing, but the deepest beginning, which reaches out the furthest and catches up with itself with the greatest difficulty."[29] The difficulty that Nietzschean thought confronts is its inability to catch up with its deepest beginnings residing in the poetic thought of Hölderlin. This triad in effect revolves as an inextricable link between poetry and thinking.

This inextricable link between poetry and thinking is deepened in returning to the response of Heidegger to Nietzsche's opening parable of the madman. In the last section of Contributions (VII), Heidegger delineates the guiding thread of deicide's deepest beginning as its guiding question, enumerated as follows: (253) The last; (254) Refusal; (255) Turning in enowning; (256) The last god. This pathmark in Heidegger's thinking parallels the aforementioned triad in the encircling of inception. Only once the inception of the last is understood within the triad of those who intimated their gods most intimately can there be any appreciation of the last god. Integral to understanding this thinking is to see how interwoven within the warp and woof of this guiding thread is the thought that:

> The last god is not an end but rather the beginning as it resonates unto and in-itself and thus the highest shape of not-granting, since the inceptual withdraws from all holding-fast and holds sway only in towering over all of that which as what is to come is already seized within the inceptual—and is delivered up to its [the inceptual's] determining power.[30]

What is at stake is not just the hold these spatial and temporal categories exude upon thought, but the circumstance of exile, of being "torn away" from origins which underlies such thinking. This circumstance and its calling both form much of the ground, albeit veiled, which ground thinking's spatio-temporal relationality:

> The end is only where a being has torn itself away from the truth of be-ing and has denied every question-worthiness, and that means every differentiating, in order to comport itself in endless time within endless possibilities of what is thus torn away.[31]

This end, in its finality and closure is differentiated from the encircling interplay of the last and the first. It is evident that just as our exploration began with the last of the triad (i.e. Nietzsche), this marking along the spatio-temporal continuum is only last in relation to the first (i.e. Hölderlin), that is, "the one who poeticized the furthest ahead."[32] The problem with conceptual thinking is that it falls into the trap of identity-thinking whereby "the end is unceasing *etcetera* from which the beginning and long since the *last* as the most inceptual has withdrawn."[33] In contrast, the inceptual thinking now being proffered reveals in concealing, grounds in passing over:

> God no longer appears either in the "personal" or in the "lived experience" of the masses but solely in the "space" of be-ing itself—a space which is held to abground.[34]

All the while "standing in the remotest remoteness to the passing of god,"[35] one must reorient and prepare anew for the "colliding of god and man in the midpoint of being."[36] It is this existential collision—later developed into a gathering of the fourfold[37]—that stands for the *Denker* as the task of thinking.

Yet to think thought in truth is a daunting, if not elusive task for the *Denker*. For thinking poetically is the task of "the one who poeticized furthest ahead."[38] Such a path is demarcated by Heidegger's elucidation of Hölderlin, revealing the truth that: "[t]o be a poet in destitute time means: to attend, singing, to the trace of the fugitive gods."[39] The *Denker* must inevitably make the turn [*kehre*] so as to envision once again the:

> lightning of being which has reached its characteristic shape as the realm of Western Metaphysics in its self-completion. Hölderlin's thinking poetry has had a share in giving it shape to this realm of poetic thinking.[40]

Again, it is the poet whose poetic statements in their ownmost saying provide the guidance, albeit veiled, along the path of thinking. For the *Denker* already realizes that "the poetic character of thinking is still veiled over . . . but poetry that thinks is in truth the topology of being."[41] Once attuned to the power of a thinking poetry, a more poetic thinking is then possible. It is precisely such an attunement being delimited here with the "last god." Given the lack of attunement to our being-toward-death [*Sein-zum-Tode*][42] "how are we then ever going to be primed for the rare hint of the last god?"[43] In attuning to this:

> time-space of decision of the light and arrival of gods, one or the other either futurizes determining the growing awaiting or enopens a completely other time-space for the first grounded truth of be-ing, also known as enowning.[44]

To be ready for this glimmer of the last requires what remains in the offing to be futurized. The other possibility is a further rupture in the temporal-spatial realm, whereby another realm opens from its interiority to reveal the concealed origin which grounds be-ing's truth. The move beyond Being to original be-ing parallels the movement away from God to the original gods. What Heidegger means by Enowning [*Ereignis*] is an enabling of an unpossessive owning, a movement all the way into without holding onto.[45] The welling up of meaning— both unpossessive and of nonidentity that takes place in Enowning [*Ereignis*]— is crucial to understanding Heidegger's "last god." In passing over all the way into and through, this unpossessive owning has no appropriatable content. Whereas the identity of "God" has seen its demise in its overwhelming appropriation and distortion of content, the unpossessive owning of the "last god" begins by being emptied of any such appropriatable content. In this sense, the "last god" passes over both identity and concept, toward emptiness.

Enowning: Adrift in Recovering the "Last God"

Part of the radical recovery in and through the "last god" is a relinquishing of owning this god in terms of form or content. Its meaning is experienced both in and of its passing through. Enowning demands a refusal to owning by way of appropriatable content. This experience of god is the last insofar as it marks the primordially eternal moment before the coming of Being from its origin in be-ing. Yet again here we have Heidegger's unique attempt in coming to terms with the Christian notion of the *parousia*. What is at stake in Heidegger's reading of the *parousia* is how this temporal index enopens to "just what is different in the Christian experience of life."[46] Whereas its Jewish-Greek (i.e. Septuagint) meaning deals with the "advent of the Lord at the Day of Judgement," in late Judaism, it means "the advent of the Messiah as God's representative."[47] What Heidegger's rereading of the *First Letter of Paul to the Thessalonians* in this 1920–1921 lecture seeks to elucidate then is why the Christian meaning of *parousia* means the second coming of the Messiah who has already appeared. Moreover, of what consequence is this second coming of the already appeared to the experience of existence, of *Da-sein*?

> One might suppose at first the basic stance towards the *parousia* would be to await it, and that Christian hope would be one special case of that. But this would be entirely wrong! Never through a mere analysis of the consciousness of a future event would we come upon the meaning of the *parousia* in its relationship to ourselves. The structure of Christian hope—which in truth is nothing but a "meaning-relationship" towards the *parousia*—is radically different from all awaiting. Time and seasons (5:1, always mentioned together) present a particular problem for explication. If the "When" were grasped as belonging to an "objective" time that we represent, it would not be understood in its primordial sense. Nor does it belong to the time of "factical life" in the fallen, average non-Christian sense. Paul does not tell them of a "when," because such an expression would not be adequate to what needed saying; it would not suffice.[48]
>
> The answer that Paul gives to the question about "When?" of the *parousia* is therefore a challenge, to keep awake and to be sober. Here is a pointed allusion to enthusiasm, against the restless curiosity of those who pursue such questions as the "When?" of the *parousia*, and who speculate about it. They fuss about the "When" and the "What," how it will be objectively; they take no authentic personal interest in it. They remain stuck in what is wordly.[49]

As Heidegger searches deeper for the pre-Christian (i.e. unsaid Jewish) content of basic theological concepts like hope, there comes the gesture of refusal, so intimately linked to the exile of God by the gods. Whereas an end is only that closing moment when a being has torn itself away from truth, the last withdraws from the bounds of inceptual thinking itself, allowing the possibility of hope to remain. Refusal of identity-thinking is the first moment in the course of this withdrawal. It is that moment yearning to be recovered by way of temporal attunement, whereby:

> [r]efusal is the highest nobility of gifting and the basic thrust of self-sheltering-concealing, revelation [*Offenbarkeit*] of which makes up the originary essential sway of the truth of be-ing. Only thus does be-ing become estranging itself, the stillness of the passing of the last god.[50]

Within this truth of be-ing as refusal dwells the futural of ensuing greatness. An abandonment by being remains so that this truth of be-ing, through its refusal, belongs to this masking of what is not-being. Not be-ing is the unboundedness and dissipation of be-ing. Such unboundedness and dissipation within be-ing brings forth the presence amidst its absence; by extension, amidst the ashes of the divine dwells the presence of the last god.

Codirection: From Religion and Philosophy to Phenomenology and Theology

These reflections of the *Denker* upon the first God and the last god provide a critical response to the proclamation of Nietzsche's "madman" that god is dead! Moreover, such a response opens again the possibility of reflections on Religion within the realm of Philosophy. The terms of engagement in Heidegger's discourse, however, early on take one step away from the broader concepts of Philosophy and Religion to demarcate a niche of Phenomenology and Theology.[51] When philosophy is working through its ontological faculty, it opens itself to the possibility of being "employed by theology as a corrective," insofar as theology can be codirective of the "factical with respect to the facticity of faith."[52] Phenomenology is merely the procedure whereby *Da-sein* is able to recover the prior moment of faith's facticity.[53] The primary direction or derivation of existence from faith's facticity is possible through the codirection of ontology. Such ontological codirection allows for the existential dimension of faith to arise out of it and to present itself within it.[54] Heidegger distills his ground within the correlation of Phenomenology and Theology in the following way:

> Philosophy is the possible, formally indirect ontological corrective of the ontic and, in particular, of the pre-Christian content of basic theological concepts. But philosophy can be what it is without functioning factically as this corrective.[55]

As regards the grounding of our *problèmatique*, it is instructive to take note of the "Addition to the Pointers," wherein Heidegger's shift into poetics from Theology and Phenomenology is more apparent:

> Poetic saying is "*DaSein*," existence. This word, "*DaSein*," is used here in the traditional metaphysical sense. It signifies: presence.
>   Poetic thinking is being in the presence of . . . and for the god. Presence means: simple willingness that wills nothing, counts on no successful outcome. Being in the presence of . . . : purely letting the god's presence be said.[56]

An earlier pre-Christian aroma of presencing that arises out of, and presents itself within, the intrinsically Jewish theological overflow, here returns from within the ontological realm. However, the site of this return that presences is now within a poetic thinking. The development of Heidegger's thinking from the time of this early essay betrays the growing inadequacy of the categories of Philosophy and Religion in general, as well as Phenomenology and Theology in particular. This shift or sharp turn [*Kehre*] in his thinking toward poetics is most apparent in hybrid works that attempt to unearth the poetic within thinking. The prelude and reprise of "The Thinker as Poet" [*Aus der Erfahrung des Denkens*] (1947), for instance, are comprised of two terse stanzas, which then open to a series of ten further fragments. These fragmented stanzas are then followed by a commentary (on the opposite page in the German edition), reflective of an inner thinking concealed within the revealed poem itself and significant in its post-Auschwitz context. Consider the refusal to submit to conventional categories of genre within the first section of this hybrid work:

> When the early morning light quietly
> Grows above the mountains . . .
>
>   The world's darkening never reaches
>   to the light of Being [*des Seyns*].
>
>   We are too late for the gods [*die Götter*] and too
>   early for Being [*das Seyn*]. Being's poem,
>   just begun, is man.
>
>   To head toward a star [*einen Stern*]—this only.
>
>   To think [*denken*] is to confine yourself to a
>   single thought that one day stands
>   still like a star in the world's sky.[57]

This refusal of genre, bespeaks a withdrawal from thinking proper while only entering into the realm of poetry in a fragmented way. Is it possible for this seeming shorthand thinking, however, to be deemed poetry? Or is there a certain *poiesis* dwelling within the refusal of such thinking in truth as it resists poetry *per se*?

Heeding the Hidden Star: Turning to Poetry

As the thinker in truth inevitably makes the turn [*kehre*] toward poetry, one realizes what poets are for. Only poets are capable of envisioning the truths which thought cannot contain. The multiplicity, which concepts cannot contain, is liberated by the realm of words. The constellation of the poem welcomes words to find their dwelling place. Thus, to truly enter into the realm of the poetic, Célan, the *Dichter* considers the act of poetic thinking to be deserving of a poet's reflection. His poem, *Todtnauberg* is but one example of a reflective response of the *Dichter* alongside the *Denker*. In contradistinction to Heidegger's aforecited call: "To head toward a star—this only," Célan poetically hovers round the ashen star in his own poem. An apparently hypostatic icon for the thinker can still yield its multiplicity as a living memory of the symbol for the poet. Whereas for the thinker:

> To think is to confine yourself to a
> Single thought that one day stands
> Still like a star in the world's sky.[58]

For the poet, reality is one of withdrawal, a revealed concealment, rather than a confinement to a single thought. This confinement to a single thought— the hypostasis of the constellation—bespeaks the larger movement toward an ontological recovery of Being. When a solitary thought is privileged above others in its standing, "Still like a star in the world's sky," the possibility of the plurality of beings is arrested and effaced. In the sharpest contrast, consider how the poet sees the selfsame star:

> Arnica, Eyebright, the
> drink from the well with the
> star-die on top,[59]

This star—perhaps adorning the spring itself[60] or seen from an intimate distance as the sky reflected upon the water—is envisioned through a perspective of multifarious reflectivity, not merely as *die Stern* but as "star-die on top" [*Sternwürfel drauf*]. While singular from its normally paired form as dice, even in its iconicity as a die, its multifaceted nature still resonates. While this icon can serve the gods, it can also give way to the experience of beings within God's constellation. Even by way of the seeming singularity in which the thinker presents it, in approaching the thinker's hut, the poet only sees the Limitless within such a given delimitation. This likeness of the star to the die is inter-twined with all creatures, including its surrounding vegetation. Seeing the breath of life in every creature, in this case for instance, is what makes Célan's poetry pneumatically rather than thematically Jewish. Yet as the singularity of thought requiring a delimitation of the Limitless persists, the poetic statement liberates an envisioning through what Adorno termed the "constellation."[61] For the poet, the breath of every living word is a *mise-en-abîme éclatée.*[62] Gadamer's elucidation of this promenade that treads over the "log-/paths in the high moor," is of the *Stübenwasen:* "forest sward, unleveled,/orchis and orchis, singly," symbolizing the unleveled path trodden by "thinkers or us who are thinking" remains most illuminating.[63] This elucidation opens up the symbolic landscape, wherein every experience reveals its shards of the Limitless adrift from the symbol itself. Unlike the rigid lexicons of Romantic landscapes and their fixed symbolic meanings, in Célan's poetry the symbol and the experience sym-bolizing it are intimately intertwined, and limitlessly adrift in a sea of meanings and trauma.

Inevitably the thinker succumbs to the delimited nature of thought in relation to the limitless facets of the poetic statement. In his opening poetic fragment, the *Denker* draws our attention to this admission by way of meandering:

When the cowbells keep tinkling from
the slopes of the mountain valley
where the herds wander slowly . . .

    The poetic character of thinking [*Dichtungscharakter des enkens*]
        is still veiled over.

    Where it shows itself, it is for a
        long time like the utopism of
        a half-poetic [*halbpoetischen*] intellect.

    But poetry that thinks [*das denkende Dichten*] is in truth
        the topology of Being [*des Seyns*].

    This topology tells Being the
        whereabouts of its actual
        presence.[64]

What is salient to the thinker here is not poetry per se, but the "poetic character of thinking," albeit veiled over. To recover such a "poetry that thinks" is akin to founding anew the foundation of Being. The presencing of Being is only possible through the knowledge intrinsic to a monolithic topology. Whereas the thinker is mapping out a destination amidst the wandering, it is the poet who envisions the constellation through poetic reflection. In the wake of the madman in the opening parable decrying: "God is dead [*Gott ist todt*]! God remains dead [*Gott bleibt todt*]!" here the thinker seeks a presencing of Being that is excised from the decomposing God.

Weeping Eyebright Exile: God is Dead, Long Live God!

The poet encounters the thinker already dwelling within the place named **Todt**nauberg—a site built upon the ruins of "God is dead" [*Gott ist **todt***] engendered by a being-toward-death [*Sein-zum-**Tode***]. Amidst this decomposition are signs of life sprouting forth. The first things that spring into the poet's line of vision are Arnica and Eyebright. Both symbols are native healing herbs growing wild in these high mountains of the Black Forest, as Gadamer has remarked. However, the poet is more than an observer of nature, seeing that both plants are intimately related to the restoration of vision.

Vision is crucial to poetic envisioning. Arnica or Leopard's Bane is a curative before and after traumatic shock, providing a path to recovery from dreams of mutilated bodies. Such horrific anxiety forever marks the imaginality of a *Shoah* survivor like Celan. This vigilance in keeping the eyes open[65] comes in the face of unbearable pain that is incessantly recalled in seeing reality. But those eyes that are unable to see such unbearable suffering within the world of beings could be said to be blind. This is where Eyebright or Euphrasia functions as a curative for diseases affecting sight.[66] What Eyebright addresses is the frequent inclination to blink as the lids burn and swell, while the eyes water incessantly.[67] This seemingly innocuous Black Forest herb conceals and salves a limitless weeping, second only to the wailing of that indwelling within godhead itself, the *Shekhinah* (Presence), in incessant exile. This weeping to the point of becoming eyeless concatenates in the Zoharic parable proffered by the old man to Rabbis Hiyya and Jose as a riddle: "Who is a ravishing maiden without eyes, her body concealed and revealed?"[68] The source of speech-thinking [*Sprachdenken*] is this ravishing maiden, the *Shekhinah* [Presence] hovering in incessant exile.

Hope Not Yet *De-Eyed*: Seeing in Truth

While there are a myriad of beings who have eyes and see, still many of this myriad move through the world veiled by blindness. Is the poet who is "not yet/de-eyed" [*noch nicht/entaügt*] then proffering that this blindness is a function of thinking? The poet, like the prophet, cries out to circumcise the eyes from their blindness to dwell in the purity of envisioning. If the myriad of beings that act to presence a Presence into the world is de-eyed, then what hope is left for thinking to envision? In the face of this blinding, traumatic decomposition of the divine within existence, the poet still envisions the possibility of:

> A hope, today,
> for a thinker's
> (un-
> delayed coming)
> word
> in the heart,[69]

While the meaning of this hope resists delimitation, its yearning is for the redemption of thinking that has remained so blind, so de-eyed to truth. While the thinker can claim: "But poetry that thinks is in truth/the topology of Being," only the poet can decry such a sacrifice of truths for the sake of ontologizing a singular truth. The hope is for a return to the plurality of effaced beings, upon which the *ab-grund* of Being is grounded. For the poet, there is still the hope of redressing the excision of God from Being by restoring the indwelling of beings within God.

But there is more that encircles the restoration of this divine indwelling within beings. For Celan, the revelation dwells in the circularity of language itself. The poem is an encounter along the impossible path toward truths, as he proffers in his remarks regarding the meridian:

> I find something that binds and that leads to encounter, like a poem.
> I find something—like language [*die Sprache*]—immaterial yet earthly, terrestrial, something circular [*etwas Kreisförmiges*], returning upon itself [*selbst Zurückkehrendes*] by way of both poles and thereby—happily—even crossing tropics (and tropes): I find . . . a meridian.[70]

Meridian: Crossing Over into Imaginality

This crossing over of the delimitations posed by tropics and tropes in the imaginal mappings of our existence is the task of the Hebrew Poet as an *'ivri* or boundary crosser. What rumbles in its unleveling experience alongside the path of thinking trodden with the thinker in the poem *Taudtnauberg* is opened to the limitlessness constellation of *der Meridian*. Why is this symbol of the meridian so crucial to the poetic experience of thinking for the poet? How might the poetics of the meridian affect a decomposed thought to renew into thinking?

In conjuring the meridian, Celan is drawing upon an imaginal symbol par excellence, rooted somewhere between existence and the imagination.

A meridian is an imaginary line joining the north and south points of the horizon, passing directly through the zenith. It thus acts, in its imaginal capacity, as a reference line for a transit. The transit is the shadow emitted by the satellites of the constellation. It traces the passage of a celestial body or a point on the celestial sphere across the meridian of an observer,[71] namely, the one who dares envisioning. At the time of transit or passage, the point on the celestial sphere must be at its highest point in the sky. It is at this very point of passing over for Celan, there is an incessant turn away from the language of thinking; a re-turn to language of words that brings forth the possibility of envisioning. The poet takes leave of the earlier unleveled path of thinkers heading toward its unity of the fourfold. From the conceptual time-space thinking of the thinker—the veritable site unifying the fourfold[72]—Celan's turn [*kehre*] is away from such a singular interrelation with beings in the world. Rather the poet's relation to the poem is more of a re-turn [*heim-kehren*] to the elemental nature of its letters that bring forth the beauty of words. It is this re-turn [*heim-kehren*] into the constellation of the meridian that opens itself as a by-path lost to the thinker:

> Then does one, in thinking of poems, does one walk such paths with poems? Are these paths only By-Paths [*Um-Wege*], bypaths [*Umwege*], from thou to thou? Yet at the same time, among how many other paths [*Wege*], they're also paths on which language get a voice, they are encounters, paths of a voice to a perceiving Thou, creaturely bypaths [*kreatürliche Umwege*], sketches of existence perhaps, a sending oneself ahead toward oneself, in search of oneself . . . A kind of homecoming [*Eine Art Heimkehr*].[73]

Eine Art Heimkehr is not merely a homecoming, but really refers to the by-path away from thought, namely the re-turn [*heim-kehren*] within poetry rather than the turn [*kehre*] away from thought. Recall that as *Denker*, Heidegger seeks the pre-Christian content of basic theological concepts of hope and the *parousia* to measure out the collision of the "last god" and the human in the midpoint of being; by contrast, as *Dichter*, Celan seeks a re-turn [*heim-kehren*] or *teshuva* to dialogue from the self, whereby:

> It was . . . myself I encountered. . . .
> I also seek—for I'm back again where I began—the place of my own origin [*eigenen Herkunft*].
> I am seeking all of what with an inexact finger because uneasy finger on the map—on a children's map, I must admit.
> None of these places [*dieser Orte*] is to be found, they do not exist, but I know where, especially now, they would have to exist, and . . . I find something![74]

A Creaturely Bypath: Turning to the Communal
Constellation of beings

To take leave of this By-Path [*Um-Wege*] seeking a re-turn [*heim-kehren*] or *teshuva* to the creaturely bypath is the Jewish content that founds a basic theological experience of exile. Being at home is to be in "the place of non-place" or *'attar d'lo 'attar* in Lurianic discourse. Yet being in "the place of non-place" is only possible once one has passed over and broken through the reality of "the place of un-being" or *'attar d'lo havai*.[75] These pre-ontological gestures take place within the intimate constellation of community.

Moreover, when moral conscience is "affected to its marrow [*atteinte dans sa moelle*]," the by-path [*Um-Wege*] is then re-oriented toward the constellation of the "objective order of the community to obtain this intimacy of deliverance [*cette intimité de la délivrance*]."[76] The set point in time, within the temporal meridian of Sabbaths, is the Sabbath of Sabbaths—the Day of At-onement. This center of centers—the true indwelling of exile—is forever enopening to the needs of "the damaged moral conscience to reach its intimacy and reconquer the integrity that no one can reconquer for it."[77] This dialectic of the intimate collective of beings maps out the constellation—"the place of un-being" or *'attar d'lo havai*—from whence the poet envisions the poem to re-turn [*heim-kehren*]:

> A poem—under what conditions!—becomes the poem of someone (ever yet) [*immer noch*] perceiving, facing phenomena, questioning and addressing these phenomena; it becomes dialogue [*Gespräch*]—often despairing dialogue.
>
> What is addressed takes shape only in the space of this dialogue, gathers around the I addressing and naming it. But what's addressed and has now become a Thou [*Du*] through naming, as it were, also brings along its otherness [*Anderssein mit*] into this present. Even a poem's here and now [*Hier und Jetzt*]—the poem itself really has only this one, unique, momentary present [*punktuelle Gegenwart*]—even in this immediacy and nearness it lets the Other's ownmost quality speak [*dem Anderen, Eigenste mitsprechen*]: its time [*dessen Zeit*].[78]

The possibility of the bypath of re-turn [*heim-kehren*] or *teshuva* that opens through the poem is derived from true discernment or *Binah* of the momentary present [*punktuelle Gegenwort*].[79] At this temporal incursion into the poem's temporality, the presencing of Presence opens in its everlasting ground through this discernment,[80] as seen in the verse "This shall be an everlasting statute for you [to make atonement for the Israelites because of all their sins once a year]" (Lev. 16.34). But re-turn [*heim-kehren*] or *teshuva* is prominent the moment its wholeness is broken into, peeling forth a meridian of ten days.[81] This encircled time is dedicated to self-restoration through attunement to alterity's temporality. Face-to-face with this alterity through the very words and their time within the poem, the cavity once filled with ground, foundation, and splendor is ruptured.[82]

To Pray *after Prayer*: Restoration through Metaphysical Atheism

Recalling then how that rupture was confronted at the opening of our reflections through Adorno's metaphysical atheism, it is now time to return to the unanswered challenge of whether prayerful poetry or even prayer itself is still possible. Adorno is challenging Wittgenstein's logical poem which closes the *Tractatus*, "Of that which one cannot know [*sprechen*], it is best to remain silent [*schweigen*]"[83] by repealing his own original *Bilderverbot* argument for silencing poetry in imagining Utopia after Auschwitz. Not only does Adorno repeal past thought but he is willing to rethink his *Bilderverbot* argument in *Negative Dialectics*, admitting that, "[o]ur metaphysical faculty is paralyzed because actual events have shattered the basis on which speculative metaphysical thought could be reconciled with experience."[84] Adorno's declaration that after Auschwitz metaphysics is no longer the same and thus more self-reflection on thinking is demanded, means "that thinking must, nowadays at any rate, in order to be true, also *think against itself*. If it does not measure itself by the extremity, which flees from the concept, then it is cast in advance in the same mold as the musical accompaniment, with which the SS was wont to drown out the cries of their victims."[85] Contemporary Jewish Thinking lapses into identity-thinking, no matter how eloquent its musicality, unable to flee the concept. Moreover, there is an unwillingness to apply negative dialectical thinking to Judaism in the Diaspora or in Israel.[86] But the deeper dilemma remains, namely, how to escape the paradox of "a critique of thinking by thinking itself;"[87] can poetry or prayer escape that paradox?

To be truly ready to think and pray with an "open-endedness of the future" with respect to what is possible[88] means confronting the metaphysical atheism necessarily articulated by Adorno.[89] Recall the metaphysical atheism as captured succinctly by Adorno in *Negative Dialectics*: "Whoever *believes* in God, therefore *cannot believe* in God. The possibility, for which the divine name stands, is held fast by those who *do not believe*." What is necessarily confronted in the Diaspora through Adorno's thinking, for example, continues to elude Jewish thinkers in Israel who remain paralyzed by the hegemony of a theology[90] which makes a causal link from Auschwitz and the rebirth of Israel. The inability and unwillingness of thinkers in Israel (as well as in much of the Diaspora)[91] to formulate what Hent de Vries calls a "minimal theology"[92]—any speculative metaphysical thought that is true to contemporary secular experience—gives birth to lamentable realities and devastating lapses into identity-thinking.[93]

Prayer *against Prayer*: Redemption from Rote Thinking Ensaring Prayer

Prayer should be on the minds and hearts of every caring, thinking, and prayerful being, Jewish or other, around the world. Daring to apply Adorno's metaphysical atheism to Jewish Thinking could inspire the true prayer that dares praying *against itself,* no longer asphyxiated by the hegemonic thinking, which may then just bring Judaism, Jerusalem and its people one step closer to redeeming itself *from itself.* How? In Auschwitz, God was tried for crimes against humanity, pronounced guilty (i.e. conceptually dead) as a prelude to the afternoon prayers.[94] It is this very daring to pray *against prayer* and its presumptions *that will open the bypath.*

In opening to the discernment of language that takes time—from one letter to the next—words in their alterity come forth in dialogue [*Gespräch*]. In the immediacy of a poem's "here and now" [*Hier und Jetzt*], the Other's ownmost quality speaks [*dem Anderen, Eigenste mitsprechen*]. Whatever is discerned to be spoken in the poem is its time [*dessen Zeit*]. This dialectic of discernment within the intimate collective of beings then maps out the constellation wherein words come to dialogue in their ownmost alterity as letters. Whereas for the *Denker,* language *is the house of being,* by contrast, here for the *Dichter,* the alterity of letters composing words opens up the dialogical *temporality between beings.* The prayerful poem is forever taking place as it discerns the grounding of each letter's temporal alterity. The temporality that takes place is the temporality of re-turn [*heim-kehren*] to a wholeness already ruptured. This is the hope for a time of discerning restoration. It is that eternal prayerful moment *against rote prayer* for the indwelling of beings within god, by way of re-turn [*heim-kehren*] to creaturely bypaths [*kreatürliche Umwege*].

Chapter 3

Thinking of Redemption/Redemption of Thinking: Toward a Metaphysics of Musical Temporality

The messiah will come only when he is *no longer necessary*; he will come only on the *day after his arrival*; he will come, not on the last day, but on the *very last.*

—Franz Kafka[1]

Thus in Judaism the Messianic idea has compelled a *life lived in deferment,* in which nothing can be done definitively, nothing can be irrevocably accomplished. One may say, perhaps, the Messianic idea is the *real anti-existentialist idea.*

—Gershom Scholem[2]

. . . the sound of *disappearance* . . . says more of the *hope of return* than would any general reflection on the essence of the *fleetingly enduring* sound.

—Theodor Adorno[3]

From the Death of Philosophy to Recuperating a Fallen Metaphysics

Despite itself, philosophy outlives its own death; so its afterlife imbues the contemporary moment. But what unknown remains to be known through the hegemony of knowledge, what thinking remains to be thought? After the demise of a more Utopian strand of dialectics already within the Hegel's philosophy of history, or within Heidegger's onto-theology, is there still a redemptive purpose or even a possibility of dialectics, or even of philosophy? Within the Frankfurt School, the voice of Adorno cries out from the void:

> Philosophy, which once seemed outmoded, remains alive because the moment of its realization was missed. The summary judgment that it had merely interpreted the world is itself crippled by resignation before reality, and becomes a defeatism of reason after the transformation of the world failed.[1]

With the passing of each redemptive moment, realizing a Utopian vision of the inner world seems more and more absurd. Recuperation of these missed moments may however begin with the musical thinkers as artists to whom we must turn for a rekindling of the flickering flame of Thinking.

This crucial questioning of Thinking is the question par excellence of the contemporary moment. The formulation of Franz Rosenzweig's "New Thinking" [*Das Neue Denken*] in October of 1925 is an underlying correlation which will inform the framework of our investigation. Rosenzweig correlates the need for time *vis-à-vis* the temporality of the thinker:

> The *thinker* plainly knows his thoughts in advance; that he "expresses" [*ausspricht*] them is only a concession to the defectiveness, as he calls it, of our means of communication; this does not consist in the fact that we need speech, but rather in the fact that *we need time.* To need time means: not to be able to *presuppose anything*, to have to *wait for everything*, to be *dependent on the other for what is ours.*[5]

To situate thought and Thinking which brings it to light, is inherently linked to this need for time. For Rosenzweig, affecting such a situatedness takes place through a new thinking called "speech-thinking" [*sprache-denken*],[6] it is this turn to the orality of language that marks a correlation of thinking in both Frankfurt and Freiburg. However, letting time be heeded and taken seriously *vis-à-vis* thinking introduces both the reality of alterity and waiting. This waiting or anti-existentialism of "a life lived in deferment,"[7] as Gershom Scholem came to critique such temporality in his 1959 Eranos lecture, reveals many concealed facets of redemptive thinking.

Redemptive thinking might be said to begin with a turning to language. It is by way of such a turning that an injection of a temporal locus within reflective thought is revealed. As one scholar of the Frankfurt and Freiburg schools has pointed out, "the focus on time and temporality was perhaps the deepest, but also the most hidden (and overtly controverted) liaison between the two thinkers."[8] The two thinkers in question, leaders of the Frankfurt and Freiburg schools respectively, are Theodor W. Adorno (1903–1969) and Martin Heidegger (1889–1976).

Peeling away further layers of this Frankfurt-Freiburg palimpsest, both thinkers offer important contributions in the unveiling of a critical correlation of temporality and thinking. Such a correlation leaves its redemptive trace through thinking. Heidegger declares in his post-Auschwitz lectures of 1954 entitled, "What is Called Thinking?" [*Was Heisst Denken?*] that: "Most thought-provoking in our thought-provoking time is that we are still not Thinking."[9] The challenge that resonates most desperately in this moment is that: "We have not yet attained to the region of that which, of itself and essentially, wishes to be pondered."[10] Attaining this region from whence thinking wishes to emanate into thought, is a bringing to bear what is left behind in memory, a presencing of the absent now recollected: "The event of withdrawal [*Das Ereignis des Entzugs*] could be what is most present [*Gegenwärtigste*] in all our present [*Gegenwärtigen*], and so infinitely exceed the actuality of everything actual [*die Aktualität alles Aktuellen*]."[11] If there is a possibility of Thinking at all, first we must confront the correlation between Thinking and Metaphysics, from which Thinking then breaks forth, especially in the post-Auschwitz rupture.

The challenge to the current state of metaphysics proffered by Heidegger is part of his project of recovering the pristine unity of "mythos" and "logos," irreparably ruptured since Plato.[12] The situatedness of contemporary chaos stems from the destruction of "mythos" by "logos." Heidegger's proposed recovery of the unity is by way of Friedrich Hölderlin's (1770–1843) poetic pathmarks, titled "Mnemosyne," a movement toward thinking as recollection. The poet remarks: "We are a sign that is not read."[13] The impoverishment of current Thinking stems from this withdrawal of "mythos," of God, of subjective experience. It is the task of the poet to envision this primordial unity so as to rectify Thinking through recollection. This recollection is a dynamic gesture of poetic swaying, such that: "[p]oetry wells up only from devoted thought thinking back [*der An-Dacht des Andenkens*], recollecting."[14] Such a recollection is evinced in language as the locus of "Being" [*Sein*].

Yet even in 1954, could language serve as such a locus amidst the ashes of Auschwitz? Does recollection include recent trauma and catastrophe? Can the region that wishes to be pondered authentically be reached without an apology? Without a critique of that thinking that informed the horrors of Auschwitz in the first place? Moreover, when the critique is spoken but unheard as early as 1938 to 1940, is the thinker still as culpable as first thought?[15] Was the initial truth of rebirthing the Nation state, its language and its people for Heidegger ultimately becoming an "unvalue" whose real truth was not heeded but betrayed?[16]

Language is the site of recollection for Heidegger in a marked re-turn to the eighteenth-century orthographic form of *Seyn*. Such a nuanced shift into the hymnal-poetics of Hölderlin is seen to indicate that "*Sein* is no longer grasped metaphysically."[17] From this site of absence springs forth a presence of Thinking, no longer a Thinking of the Being of beings, rather it is now

possible to engage in the pure thinking of Being itself. This is articulated aphoristically as follows:
Here lie the boulders of a quarry, in which primal rock is broken:

Thinking.
Intending being.
Being and the difference to a being.
Projecting be-ing open.
En-thinking of be-ing
Essential swaying of be-ing.[18]

This is a swaying away from the intentionality of *thinking being* toward the experience of *en-thinking be-ing*. Such a reflexive gesture is by way of recollection. Such a recollection, however, is not merely a backwards-looking motion, nor does it impute an atemporal meaning of being.[19] It is crucial to remember that Heidegger's ontological inquiry into the temporality of origins, for instance, is a "forward or forward-directed" inquiry, a "commemorative anticipatory thinking [*andenkenes Vordenken*]."[20] However, it is precisely at the apex of its catastrophic moment that "[t]his kind of Thinking has its solidarity with Metaphysics upon its collapse."[21] It is within a self-critical modality that Thinking has the ability to enter into the dynamism of dialectics, allowing for an afterlife beyond Metaphysics. A negative dialectics, then, is a dynamics of response to what has "not yet attained to the region of that which, of itself and essentially, wishes to be pondered"[22] in a nonessential rather than "essential sense [*wesentlichen Sinne*],"[23] in a nonconceptual rather than conceptual sense. Adorno's method of dialectics then clarifies in its negative turn:

The name dialectics says no more, to begin with, than that objects do not go into their concepts without leaving a remainder [*die Gegnstände*] . . . That which is differentiated appears as divergent, dissonant, *negative,* so long as consciousness must push towards unity according to its own formation: so long as it measures that which is not identical with itself, with its claim to the totality. This is what dialectics holds up to the consciousness as the contradiction.[24]

In the dialectical process there is always the overflow of the "remainder" [*die Gegnstände*] which cannot be totalized within the concept, and so Thinking reveals its negated desire. Whereas Heidegger claims that: "We have not yet attained to the region of that which, of itself and essentially, wishes to be pondered"[25] there is a subtle shift from what "wishes to be pondered" to "need" proper [*das Bedürfnis*]. For Adorno, the need of thinking as rigor becomes its raîson d'être, namely that "The need [*das Bedürfnis*] of thought [*im Denken*] is what makes us remember [*gedacht*]."[26] Adorno's critique decries the reduction of thought to the vulgar needs of the organism. What needs to be reconfigured is precisely how thought and needs are correlated. Strikingly, while avoidance of vulgar needs suggests an aversion to the body, Adorno's focus on a reflective embodiment will prove important further along in our thinking.

For the moment, the interplay of need and its negation is a pathmark of departure for Adorno. However, crucial this "need [*das Bedürfnis*] of thought [*im Denken*]" will shortly prove within Adorno's Thinking, it remains enveloped in ineffable catastrophe. Despite this concealment and distance of need, the urge to think it and write it lives on. The danger of an idolatrous reductionism—by way of naming what cannot be named—looms forever in the foreground of any philosophical investigation toward truth(s) at this post-Auschwitz moment. Adorno is continually turning away from the philosophic corpus, rather relying upon the aesthetic impulse within art as a source of inspiration for envisioning new thought amidst catastrophe. Artistic impulse cannot, however, distance itself from the concept; rather reflection is achieved "by thought's turning towards it."[27] Adorno proffers this approach of turning toward a catastrophe's dimunition of life most poetically with the example of the moment before the close of the first movement of Beethoven's sonata *Les Adieux*:

> an evanescently fleeting association summons up in the course of three measures the sound of trotting horses, the swiftly vanishing passage, the sound of disappearance . . . says more of the hope of return than would any general reflection on the essence of the fleetingly enduring sound.[28]

Such an exemplar in what we shall call the metaphysics of music is crucial to Adorno's thinking as it is followed by his recurrent correlation that:

> Only a philosophy that could grasp such micrological figures in its innermost construction of the aesthetic whole would make good on what it promises. For this, however, aesthetics must itself be internally developed, mediated thought.[29]

Moreover, such micrological inspiration also abounds within the artistic details of *Théâtre de Catastrophe*, exemplified in the oeuvre of that one playwright, who according to Adorno understood the purpose of art as action after Auschwitz:

> Beckett reacted to the situation of the concentration-camps, which he does not name, as if there were a ban on such like that of the graven image [*Bilderverbot*], in the only befitting manner. What is, is like the concentration-camp. Once he speaks of a lifelong death-sentence. The only hope, faintly dawning, is that there would be nothing anymore. This too he rejects. Out of the fissure of inconsistency formed by this, the image-world of nothingness appears as something which tethers his poetry. . . . The most provocative dictum from Beckett's *Endgame*: that there would no longer be anything to

really be afraid of, reacts to a praxis, which delivered its first test case in
the camps and in whose once honorable concept [*Begriff*] already lurks
teleologically the annihilation of the non-identical. Absolute negativity is
in plain view, is no longer surprising.[30]

The catastrophic experience of the Nazi death camps in this century and in
particular how the dialectic continues in its infinite horror to respond through
the *Bilderverbot*, in theatre, music and in writing remain our focus. For the
moment, if neither a Fackenheimian 614th commandment to never grant
posthumous Nazi victory[31] nor a "[n]ew categorical imperative . . . imposed
by Hitler upon unfree mankind"[32] can escape the impending threat of aesthe-
ticizing into a concept, lapsing into identity, then where to go from these
beginnings in the aftermath of catastrophe?

One path open to counter the concept is from the perspective of historical
materialism. Against the hegemony of the concept, there is the "exemplar."
By way of homage to Walter Benjamin's (1892–1940) lifework, here Adorno
demarcates the final part of *Negative Dialectics* with reference to the role of the
"exemplar" in shattering through the concept in thought:

> The need in thinking wishes, however, that there would be thinking. It
> demands its negation through thinking, it must disappear into thinking, if it
> is really supposed to be satisfied, and in this negation it lives on, representing
> in the innermost cells of thought, what is not the same as the latter. The
> smallest innerworldly markings would be relevant to the absolute, for the
> micrological glance demolishes the shells of that which is helplessly com-
> partmentalized according to the measure of its subsuming master concept
> and explodes its identity, the deception, that it would be merely an exem-
> plar. Such thinking is solidaristic with metaphysics in the moment of the
> latter's fall.[33]

This micrological approach to the exemplar is jarringly recontextualized
earlier as explicitly identifying Adorno's materialism with embodiment:

> With the murder of millions through administration, death has become
> something which has never yet been so feared. No possibility anymore, that it
> could enter into the experienced lives of individuals as something somehow
> concordant with its course. The individuated is expropriated of the final and
> most impoverished thing which remained to it. That the individual [*Individuum*]
> no longer died in the concentration camps, but rather the exemplar, has to
> affect the dying of those who escaped the administrative measures.[34]

At the risk of falling prey to its reification in the concept, one may venture
along with Adorno to declare, that after Auschwitz, "[o]ur metaphysical faculty
is paralyzed because actual events have shattered the basis on which speculative

metaphysical thought could be reconciled with experience."[35] If any rehabilitation is possible from this paralysis of our metaphysical faculty, then the painful path begins in "the *self-reflection* of thinking,"[36] an experiential process of critique that Frankfurt School thinkers Theodor W. Adorno and Max Horkheimer came to call "Negative Dialectics." The act of thinking is merely a gesture turned against itself so as to engage in critical self-reflection:

> If negative dialectics demands the self-reflection of thinking, then this implies in tangible terms, that thinking must, nowadays at any rate, in order to be true, also *think against itself*. If it does not measure itself by the extremity, which *flees from the concept*, then it is cast in advance in the same mold as the musical accompaniment, with which the SS was wont to drown out the cries of their victims.[37]

By way of such a debilitating movement beyond the concept in thinking and beyond the horrifying musical accompaniment of extermination, do the birth pangs of redemption come to light. How then is this possibility of redemption envisioned vis-à-vis the metaphysics of musical thinking? Moreover, what is left to be recuperated[38] from a paralysis within the metaphysical faculty of the experience itself?

Metaphysics of Music as Negative Theological Dialectics

The redemptive gesture consistently brought to light in the oeuvre of German Jewish thinker Adorno is a bridging of the abyss between the metaphysical experience encountered in existence versus music. His reflections on music, often titled philosophies of music, are frequently a sliding in and out of a flickering metaphysical experience. Having always just passed over, the metaphysical experience leaves its trace upon Thinking. Despite the near impossibility of resuscitating a metaphysical experience in paralysis, Adorno continues on with a most "desperate and negative recuperation." What is most intriguing about this seemingly hopeless gesture is that the "negative recuperation" of metaphysics itself then "turns into something else—namely theology."[39] Uncovering the theological within the dying metaphysical experience will have to inform the course of our thinking by drawing on some of that tradition in Jewish and Christian sources. For the moment, the inexorable link between the metaphysical experience and the theological is now articulated, most prominently in the negative.

Adorno's movement toward this negative dialectical link is most explicit in his philosophic writings' allusions to his more sustained reflections on music. Why is it that the language of philosophy conceals in its concealment, while the language of music conceals in its revelation? Recollection of what has already passed over—the metaphysical experience's revelation—is anticipated in the presencing experience of music. Any such revelation then would unveil both a linguistic and acoustic experience. A philosopher of aesthetics like Mikel Dufrenne (1910–1995) dedicates an entire study to this need for recovering the primacy of acoustic perception in aesthetics. Hearing then for Dufrenne is an interiorization of sound. The source of sound cannot be determined, per se, rather it exceeds its categorical envelope, as Dufrenne indicates: "There is more: I am myself a sonorous being."[40] This overflowing the boundaries of the external and the internal is evident in how the subject is constituted vis-à-vis sound: "I resonate in it as it resonates in me, I vibrate."[41] Such a reformulation of subjectivity underlies much of Adorno's writings on music, albeit in an unsaid manner. A closer companion in dialogue with Adorno on Jewish mysticism, Gershom Scholem (1897–1982), also alludes to this path of recollecting the primacy of acoustic revelation when he writes:

> Under the system of the synagogue, revelation is an acoustic process, not a visual one; or revelation at least ensues from an area which is metaphysically associated with the acoustic and the perceptible (in a sensual context).[42]

Sound is no stranger to revelation of the metaphysical experience, found for instance, within reflections on the Sinaitic revelation: "And the Name spoke to you from within the fire, the sound of things did you hear, seeing no similitude; nothing but a voice."[43] This focus on the acoustic aspect of revelation finds further resonance within the Psalms. Whereas the locus of polytheistic revelation, for instance, is upon the mighty words of Enlil and Marduk in the Babylonian hymnic tradition, the locus of monotheistic revelation is upon the sound of the Name:

> The sound of the Name over the waters!
> . . . The sound of the Name resounds with power,
> the sound of the Name with majesty!
> The sound of the Name shatters cedars,
> The Name shatters the cedars of Lebanon . . .
> The sound of the Name flashes flames of fire.
> The sound of the Name makes the desert quake,
> The sound of the Name makes the desert of Kadesh quake.
> The sound of the Name brings the hinds to birth pains,
> Makes the kids squirm with pain.
> And in his palace all cry out: Glory![44]

Moreover, the soundings of this Psalm become the locus of mystical contemplation of the ineffable Name. In the prayer book of Rabbi Shalom Sharabi,[45] for instance, an extended meditation on the seven primordial soundings of the Name is embedded within the aforecited Psalm 29. For each one of the seven soundings, there unfolds a mystical shape of the Godhead filling an entire page. This is not by any means unusual within a mystical tradition that sees the entire Torah as one continuous Name: "The whole Torah is a unique holy and mystic Name."[46] The paradoxical relationship of the plethora of these letters vis-à-vis the form of the formless, ineffable Name, will be discussed shortly regarding the *Bilderverbot* in Schoenberg. This is one example of many within the Jewish mystical tradition which supports Adorno's inexorable link between the metaphysical experience and the theological as being contingent upon the acoustic.

The acoustic, as matrix for revelation of the metaphysical experience, then finds deep resonance in Adorno's reflections on music. Great pains are taken in Adorno's writings with regard to the language of music to differentiate it from the language of philosophy:

> Music resembles a language in the sense that it is a temporal sequence of articulated sounds which are more than just sounds . . . But what has been said cannot be detached from the music. Music creates no semiotic system.[47]

The inherent mediation of any semiotic system, in its web of composed signifiers and signifieds, cannot be overcome. Linguistic conceptualization, since Ferdinand de Saussure (1857–1913), like denotation (signifier) and connotation (signified), cannot in and of themselves be extricated from their conceptual natures. Adorno, however, proffers that extrication from the concept begins by its very elusion—engaging in a self-reflection that turns the concepts of the system *against themselves*. In this self-reflexive turning, a parallel process is reiterated by Adorno in his delimiting it as *vers une musique informelle* that should be a "music whose end cannot be foreseen in the course of production . . . the idea [*Vorstellung*] of something not fully imagined [*vorgestellt*]."[48] Imagining the unimaginable or ineffable is a paradoxical movement toward the immediacy of the metaphysical experience of music which will remain "as yet undreamt of"[49] and which must always "leave possibilities unused [*Möglichkeiten ungenützt*]."[50] Within this movement, the very intentionality framing the idea itself is under self-reflection. The groundwork for this self-reflection is already apparent in Benjamin's iteration from 1916–1925 in *Ursprüng des deutschen Trauerspiels*, namely that: "Truth is the death of intention."[51] Is it possible that this death of intentionality indicates a shift toward a *philosophie informelle*, a veritable "open thinking"[52] of sorts?

Regarding the correlation of the theological core negatively recuperated within the husk of the metaphysical experience in paralysis, Adorno makes a case for the possibility of music as the house for this experience. Distinctly set apart from the language of intentionality, experiencing the language of music:

> contains a theological dimension. What it has to say is simultaneously revealed and concealed. Its Idea is the divine Name which has been given shape. It is

demythologized prayer, rid of efficacious magic. It is the human attempt, doomed as ever, to name the Name, not to communicate meanings.[53]

This attempt at naming the Name would appear to be an allusion to the body of Jewish mystical literature which dedicated itself to this very task, namely, the Kabbalah. One such iteration is found in the prolific Book of Splendor [*Sefer ha'Zohar*]. In search of a manifestation of such an intentionless metaphysical experience, akin to a musical naming, Adorno was in frequent dialogue and correspondence with another fellow German thinker and specialist in Jewish mysticism, Gerhard [Gershom] Scholem who had emigrated to Palestine. Already in a letter dated April 19, 1939, an early stage in their correspondence regarding the Zohar, Adorno inquires into the possibility of a negative recuperation of an intentionless metaphysical experience. This segment of the correspondence is quoted at length to recapture a sense of the dialogue in process:

> Dear Herr Scholem, It is not just an empty phrase if I tell you that the translation of the extract from the Zohar which you sent me gave me the greatest pleasure I have had from any gift in a very long time . . . its undecipherable aspects form part of the pleasure it gave me . . . The other question is of a somewhat epistemological nature, of course, it is factually connected to the mythical form of absolute spiritualism. . . . [T]he language into which the symbol is translated is itself a mere symbolic language, which calls to mind Kafka's statement that all his works were symbolic, but only in the sense that they were to be interpreted by new symbols in an endless series of steps. The question I would like to ask you is as follows: Has this series of steps got a bottom, or does it fall into a bottomless void? Bottomless because, in a world which knows nothing except spirit and in which even differentness is defined as a mere self-divestment of spirit, the hierarchy of intentions has no end. One might also say that there is nothing but intentions. If I may go back to Benjamin's old theorem of the intentionless character of truth, which does not represent a last intention but calls a stop to the flight of intentions, then, in face of the Zohar text, one cannot escape the question as to the role of myth as blinding. Is not the totality of the symbolic, however much it may appear as the expression of the expressionless, subject to the natural order because it does not know the expressionless—I would almost like to say, because it does not know nature in the true sense?[54]

Throughout the course of his writings, Adorno returns to this question of the Kabbalah[55] posed to Scholem and one of its manifestations, the Zohar, to peel away further at the possibility of attaining Benjamin's theorem of the intentionless character of truth. If such a call to arrest the flight of intentions could be heard within the Zoharic text, one might be able to escape the indictment of its overwhelming "mythos" being other than utterly blinding. Adorno's challenging the Kabbalah of the Zohar as being nothing but intentions clouded by blinding myth continues to resonate in Scholem's breathtaking address delivered in 1970 at the Eranos meeting in Ascona. It concludes with the following query, which in many ways responds to Adorno's earlier challenge, now being addressed by way of Scholem's own linguistic and acoustic correlation of the Name:

> In conclusion, let me return once more to the central thought which we have tried to trace here. The name of God is the "essential name," which is the original source of language. . . . For the Kabbalists, this name has no "meaning" in the traditional understanding of the term. It has no concrete signification. The meaninglessness of the name of God indicates its situation in the very central point of revelation, at the basis of which it lies. Behind every revelation of a meaning in language, and, as the Kabbalists saw it, by means of the Torah, there exists this element which projects over and beyond meaning, but which in the first instance enables meaning to be given. It is this element which endows every other form of meaning, though it has no meaning itself. . . . Its radiation or sounds, which we catch, are not so much communications as appeals. That which has meaning—sense and form—is not this word itself, but the tradition behind this word, its communication and reflection in time. This tradition, which has its own dialectic, goes through certain changes and is eventually delivered in a soft, panting whisper; and there may be times, like our own, in which it can no longer be handed down, in which *this tradition falls silent.* This, then, is the great crisis of language in which we find ourselves. We are no longer able to grasp the last summit of that mystery that once dwelt in it. The fact that language can be spoken is, in the opinion of the Kabbalists, owed to the name, which is present in language. What the value and worth of language will be—the language from which *God will have withdrawn*—is the question which must be posed by those who still believe that they can hear the echo of the vanished word of the creation in the immanence of the world. This is a question to which, in our times, *only the poets presumably have the answer.* For poets do not share the doubt that most mystics have in regard to language. And poets have one link with the masters of the Kabbala, even when they reject Kabbalistic theological formulation as being still too emphatic. This link is their belief in language as an absolute, which is as if constantly flung open by dialectics. It is their belief in the *mystery of language which has become audible.*[56]

The immediacy of naming meanings in a Name as opposed to the mediacy of communicating meanings in names is again a step toward recollecting the primordial act of Edenic naming. To correlate the comment of Scholem back to that of Adorno, the mystery of the Name becoming more audible is the key provided by the dialectics of music:

> Music aspires to be a language without intention. But the demarcation line between itself and the language of intentions is not absolute; we are not confronted by two wholly separate realms. There is a dialectic at work.[57]

In its ability to "find the absolute immediately"[58] music seems to be the way out of the albatross of a dying metaphysical experience. Yet "at the moment of discovery it becomes obscured, just as too powerful a light dazzles the eyes, preventing them from seeing things which are perfectly visible."[59] It is the need to move beyond intentionality which is so crucial to this turn in Adorno's Thinking, for "[w]ith music intentions are broken and scattered out of their own force and reassembled in the configuration of the Name."[60] Such a reunification indelibly links the metaphysical experience's shattering vessel with the possibility of a redemptive thinking. This link is possible only through the hidden temporality[61] by which music is continuously nourished:

> [T]he congealed time contained in musical texts can be actualized in every performance or reading, and hence is not identical with empirical time . . . As soon as the notation is actualized—that is to say, the piece is played—it merges with empirical time and possesses chronological duration, even while appearing simultaneously to belong to another order of time, namely that of the work which is immortalized, as it were, by being written down.[62]

Indeed, this zone between temporalities, both empirical and immortal, is where music dwells. This nexus of dwelling, between the immanent and the transcendent, is what allows for a gesturing toward Utopia:

> What the musician longs for, because it would be the fulfillment of music, has not yet proved capable of achievement. . . . Kant himself thought of this [eternal peace] as an actual concrete possibility which is capable of realization and yet is nevertheless just an idea. The aim of every artistic utopia today is to make things in ignorance of what they are.[63]

Yearning for the fulfillment of what remains unfulfilled in music is the artistic Utopia to which we must now turn our attention.

Nowhere is Utopia more explicitly confronted than in Adorno's reflections on music. Yearning for the fulfillment of the unfulfilled in music finds its most lucid expression for Adorno prominently in both the Utopias and apocalypses of the following three composers: Richard Wagner (1813–1883), Gustav Mahler (1860–1911), and Arnold Schoenberg (1874–1951). Adorno's reflections on each of these three composers as musical thinkers reveal a most lucid articulation of the possibilities and concomitant dangers of a Redeemer and ensuing Redemption. Each of Adorno's reflections will be approached from its standpoint on Redemption, respectively as Phantasmagoric, Near, and Negative.

Phantasmagoric Redemption

Death, as the salvational nexus upon which Wagner's Redeemer and Redemption turns, is laid bare from the outset by Adorno in his 1952 study, *Versuch über Wagner*:

> Even in Schopenhauer there was a foretaste of the Wagnerian practice of dressing up death as salvation and of the inflated concept of the "redeemer of the world" *oeuvre* . . . With the concept of redemption of the world, the particular reflective mind, the self-knowledge of the individual, contrives to smuggle in a speculative, substantive principle of the sort that Schopenhauer had repeatedly condemned in Hegel. The concept of redemption, born of the indifference of the conscious towards the unconscious, extends the ideology of pessimism to its logical conclusion in Wagner. Under the title of redemption both the negativity of the bourgeois world and its negation are deemed equally positive. The destruction of the world at the end of the *Ring* is also a Happy End.[64]

Destruction as a Happy End is the culminating moment of Redemption. It is here that Adorno is able to draw on the ultimate fantasy of horrifying proportions. It is evident that any redemption "born of the indifference of the conscious towards the unconscious"[65] is dangerous in its blurring and consequent totalization of the thinking subject. But the category of the phantasmagoria that Wagner's music occupies is lodged in an absurdity more dangerous than Beckett's theatre. Whereas Samuel Beckett (1906–1989) lays bare the absurdity of existence in the face of catastrophe spawned by genocide, Wagner idealizes this catastrophic ending as happy, to mythic proportions:

> Wagnerian redemption . . . is the ultimate phantasmagoria. For true transcendence it substitutes the mirage of the enduring upwards-soaring individual who vanishes into thin air at the moment of his annihilation. Nothing could reconcile the spectator with an apparent reconciliation but the perfection of that manifest appearance itself, the element of a *promesse de bonheur* in a situation of complete absurdity, in cheap fiction or a circus finale. In the innermost core of Wagner's idea of redemption dwells nothingness. It too is empty. Wagner's phantasmagoria is a mirage because it is the manifestation of the null and void. And this defines the impulse underlying

Wagner's style. It is the attempt to conjure up out of mere subjectivity a being superior to and with authority over that subjectivity, just as if it were a being that could reflect something greater than itself.[66]

Moreover, what stands out as a key violation in Adorno's eyes is the appearance of deceptive solace in the face of an abandoned theology, which such musical compositions invite so seductively:

> The category of redemption is stripped of its theological meaning, but endowed with the function of giving solace, without however acquiring any precise content. It is a homecoming without a home, eternal rest without Eternity, the mirage of peace without the underlying reality of a human being to enjoy it. The reification of life extends its domain even over death, since it ascribes to the dead the happiness it withholds from the living. In exchange, it reserves for itself its property rights over existence without which the title of happiness is doomed to remain a lie and an obscenity. It could be said that in the name of redemption the dead are cheated of lives twice over.[67]

Appearing as a boundary between something and nothing, the nothingness which Wagner deceptively ornaments with "the chimera of utopia"[68] is an abuse of "the concept of negativity to gain a purchase on reality that was slipping between his fingers."[69] Despite his severe polemical stance against the seductive redemption of phantasmagoria proffered by Wagner, still Adorno is able to hear within the compositions that undying protest of music. As Adorno was wont to quote Benjamin's dictum, that hope is for the hopeless, indeed in Wagner resonates hope's negative recuperation:

> By voicing the fears of helpless people, it could signal help for the help-less, however feebly and distortedly. In doing so it would renew the pro-mise contained in the age-old protest of music: the promise of a life without fear.[70]

Through the negative dialectical process, what Adorno is able to recover in Wagner are the negative acoustical traces of Utopia. It is precisely amidst the phantasmagoric mythos of Wagner that Adorno is able to discern the cries of the helpless against which Redemption must issue forth.

Near Redemption

By contrast to the phantasmagoric Redemption of Wagner, there is a Redemption which appears to edge closer to Adorno's nonidealized ideal. It is with the musical compositions of Mahler, wherein one remains on the edge of Utopia, all the while attuned to the very danger which the harbinger of Redemption poses:

> Enigmatically enough. Mahler gave the text something of the color of the [k]abbalistic *Gevura*. That throughout the piece he mutes the gigantic orchestra to an accompaniment furthers the disintegration of the sound by a certain caustic sharpness, and by soloistic mixtures; the second part of this work, notorious for its mass forces, is poor in cumulative mass effects; there can be no question in it of an excess of external means . . . All is poised on a knife-edge, uncurtailed Utopia and the lapse into grandiose decorativeness. Mahler's danger is that of the redeemer.[71]

Being "poised on a knife-edge" between, on the one side, "uncurtailed Utopia" and, on the other side, "the lapse into grandiose decorativeness" is troped through the recontextualization of *Gevura*. According to the Kabbalistic system of mapping the godhead, the Redeemer occupies the sixth gradation, *Tifereth* (mediating splendor), which is the equilibrating response to the fifth gradation, *Gevura* (power of stern judgment or punishment), and the fourth gradation, *Hesed* (power of grace). Adorno captures the tenuous position of *Tifereth* as the link of consciousness about to undergo transmutation. This transmutation is one whereby the upper realms of consciousness are revealed below, namely that the endless light of the first gradation, *Keter* (Crown), is filtered down all the way through to the mundane existence of the tenth gradation, *Malkhuth* (Sovereignty). Seeing Mahler's "disintegration of the sound by a certain caustic sharpness" as *Gevura*'s acoustic power is a brilliant translation by Adorno. While this serves as an explicit recasting of the Kabbalistic system of mapping the godhead in the metaphysics of musical time, Adorno's entire focus on Redemption is a most subtle translation of *Tifereth* into musical time.

Moreover, Adorno reveals the acoustical element of Mahler's metaphysics to be further entangled with the ocular. This fascinating enmeshing of the ocular within the acoustic raises signs of danger for Adorno's Redeemer. The acoustic appears to be so saturated with the ocular that it is only through the ocular that the acoustic is recovered. This dangerous lack of equilibration is troped in terms of the general and the particular, such that:

> [T]he general is so saturated with the particular that it is only through the particular that it can recover a compelling generality. The girl in *Das Lied von der Erde* throws her secret lover a "long yearning look." Such is the look of the work itself, absorbing, doubting, turned backwards with precipitous tenderness.[72]

It is the very turning backwards toward childhood memories that fills the field of vision of the secret lover with the "long, yearning look." The danger is an imbalanced giving of oneself over to memory's ocular rather than acoustic texture:

> Mahler's music holds fast to Utopia in the memory traces from childhood, which appear as if it were for their sake that it would be worth living. But no less authentic for him is the consciousness that this happiness is lost, and only in being lost becomes the happiness it itself never was.[73]

The memory of unrealized happiness is realized in its unrealization. This has ramifications, then, as to how redemptive temporality is experienced, whereby lost time is redeemed through temporality. As a result of this imbalance of the ocular over the acoustic,

> [Mahler] rediscovers time as irrecoverable . . . unfettered joy and unfettered melancholy perform their charade; in the prohibition of images of hope, hope has its last dwelling-place. This place is . . . , however, the strength to name the forgotten that is concealed in the stuff of experience.[74]

In realizing the loss of time inherent to existence there is an ensuing irruption of redemptive temporality into the mundane. Moreover, hope's dwelling place is revealed in the concealment of images. This theme of image prohibition will become more pronounced within Adorno's reflections on Schoenberg.

Negative Redemption

> When Schoenberg was once asked about a piece that had not yet been performed, "So, you haven't heard it yourself?," he replied, "Yes, I have. When I wrote it." In such a process of the imagination, the sensuous is directly spiritualized without losing any of its concrete specificity. What was realized in the imagination thereby became an objective unity.[75]

Apparently a random anecdote on Schoenberg, Adorno brings it to bear on the danger of imbalance previously discussed in Mahler. Schoenberg presences a proximity of Redemption in its distance by way of complete focus on the acoustic, disintegrating the ocular. The metaphysical experience is possible if "such a process of the imagination, the sensuous is directly spiritualized without losing any of its concrete specificity."[76] Music's power as a language devoid of mediating intentionality is evident in its ability to directly spiritualize the sensuous. Such acoustic "objective unity," however, is broken with even the encroachment of the ocular. Accordingly, Schoenberg's composition of *Moses und Aron*, for example, mirrors the broken Tablets of the Law which Moses has smashed. Here we are introduced to the concept of *Bilderverbot* in relation to music:[77]

> Music is the imageless art and was excluded from that prohibition . . . Aaron, the man of images and mediation, has to sing in the opera, but makes use of language without images. Moses, on the other hand, who represents the principle of the ban on images [*Bilderverbot*], does not sing in Schoenberg, but just speaks . . . But the intractable task of the music to provide an image of the non-pictorial could well overcome the master's matter-of-factness. To that extent matter-of-factness is his metaphysics. Music should not be an ornament.[78]

This nonpictorial composition proves pivotal for Adorno's claims to its theological foundation, namely, an acoustic re-creation of the Israelite's idolatrous worship of the image embodied in the *Egel ha'masseikha* (known as the Golden Calf, but a more literal rendering of Exodus 32:4 brings forth, the Molten or Masking Calf). The chaotic scenario recalls the community's abandonment of the acoustic revelation in favor of worshipping the ocular, which appears more tangible. The loss of control in the face of the ocular is evinced by Moses' confronting of Aaron and his response regarding the creation of the Masking Calf from the people's gold: "They gave it to me and I hurled it into the fire and out came this calf!" (Exodus 33:24). This encounter reinforces the prohibition on image-making (Exodus 20:4), which Adorno recalls in Schoenberg as the *Bilderverbot*:

> The prohibition on graven images [*Bilderverbot*] which Schoenberg heeded as few others have done, nevertheless extends further than even he imagined. To thematize great subjects directly today means projecting their image after the event. But this in turn inevitably means that, disguised as themselves, they fail to make contact with the work of art.[79]

The resonance of Schoenberg's *Bilderverbot* extends as far as the present moment's attempt to thematize subjects directly. After the sensuous event is spiritualized "without losing any of its concrete specificity," only then is an image projected backwards to what has already passed. As such, themes are temporally devoid of images, as a missed nexus.

Such a loss from the perspective of images challenges the foundation of a pictorial theology. It is indeed telling that Adorno makes note of Schoenberg's composed setting for Rilke's poem from *The Book of Hours* [*Das Stundenbuch*] in the songs of Opus 22, building further upon the *Bilderverbot*:

Alle, welche dich suchen, versuchen dich.	All who seek you, tempt you.
Und die, so dich finden, binden dich	And those who find you, bind you
An bild und Gebärde.	To image and gesture.[80]

Building on Schoenberg's *mise-en-musique*, Adorno's commentary to the Rilke verses is instructive, in further understanding this impulse toward the negative Utopia:

> Thus God, the Absolute, eludes finite beings. Where they desire to name him, because they must, they betray him. But if they keep silent about him, they acquiesce in their own impotence and sin against the other, no less binding, commandment to name him.[81]

The warning, which Schoenberg's compositions so scrupulously heed, is to beware of even contemplating an image of Utopia. For in the act of cognitive contemplation, Adorno seems to suggest, the cognomen's molten form will jump out of the fire and cause the collective to err in its idolatrous thinking. But the roots of the prohibition stem from a far greater one, namely that just as God cannot be imaged, so too is it forbidden to image Utopia. Or inversely, so as not to betray the infinite through finite cognition, one can only name the Name negatively in inscribing its erasure. One can only name Utopia negatively by inscribing its erasure. Just as the absolute metaphysical content of Schoenberg's *Moses und Aron* "would prevent it from becoming an aesthetic totality," so too does the absolute metaphysical content of Adorno's Utopia prevent it from becoming a social totality.

Furthermore, the aforementioned correlation between the music and metaphysics is becoming more heightened, whereby the immediacy of aesthetic experience draws us into the immediacy of the lived experience. What is being called for through this direct spiritualization of the sensuous is a complete reconfiguration of the quotidian. It is realizing that the imageless image makes way for the indwelling of hope according to Adorno's redemptive thinking:

> The absolute which this music sets out to make real, without any sleight of hand, it achieves as its own idea of itself: it is itself an image of something without images—the very last thing the story wanted.[82]

If the absolute of the imageless image is made real in Schoenberg's compositions, however, has not the system fallen prey to its very own prohibition? For the absolute made real implies a monolithic image which brings forth that reality. This necessitates a modal shift, albeit momentarily, within the very metaphysics of musical time into the realm of a kind of integrative theology, whereby:

> Schoenberg's conversion to theology means that he would like to negate the message of negation which the historical conjuncture proclaimed to him. The element of truth in this is that by defining itself as negative, his approach implicitly postulates the positive. . . . The integrative power of the work does not resolve the contradictions inherent in the situation.[83]

It is evident, the further we delve into Adorno's reflections on Schoenberg, that the realization of a veritable *Bilderverbot* is only possible through the intentionless language of music:

> Schoenberg's own need to express is one that rejects mediation and convention and therefore one which names its object directly. Its secret model is that of revealing the Name.[84]

The imageless image of the Name's negative engraving serves the one engaged in contemplation with the paradoxical nonpictorial image. In the act of mystical contemplation, the Name is inscribed to vision through its erasure, a negative engraving[85] of sorts through the mind's eye. However, what Adorno hears in Schoenberg's compositions is the path of contemplating the Name through, as it were, the mind's ear. This shift from the mind's eye to the mind's ear evokes another paradox, to be discussed shortly, which Adorno reveals in its concealment as the "transfigured body" [*den verklärten Leib*].[86] For the moment, however, contemplation of the Name is achieved through a simultaneity of a negative imaging and an oral unnaming of the Name's linguistic stability.[87]

Variations on Pre-redemption in *Minima Moralia*

The structural mapping of Adorno's masterpiece essays in *Minima Moralia* evinces a concern for Redemptive Dialectics. The closing aphorisms of each section are "intended to mark out points of attack or to furnish models for a future strain of thought [*Anstrengung des Begriffs*]."[88] These closing aphorisms as well as the particular "possibilities unused"[89] are then soldered into a broken universal tripartition.[90] A fragmented temporality interrupts a seemingly cohesive tripartite division, as evinced first in the epithets of Ferdinand Kürnberger (1873–1943), F. H. Bradley (1846–1924), and C. Baudelaire (1793–1871) respectively:

I.   Life does not live
II. Where everything is bad it must be good to know the worst
III. *Avalanche, veux-tu m'emporter dans ta chute?*

Each despairing station of epithets acts as an *in absentia* guide through the descent into the apocalypse. A veritable descent for the sake of ascent, this dialectical journey through this hell of the materialist world may reveal fragments of redemptive thinking. For Adorno, such materialism is integrally linked to embodiment, whereas for Benjamin redemption is only possible when one "takes up the struggle against dispersion"[91] of the commodified objects. Reunion of infinite objects is recontextualized into the Utopian collection that is impossibly realized into "[a] sort of productive disorder"[92] which becomes the "canon of the *mémoire involuntaire*."[93] While the Marxist undertones of Benjamin's gesture are evident, this is a form of the aforementioned "commemorative anticipatory thinking [*andenkenes Vordenken*]."[94] Further, for Benjamin this uncovering of the "afterlife" takes place after the life of his 18 theses.[95] However, as Benjamin's 18 theses begin their denouement in Adorno it gives way to a somewhat more masked numerological structuring. Adorno's tentative systematization, however, is reminiscent of Benjamin's structuring of *Theses on the Philosophy of History*,[96] where a numbering by Roman numerals I–XVIII then allows for the "afterlife" of the theses to reveal themselves with sections A and B. Whereas Benjamin, through implosion, is explicitly resuscitating the primordial naming power of language hidden in "an enormous abridgement"[97] by placing A and B after Roman numerals I–XVIII, Adorno continues his composition of *Minima Moralia* strictly with numerals, both Roman and Ordinal. Within parts I, II, and III there are sections respectively numbered as 50, 100, and 150:

I.	1944	50. Gaps
II.	1945	100. *Sur l'Eau*
III.	1946–1947	150. Late Extra

Although part III technically ends in its published form with *Zum Ende*, deceptively translated as "Finale"[98] the pattern of this composition thus far would rather point to 150[99] as its most logical end point. Thus section nos. 151, 152, and 153 remain as the three "unused possibilities" which are crucial reflections that "out-live" the end, just as A and B glow in the "afterlife" of Benjamin's *Theses*. Our approach to unraveling the thematic of Redemption embedded within these concluding aphorisms will be to follow the initial chronology of nos. 50, 100, and 150, and only then reflect on nos. 151, 152, and 153.

"Gaps" [*Lücken*][100] reveal themselves as the ground from which thinking is thought, and action can catalyze the praxis of rectification. "If a life fulfilled its vocation [*Wegs seine Bestimmung*] directly, it would miss it."[101] Unfulfilled fulfillment along one's path then is the lived experience of the thinker. Thought and action, however, ensue from a given teaching. Thought cannot be traced toward its reified conclusion, nor can such a tracing lead to its duplication. Such potential duplication becomes problematized as a principle of representation:

> For the value of a thought is measured by its distance from the continuity of the familiar. It is objectively devalued as this distance is reduced.[102]

Rather than falling prey to reproducing the exact process of thought, knowledge is to be conveyed as it comes through us, that is, "through the dense, firmly-founded . . . medium of experience."[103] It is by way of the lived experience that the dynamism reaches Thought proper. This dynamism is crucial for the Redemption of Thought, seeing that:

> Every thought which is not idle, however, bears branded on it the impossibility of its full legitimation, as we know in dreams that there are mathematics lessons, missed for the sake of a blissful morning in bed, which can never be made up.[104]

Thinking, then, is the bridge between what has been missed and what is *not-yet* thought. The *not-yet* thought that lies in wait gives way to a certain anamnesis. Forgetting what one has forgotten to think is the call to awaken Thinking:

> Thought waits to be woken one day by the memory of what has been missed, and to be transformed into teaching.[105]

Thought could not be aroused into a thought-provoking teaching without this importance placed on the negative spaces. Such a focus on gaps is embedded deep within the Jewish mystical tradition of thinking, for example:

> The Infinite, the King, King of Kings, who rules all: for His essence penetrates and descends via the Gradations and between the Gradations, and between the Chariot and within the Chariot, and within the angels, and within the celestial spheres and between the celestial spheres, and within the elements and between the lowly elements, and within the land and between the land and its offspring, down to the final point of the abyss—the whole world is full of His glory.[106]

The emphases on gaps are crucial, as oscillation both "between" and "within" the dialectic of truth. This space of oscillation is a veritable *Zweischenraum*. It is projecting to a nearing of farness from the "between" [*Zwischen*] to the "between-space" [*Zwischenraum*]. Once the *Zwischenraum* is grounded, a "surging-over" from time to temporality is experienced.[107] This frenzied to and fro oscillation, from time to temporality, colors each of these fragments respectively, nos. 50, 100, and 150.

From the foundational gaps necessary for Thinking to redeem Thought, Adorno now shifts to a seemingly incongruent pastoral scenario. The incongruence is even sharper when the aforementioned *Bilderverbot* of Schoenberg is recalled. Gaps resonate here with the call to "leave possibilities unused" [*Möglichkeiten ungenützt*].[108] However, one is led to wonder just how ironic an intention underlies Adorno's description of the Utopian scenario:

> *Rien faire comme une bête,* lying on water and looking peacefully at the sky, "being, nothing else without any further definition and fulfillment," might

take the place of process, art, satisfaction, and so truly keep the promise of dialectical logical that it would culminate in its origin.[109]

Although Adorno seems to initially admire the "onlookers of progress" [*Zaungäste des Fortschritts*][110] like Maupassant and Sternheim and their singular abilities as artists to envision the Utopia with such "fragility" [*Zerbrechlichkeit*],[111] the *Bilderverbot* looms in the horizon. In recollecting this scenario of Maupassant, is Adorno succumbing to this very betrayal by way of the image? "None of the abstract concepts [*den abstrakten Bergen*] comes closer to fulfilled utopia than that of eternal peace [*Frieden*]."[112] Returning to this section's opening ban on any inquiry into the nature of the emancipated society puts the final scenario into the context of an outright betrayal:

> He who asks what is the goal [*dem Zeil*] of an emancipated society [*der emanzipierten Gesellschaft*] is given answers such as the fulfillment of human possibilities [*die Erfüllung der menschlichen Möglichkeiten*] or the richness of life. Just as the inevitable question is illegitimate, so the repellent assurance of the answer is inevitable.[113]

The illegitimacy of questions and answers surrounding the Redemption presupposes an ideal. The ideal cannot be separated from its image. Once thought becomes manifest as singular in its "destination" [*dem Zeil*], it is already reified, raising the wall between Thought and Thinking. This is the fine line that must be danced by Adorno in appropriating such a concept as Redemption. For even the concept of "abstract concepts" [*den abstrakten Begriffen*] is both "the organon of Thinking [*Organon des Denkens*], and yet 'the wall' [*die Mauer*] between Thinking and 'Thought' [*Denkenden*]."[114] This interposition between Thinking and Thought affects the intrinsic "yearning" [*Sehnsucht*][115] for Redemption. If the division is inflexible and opaque, yearning is fully negated, whereas if the interposition is porous and transparent, the yearning of unfulfilled fulfillment continues to take place. But the proximity of this "yearning" [*Sehnsucht*][116] for Redemption to "the element of wish" [*das Element des Wunsches*][117] in "wishful thinking" is remarkable. In attempting to redress the bifurcation of Thought into feeling and understanding, Adorno attempts to redeem "wishful thinking" from its usual severance. In contrast to "gaps" in Thought, here there is a rupture beyond repair. This rupture in Thought holds the very key to its own healing within itself by way of:

> self-conscious reflection [*Selbstbesinnung*] on the element of the wish [*des Wunsches*] that antithetically constitutes Thinking as Thinking [*Denken als Denken*]. Only when that element is dissolved purely, without heteronomous residues, in the objectivity of Thought [*Objektivität des Gedankens*], will it become an impulse towards Utopia.[118]

Finally, "Late Extra" [*Extrablatt*] is an insertion true to its namesake. Reaching its crescendo like the highly musical finale of the 150th in the Book of Psalms, this apparent ending of no. 150 for *Minima Moralia* is the very precipice of being already too late to search for the new. Yet it is "into the depths of the unknown to find the new" [*au fond de l'inconnu pour trouver du nouveau'*][119] that Adorno leads his thoughts. Following Benjamin's lead to take a Baudelairean path through "the cult of the new," Adorno admits that:

> [t]he layer of unpremeditatedness [*Vorgedachten*], freedom from intentions, on which alone intentions flourish, seems consumed.[120]

That layer of the intentionless seems accessible only through music in our earlier discussion. In this regard, Adorno evokes the aforementioned phantas-magoric [*phantasmagorisch*][121] redemptivity of Wagner,[122] as exemplary of this perverted quest for newness. Once the "veil of temporal succession" [*der Schleier der zeitlichen Sukzession*] is rent, then newness reveals "the archetypes of perpetual sameness" [*der Immergleichkeit*].[123] Such damnation interposes a linear time in the way of a true temporal Redemption. Such interposition seems to recur with this "wish for survival" [*den Wunsch des Überlebens*], leading to the unconscious projection into "the chimera of the thing never known [*die Schimäre des nie gekannten Dinges*], but this resembles death."[124] The difference in the aforementioned proximity now comes to the fore. It is "the element of wish" [*das Element des Wunsches*][125] that constitutes the illusory chimera, whereas only "yearning" [*Sehnsucht*][126] is sound guidance toward the path of redemptive thinking.

Variations on Redemptive Thinking

Of all the nine theses in *Theses gegen den Okkultismus*, it is no. VII that brings forth guidance along the path to redemptive thinking. Thesis no. VII revisits the *Bilderverbot*, explored more fully in Adorno's aforementioned reflections on Schoenberg. Here the dialectic is posed between:

> the ban on graven images veiled in the silence of the salvation of the dead [*die Rettung der Toten nach dem Bilderverbot mit Schweigen bedacht*], or the preached resurrection of the flesh [*die Auferstehung des Fleisches gelehert*].[127]

There is no way to extricate the spirit from the flesh or *vice versa*. The body serves as the vessel giving form to the spirit, for "[o]nly in the parable [*im Gleichneis des Leibes*] of the body can the concept of pure spirit be grasped at all." Yet, true to redemptive form that forbids any such flagrant imaging, Adorno concludes the above statement: ". . . and is at the same time cancelled."[128] In a similar turn of negation, Adorno proffers the vision of final hope [*Hoffnung*] that clings to the "transfigured body" [*den verklärten Leib*].[129] Are buffers of metaphor and parable enough for a complete cancellation, or has the *Bilderver-bot* been broken? Moreover, must not the absolutism of the *Bilderverbot* be nuanced or subverted so as to allow for this final hope to shimmer on? If not, the looming danger of falling back into the concept returns with force.

The corruption and reification that result from violating the inseparability of body and soul into disparate concepts is reiterated elsewhere, specifically in *Negative Dialectics*, as follows:

> All metaphysical ones however are pushed fatally into the apocryphal. The ideological untruth in the conception of transcendence is the separation of body and soul [*die Trennung von Leib und Seele*], reflex of the division of labor. It leads to the idolization of the *res cogitans* [thinking substance] as the principle which exploits nature, and to the material denial, which would dissolve in the concept of a transcendence beyond the context of guilt. Hope [*Hoffnung*] however clings, as in Mignon's song, to the transfigured body [*den verklärten Leib*].[130]

The question arises as to exactly what Adorno is referring to if not an image in this passage. What is the experience of such a "transfigured body" such that it remains all the while imageless?

Adorno has in mind an experience redolent in the early Jewish mystical sources. For instance, Scholem's research on the mystical shape of the godhead or *Shi'ur Komah* would have been accessible and read by Adorno in light of their aforementioned correspondence. Scholem's comments on the *Shi'ur Komah* literature end with a remark of Benjamin's, strongly echoing and encapsulating Adorno's thesis thus far:

> But the [mystics] were also inspired by the certainty with which, in the course of comparing the theory of emanation with the mystical linguistic theory of the name of God, they grasped the imageless which . . . is the refuge of all images.[131]

What such mystics revel in is the ability to live and experience the contradiction, in this case of imaging the imageless body, leading to its transfiguration.

The esoteric enigma of the "transfigured body" is revealed in varying forms of concealment in the mystical traditions.[132] This vision of the redeemed community as transfiguring into the divine body is most astonishing in the *Shi'ur Komah* corpus in its unabashed violation of the *Bilderverbot.* For the individual to be emancipated, subsumption within the identity of the singular collective imaged as the body is crucial. Scholem's interpretation of this experiential vision stemming from the extant fragments of the *Shi'ur Komah* literature presents matters as follows: "God's shape is conceived of, not as a concept or idea, but as names."[133] This interpretation turns on Scholem's astute interlocking of tactile and linguistic anthropomorphism, which resonates deeply with Adorno's allusions to the "transfigured body." In the eyes of these mystical confraternities, Redemption remains a tangible, audible mode of contemplation. It is a contemplative modality that is rooted in Thought but transcends it toward the root of Thinking itself. Adorno in many ways is in search of such an origin as well as a way of equilibrating the proximity of this "yearning" [*Sehnsucht*]¹³⁴ for Redemption. This stands in contrast to seduction of "the element of wish" [*das Element des Wunsches*]¹³⁵ in "wishful thinking." As Benjamin declared, this "more or less ascetic apprenticeship,"¹³⁶ rather than being a denial of yearning, transforms it into the root of unfulfilled fulfillment, arousing the search toward the root of its roots.

Adorno challenges those who claim this lived experience is merely a parable, rather it is "[o]nly in the parable of the body [*im Gleichnis des Leibes*] [that] the concept of pure spirit [can] be grasped at all." The challenge raised by the *Shi'ur Komah* teachings in light of Adorno's contemporary gloss, is whether such anthropomorphism, read "only in the parable [*im Gleichnis des Leibes*]," gives way to the spiritual, or if the parable itself is not to be fully discarded en route to the spiritual? It is at this point that the monolithic wall of the *Bilderverbot* gives way to a more porous division between Thinking and Thought.

Despite his scathing critique of its pseudoscientific occultation, the role of "the astral body" [*der Astralleib*]¹³⁷ for Adorno resonates with the *Shi'ur Komah* mystics as the "body of splendor" [*guf ha'kavod*] or the "body of the Indwelling Presence" [*guf ha-Shekhinah*]. Both instances are an imaging of the imageless, negating the negation. Scholem articulates that within the *Shi'ur Komah* teachings it is only by way of a strident anthropomorphism that a clearing is made for the spiritual beyond it, as:

> [T]here is no thoroughly shaped image that can completely detach itself from the depths of the formless: this insight is crucial for the metaphysics of the Kabbalah. The truer the form, the more powerful the life of the formless within it. To delve into the abyss of formlessness is no less absurd an undertaking for the Kabbalists than to ascend to the form itself; the mystical nihilism that destroys any shape dwells hand in hand with the prudent moderation struggling to comprehend the shape.¹³⁸

Adorno's redeeming of this neglected pathmark within mystical thinking is an attempt to transfigure "the hopeless" [*der Hoffnungslosen*] embodying an unemancipated society into the body of "Hope" [*die Hoffnung*].¹³⁹ This transfiguration, according to Adorno's innovative turn, begins within the source of a thinker's Thinking prior to the collective Thought of the communal body.

Turning full circle "Toward Ending" [*Zum Ende*], there is in no. 153 a return from the death of philosophy (where we began) to the conditions of its rebirth. The only responsible philosophy worthy of Redemption in the face of despair is one that will "contemplate [*betrachten*] all things as they would present themselves from the standpoint of Redemption [*vom Standpunkt der Erlösung aus sich darstellten*]."[140] Such a radical standpoint sees the contemplation necessary for redemptive thinking, in no. 152, not as the mastery of a Dialectic, "instead of giving himself [*sic*] up to it [*anstatt an sie sich zu verlieren*]."[141]

If knowledge has no autonomous light except that which is cast upon the world by way of Redemption, then the task of the thinker is to seek out the source of this light. The whole question of epistemology comes to light as the normative limitations of knowledge and knowing are surpassed by this return to the origin of Thinking beyond such limitations. However, refracting this light from Redemptive Thought back into the world of knowledge necessitates a distortion, perhaps through buffers like epistemology:

> Perspectives must be fashioned that displace and estrange the world, reveal it to be, with its rifts and crevices [*ihre Risse und Schründe*], as indigent and distorted as it will appear one day in the messianic light [*im Messianischen Lichte*].[142]

Such a self-reflexive perspective recalls the earlier "Gaps" [*Lücken*] in these "rifts and crevices" [*ihre Risse und Schründe*] of Thought. This reiteration of self-reflection, albeit distorted through the messianic light, is a movement through the hegemony of the concept to move beyond it: "Reflection upon its own meaning is the way out of the concept's seeming being-in-itself as a unity of meaning."[143] Such reflection is possible in a "consummate negativity, once squarely faced" to delineate "the mirror-writing [*Spiegelschrift*] of its opposite."[144] Adorno is discerning as always in his word choice here such that the reflection of the "mirror-writing" [*Spiegelschrift*] suggests a contemplation of letters rather than images per se. Again, in line with the mystical contemplation of letters, as opposed to images, which then retain an ontic reality prior to the ontological seduction posed by images. Regarding this stance toward the reflection confronted in the "mirror-writing" [*Spiegelschrift*], Adorno necessitates a complete revisioning of the classic exegetical teaching on the sign of the times for Redemption:

> The only difference between this-worldly-temporality and a redemptive-temporality is political enslavement, as Scripture teaches, "For there will never cease to be needy ones in your land: open your hand to the poor and needy kinsman in your land." (Deut. 15.11)[145]

This "mirror-writing" [*Spiegelschrift*] brings forth a bridge between letters as the ontic ground for existence and their temporal existence. Redemption within a "this-worldy-temporality" is now intimately linked to the building blocks of language and their ontic reality within existence. The aforecited Deuteronomy prooftext is the "mirror-writing" [*Spiegelschrift*] that is necessarily confronted in an awakened existence. If "everything would be in its right place" then the concept of suffering would not be eliminated, but its experience could be responded to immediately, rather than lingering for an eternity filled with despair. Like in that renowned vision of Redemption wherein the leper Messiah at the Gates of Rome[146] ensures that its humanity, albeit punctured, would not be inalterably delayed in tending to the wounds of others.

A final reflection on this tension between the individual and community is warranted as found within the dedication of *Minima Moralia*. This comment sheds further light on the conceptual experience of a "transfigured body" (politic), as Adorno remarks that:

> [I]n an individualistic society [*der individualistischen Gesellschaft*], the general not only realizes itself through an interplay of particulars [*Zusammenspiel der Einzelen*], but society is essentially the substance of the individual [*die Substanz des Individuums*].[147]

From the foundational Thinking of the thinker springs forth the Redemptive Thoughts that make communal existence possible. The interplay of the particulars now coming to light are in constant transformation through moments of somatic intervention. Only through somatic awareness can one come to know anything embodied in existence:

> But in it the somatic moment trembles epistemologically [*Mal das somatische Moment erkenntnistheoretisch*] for one last time, before it is completely driven out. In cognition it survives as its disquiet, which brings it into motion and reproduces itself unpacified in its course; unhappy consciousness is no deluded vanity of the Spirit but inherent to it, the sole authentic dignity, which it received in the separation from the body. This reminds it, negatively, of its corporeal aspect; solely that it is capable of this, lends it any sort of hope. The smallest trace of senseless suffering in the experienced world condemns the whole of identity-philosophy, which would like to talk experience out of this, as a lie: "So long as there is even a single beggar, there will be mythos"; that is why identity-philosophy is mythology as thought.[148]

The societal impulse toward Redemption finds its origin within the thinking thinker:

> The corporeal moment registers the cognition, that suffering ought not to be, that things should be different. "Woe speaks: go." That is why what is specifically materialistic converges with what is critical, with socially transforming praxis. The abolition of suffering, or its mitigation to a degree which is not to be theoretically assumed in advance, to which no limit can be set, is not up to the individual who endures suffering, but solely to the species that it belongs to, even where it has subjectively renounced the latter and is objectively forced into the absolute loneliness of the helpless object.[149]

Adorno is inexorably linking the societal task of redeeming physical suffering with the individual task of Thinking. Just as the group of lepers squatting at the City Gates collectively unbind and rebind their wounds, this is a motion of a collective body (politic) composed of thinking individuals, who can think the Thought to then say: "If we are called upon then we would not be delayed."

To truly move toward ending is to grasp the question in its depth, allowing a clearing to shine forth for the Thinking in need of being remembered into Thought. Recall that in Heidegger: "We have not yet attained to the region of that which, of itself and essentially, wishes be pondered."[150] We noted there to be a subtle shift from what "wishes to be pondered" to what the "need" [*das Bedûrfnis*] of thought is, as Adorno proffers: "The need [*das Bedûrfnis*] of thought [*im Denken*] is what makes us remember [*gedacht*]."[151] Benjamin's closing comment to his *Thesis B* sheds further light on this very futural remembrance within Thought that allows for time to be pregnant with possibility, "For every second of time was the strait gate through which the *Messiah might* enter."[152]

The object of critique for Adorno then remains the relation between Thinking (as a vital need in itself) and Thought (as action, realized in one's metaphysical experience of musical time). The reconfiguration of Thought and "need" now comes into a new correlation of ancient echoes. It is a call for a self-reflection upon embodiment, for: "what hope [*Hoffnung*] clings to . . . is the transfigured body [*den verklärten Leib*]."[153] What Adorno is time and again referring to by this *den verklärten Leib* is the focus of Scholem's investigation on the mystical shape of the godhead [*Shi'ur Komah*]. Proffered by Scholem, Thinking along this path is marked by its paradoxical trajectory, since:

> [O]ne may say that there is no thoroughly shaped image that can completely detach itself from the depths of the formless: this insight is crucial for the metaphysics of the Kabbalah. The truer the form, the more powerful the life of the formless within it. To delve into the abyss of formlessness is no less absurd an undertaking for the Kabbalist than to ascend to the form itself; the mystical nihilism that destroys any shape dwells hand in hand with the prudent moderation struggling to comprehend the shape.[154]

Hope is more than for the hopeless; hope is the freedom to move between Thinking and Thought. To encircle the wall separating Thinking from Thought—the veil between need and action—is to dance through Thought toward the light of Redemptive Thinking.

Part II

Reconstruction

Chapter 4

Exile on *Ben Yehudah Street*: How Reification of Israel Forgets to Re-Member Zion

Even after the murder
of the child Muhammad on *Rosh HaShanah*,
the paper didn't go black.
For that's how it's always been—
the murderers murder,
the *intellectuals* make it *palatable*,
and the *poet sings*.

—Aharon Shabtai[1]

(A wanderer, I make a prayer
of dust).
      Exiled, I sing
my soul until the world
burns to my chants
as to a miracle
            Thus am I
risen.
      Thus I am *redeemed*.

—Adonis[2]

Political Zionism, then, is another name for the *beginning* and the *end* of the "Semite," its paradoxically double *internalization* and *exteriorization*.

—Gil Anidjar[3]

Hebrew and Arabic: Inescapable Revolutions of Language in Exile

Is it possible for the recent declaration of National Hebrew Day on the 21st of *Tevet*, commemorating the birthday of Hebraicist, Eliezer Ben Yehudah

(1858–1922), to escape the perceived hegemony of the prime minister's proclamation of honoring this linguistic "cornerstone of the revival of Israel in its own land"?[4] By contrast, is it possible for the recent declaration of Arabic Language Day on March 22 at a school in Jerusalem to promote a revolutionary vision for integrated, bilingual community models where Jewish and Arab children learn together? The reality in need of redressing is that while Arab parents speak Hebrew to their children, few Jewish parents speak Arabic to their children anymore.[5] Elevating language is also about elevating relations and re-examining the nature of relations on the ground, in the Holy Land of Israel. What are people, once Semites, now Jew and Arab, to do about this challenge in their land? How can Jew and Arab feel at home with these competing languages and competing narratives swirling about amidst the landscape of the Holy Land? If Zionism, after Anidjar,[6] marks the end of the "Semite" then it also catalyzes an exilic state of being—especially while living in Israel.

A perception of a certain brand of Hebraic hegemony permeates Israel, even for Zionists, as the project of rebirthing the language becomes more one of secularization than integration of the sacred within the mundane. If Hebrew could be experienced in a more unified way, encompassing the holy and the profane through what Scholem saw as the "inescapable revolution of language" [*diese unausbleibliche Revolution der Sprache*],[7] how different would relations between peoples and the land be? Moreover, how will the poet sing a redemption song, in Hebrew and Arabic, when the land and people are so divided, when the language invoking the divine a thousandfold into our life will never allow God to stay silent?[8]

Adorno and Israel: Thinking Critically about Zionism

In attempting to think critically about Zionism and the Jewish state today, it becomes more and more apparent the degree to which I am writing about an exile on *Ben Yehudah Street*. While critical theorists in Israel remain divided over the semantics of "occupation" versus "internal-external colonialism," there remains a marginal realization that a "creative and more egalitarian alternative to the formula of a Jewish and democratic state"[9] is critical, even if it remains far in the offing. As a result, the dreams of Zionism are in exile, while its remains reign harshly over free discourse under the current regime.[10] Thus I argue that through exile, Zionism has given birth to a fragmented reality whereby race and religion have been separated to the point of no return. Rather than Adorno's critical thinking influencing Israel directly,[11] Hannan Hever[12] and Yitzhak Laor[13] are presently engaging in the most sustained critical thinking about Zionism today in Israel, through poetry, poetics, and political critique.

In the realm of the political, Zionism reinscribes what was already at work in the early invention of the Semites. It is this very turn away from religion, the distancing from "its Semitic, monotheistic, and desertic origins," that allows for the separation of "race from religion, and religion from (modern) politics, separat[ing], finally, the Jew from the Arab."[14] If Critical Theory has anything to contribute to the evolution of discourse of Israel and Palestine, it must begin by recognizing that more than a "self-occupation," this exile is embedded throughout language, land and people.[15] Unifying theory and praxis requires a complete undoing of the reification of concepts that has been settling in since 1948.

Ever-Changing Street: *Zion* as Marking

I have chosen a street named after the rebirthing agent of Hebrew language and identity as a semiotic marker, to locate both the lamentable reification as well as the intrinsic tension amidst the landscape that is contemporary Israel. Given that with street names in Israel "[t]he very act of naming something is indeed a political act,"[16] the Zionist project has attempted to achieve symbolic integration of a political struggle, a political-bureaucratic means of symbolic violence, and an ideological imprimatur onto collective memory.[17] If semiotic analysis of street names in Israel yields the realization that "urban space is being canonized, making the ordinary sublime and vice versa in a dialectal manner," then the markings, those very *ziyunim* of Zion, left upon the city's streets reveal an "ossified state of the ever-changing production and reproduction of collective memory."[18] It is that very state of ossification which will concern this reflection. Moreover, can the newly named activists and their streets within the Diaspora found in AIPAC and J-Street move the discourse beyond a reification of categorical thinking? This question from the Diaspora is asked with a deep yearning for Zion to catalyze a redemption of theory and praxis amidst reification, returning rather to recognition and caring.

Dark Hope of Returning Home: An Activist Memoir as Critical Thinking

In his imaginal vision of returning home to Talbiya, Jerusalem, poet Mahmoud Darwish realizes the absurdity in asking permission to sleep in his own bed, "And they would tell me: There is no place for two dreams/in one bedroom?"[19] As the dream of a two-state solution fades rapidly, and calls for a one-state solution concatenate forth, that lamenting sense of loss is conveyed by Darwish when he writes: "I could not meet loss face to face. I stood by the door like a beggar."[20] In his imaginal farewell to Edward Said (1935–2003), Darwish evokes the poet's call to freedom: "Invent a hope for speech,/invent a direction, a mirage to extend hope./And sing, for the aesthetic is freedom."[21] As the critic is charged to "invent a direction, a mirage to extend hope," it is the exilic poet who understands how poetry brings forth freedom.

In contrast to this bright hope beyond the mirage which critic and poet of Palestine both seek, there is the tenebrous hope that pervades the critic and poet of Israel. Turning to critic David Shulman's recent activist memoir, *Dark Hope: Working for Peace in Israel and Palestine*,[22] there is a deeper sense of exile operative within the word "peace" and the land of Israel itself. Exile of word and place permeates this intimate memoir, brimming with righteous indignation and yearning for a resolution through activism. Sharing "my own small slice of the reality in Israel and occupied territories in the unhappy years of 2002–2006,"[23] Shulman describes his exilic reality in Israel as follows:

> Throughout this period I did as many others did: I went to demonstrations; wrote letters to the minister of defense and the chief prosecutor of the army and the prime minister; went on convoys bringing food and medical supplies to Palestinian villages; was beaten up by settlers—the usual protocol for those active in the Israeli peace camp. I also read newspapers, taught my classes at the university, went to India, listened to music. Life went on as it always does, even in the midst of worsening disaster.[24]

What strikes the reader of the memoir in these introductory remarks are the final moments of what rounds out his dialectical existence, namely, taking on a self-imposed exile by going to India and listening to music in Israel as another exile of sorts. As an activist serving in the ranks of an Arab-Jewish Partnership called *Ta'ayush* (Arabic for "Living together," or "Partnership"), Shulman once again becomes capable of recovering a "certain sober hope" amidst the terror and cruelty of life in Israel-Palestine.[25] It is through the re-emergence of this sober hope being shared in *Ta'ayush* as well as in other activist realms that an Israeli is able to become more self-reflective about his exile. This disconnect is one whereby the Israeli lives in the Land of Israel while feeling "a kind of internal exile"[26] from it:

> There is a mystery, a historical conundrum, embedded in the fact that Israel, once a home to utopian idealists and humanists, should have engendered and given free rein to a murderous, also ultimately suicidal messianism. Did our deepest values, the humane heart of the Jewish tradition, always contain with them these seeds of self-righteous terror? Do these two modes inevitably intersect?[27]

This kind of cumulative, self-reflective questioning opens again the possibility of dialectic and the danger embedded within it. Seeing his own existence as framed by both the hope and empathy juxtaposed with a dark hatred and polarization of the world,[28] Shulman chooses to act and push this dialectic toward life.

The theme of exile returns again at the conclusion of Shulman's memoir. This sense of exile within Israel is deeply felt, especially regarding the need of Israelis like himself to leave for India in order to retain the rational option of continuing to live within Israel, no matter how fragmented that existence may be:

> Distance and the passage of time may impart a certain clarity. I spent the last seven months in India, blissfully removed from the ongoing tribal wars in Israel-Palestine. I lived and thought in another language—Telugu—and I can assure you that Telugu sees the worlds quite differently from how it looks, say, in Hebrew. Distance exposes the imbecility of tribal war.[29]

The distance of space, language, and culture, Shulman notes, is the necessary perspective that exile brings through critical thinking. Writing poetry and teaching Sanskrit in an Israeli university already puts Shulman in a unique position to attempt overcoming, as Palestinian poet, Darwish renders it, being in a state where "[t]he outside world is exile,/exile is the world inside."[30] A first step out of this cultural self-reification is recognizing how fragmented reality is and that the world inside need not remain disconnected from the reality on the outside.

Reification of Hope: Religious Zionism on Tour

To continue this exploration of redeeming Zionism from reification, it is necessary to delve into one of its current ossifying iterations. If there is a just and redemptive value to be reawakened in Zionism, then its underlying purpose needs to be articulated anew. Who then in Israel has the visionary power to articulate a Zionism grounded in critical thinking and praxis? When looking to the secular or religious Zionist camps for cues, it is difficult not to concur that critical Zionist thinking in Israel is currently in exile,[31] especially when religious Zionism is articulated by Diaspora Jews on tour.[32]

Some would argue that indeed it is American *émigré* Daniel Gordis who does just that with his most recent work, *Israel: How the Jewish People Can Win a War That May Never End.*[33] One can agree with many of the preliminary arguments presented, for example, that Israel is more than a theological response to the *Shoah* or anti-Semitism.[34] But clarifying the purpose of the Jewish state, "about what sovereignty enables the Jews to do and to become", remains an urgent concern. Again, one can agree that the purpose of the Jewish State is indeed to transform the Jews, *but into what?* What kind of transformation is taking place amidst poverty, discrimination, and racism accompanying massive waves of immigration?[35] While compassionate enough to acknowledge these difficult factors plaguing existence in Israel, the shift from socialism to free-market economy is seen uncritically as being incidental.[36] This kind of uncritical stocktaking continues unabated throughout Gordis' study, except in his noting that Israel is desperately in need of fulfilling its commitment to drafting a constitution.[37]

The lack of consensus in such a deeply divided society does not make space for the realization of the Constitution intended to follow the Declaration of Independence by October 1948. Why is it that 60 years later there remains no constitution, no consensus? Is this a sign of a vibrant liberal democracy or a nation-state in the throes of a dysfunctional and ever-dying democracy?

What the nature of Israel's democracy *is* and what it should *strive to be* need further critical reflection. The question then arises as to whether Israel is capable of critical thinking and if so, what aspect of society is willing and able to do such thinking and bring it into action? Undoubtedly, think-tanks in Israel abound, spanning the spectrum, for example, from the New Israel Fund (NIF) to the Shalem Institute. While it is reassuring that Shalem Institute president Daniel Polisar remarks how it is precisely "the power of ideas [that] has again galvanized the Jewish people" for the task of realizing "a thriving Jewish democracy in the heart of the Middle East," by what measure is this Jewish democracy thriving? Moreover, Polisar's description of the fruits of Zionism as combining "the rekindled spirit of nationhood with a fierce longing for freedom and the creation of a political community dedicated to justice"[38] necessarily leaves open the profound gap between yearning for ideals and their near non-action in reality that defines the quotidian in Israel. By contrast, there is the longstanding NGO in America and Israel, called the NIF, now headed by former MP, Naomi Chazan. Since 1979, "NIF has fought for social justice and equality for all Israelis," and it is a conviction nascent to Zionism that drives their mission, namely that: "Israel can live up to its founders' vision of a state that ensures complete equality of social and political rights to all its inhabitants, without regard to religion, race or gender."[39] Their commitment to performing justice stems from a vision that taking action against "inequality, injustice and extremism," is a kind of thinking that understands justice "as the precondition for a successful democracy—and the only lasting road to peace."[40]

In reaction to the critical rebalancing act performed by NIF in Israel, a country that continues to yearn for justice but too often fails to realize it through its existing governmental programs, comes the latest iteration of weak thought in the form of self-reification at its extreme. Rather than follow the other realm of anti-street signs, namely the graffiti trail around Israel that continues to read "Kahane was Right" or "No Arabs, No Explosions," this think-tank chooses to go down the road of countering those chants against democracy that preceded the assassination of Israel's prime minister, like *"Rabin traitor, Rabin murderer."*[41] This kind of action signifies the utter paucity of thinking, namely that there is no dialectic operating and that murder is the only way out of this *huis-clos.* So when a think-tank claims its namesake from Herzl's clarion call to Zionism, as *Im Tirtzu* (i.e. If you desire, it is no dream, *Im tirtzu, ain zo aggadah*), and fancies itself as the "Second Zionist Revolution,"[42] one must seriously question whether this is indeed a Jewish or a Christian Evangelical revolution.[43] While its goals are clearly stated, namely that: "*Im Tirtzu* is a centrist extra-parliamentary movement that is working to strengthen the values of Zionism in Israel, to

renew and reinstate Zionist discourse, thinking and ideology in order to secure
the future of the Jewish people and the State of Israel and strengthen Israeli
society *vis-à-vis* the challenges it faces," its actions in the sphere of public discourse beckon the question as to whether any discourse is really possible when
it is coercive, scapegoating and nothing near centrist. Moreover, its recent
spate of *agitprop* against dissenting voices within the context of an apparent
democracy do little to assure the skeptics of "centrist" thinking.[44] All this really
bespeaks a deeper denial facing Zionism today. Demonizing the other is a tell-
tale sign of the antithesis of "renewal" of anything except the most base, trium-
phalist messianism that Zionism needs to shed if it is to evolve. Irony of ironies,
it takes America to step in, once again, to squash the antidemocratic tendency
that brews in the *Knesset*, from stopping a ban on the free speech and activism
of NIF in Israel![45]

Reification of Zion: Loss of Center as Loss of Ground

Is there then a true "centrist" ground that remains in any of the think-tanks in
Israel, like the Israel Democracy Institute (IDI)? While the IDI realizes that
"Israel's 'great leap forward' has come at a price" is it truly poised to address the
reality on the ground of profound inequality existing within a democratic state?
As IDI's president, Dr. Arye Z. Carmon, remarks: "The atmosphere of constant
crisis has stunted the evolution of Israel's institutions of government and pre-
cluded serious discussion of the Jewish and democratic values underpinning
the State. The longstanding divisions within the Jewish majority and between
Jews and Arabs have eroded solidarity and bred inequality. Buffeted by the
international winds of globalization, terrorism and post-nationalism, Israel faces
the urgent need to reinvent the Zionist ideal in order to meet the realities
of the twenty-first century."[46] The danger facing the aforementioned think-
tanks is their succumbing to a process of self-reification, as Honneth remarks:
"Institutions that latently compel individuals merely to pretend to have certain
feelings, or to give them a self-contained and clearly contoured character, will
promote the development of self-reifying attitudes."[47] Nothing could be closer
to the truth of the moment.

While Gordis rightly attempts an interrogation into the nature of democracy
and its boundaries, he does so only to close that interrogation, lapsing into
self-reification, claiming that: "[i]f the Jewish character of the country is to be
safeguarded, Israel's supporters will have to accept that Israel's democracy
can never be the model of pure liberal democracy that political life in the
United States approximates."[48] Despite the fact that Gordis spills much ink on
the disparities between these two models of democracy, it is clear that cutting
off any alternative to these stark polarities eliminates the possibility of any dialectical process. Ultimately it leads to further ossification rather than evolution
or possible insight. In lieu of a caricature whereby "Israel is going to have to

shed its self-image as an American-wannabe,"[49] there is no critical engagement with the nature of the nation-state and the evolution necessary if it is to ultimately realize any true form of democracy.

Such a simplistic comparison on the part of Gordis between these different models of democracy is deserving of the scathing critique of Israeli poet and political activist Yitzhak Laor when he writes:

> I do not want to talk about the differences between United States and Israel. Seemingly nothing is easier. Take, for example, the cornerstone of American democracy and its pride and glory, the Constitution, and compare it to Israeli ethnography, which refuses, precisely because it is an ethnocracy, to bind itself to the Law, to a constitution that would guarantee equality before the law to all the nation's citizens . . . If one takes just that example, there is seemingly no need to explain further differences. But that is too easy. After all, Americans, even the most extreme pro-Israel individuals among them, value their Constitution above all else yet they know too that Israel does not have a constitution and nevertheless identify "us" with "you," over and over again.[50]

What remains however is a deeper sense of hope amidst hopelessness. Even Gordis admits early on that Israelis may be giving up hope for peace without giving up hope.[51] But what is now manifesting is a deeper self-loathing that characterizes Israeli life that really began the dystopian morning after June 1967. Ever since awakening the morning after that messianic moment, the moral fiber of the country has been delving into a gradual state of corrosion, as Yeshayahu Liebowitz (1903–1994), Israel's self-proclaimed Adorno,[52] warned in colonizing another people. Gordis is not fully immune to the entire impact of the occupation on one's humanity, when he reflects that:

> Occupation, regardless of its origins, exacts terrible tolls on both sides. It demeans the occupied. It can make the occupier callous, insensitive to the impact of occupation on those to whom he is just a soldier, not a human being.[53]

Yet despite the dehumanization that takes place, which "centrist" think-tanks like *Im Tirtzu* are simply incapable of witnessing, occupation trumps the humanitarian concerns at hand. Gordis seems more concerned with the lost humanity of the occupying soldier than with the occupied. To add insult to injury, Gordis persists in ambivalent apologia by claiming "complicated reasons" as disallowing a trading of captured territories for peace.[54] To claim that occupation is justified "regardless of its origins" is to ignore the protomessianic triumphalism that has metastasized since the morning after 1967. That messianic triumphalism has morphed into the normative messianism of religious Zionism in post-1967 Israel.[55] Weak thinking and strong apologia lead to this kind of uncontrollable spread of messianic triumphalism, no matter how unpragmatic.

What gets lost in the fog of this messianic triumphalism, however, is that regardless of the broad consensus about the applicability of the Geneva Conventions to the Israeli occupation it in no way implies that the occupation itself is *legal.* "[T]he question about whether an occupation itself is legal (a question for *jus ad bellum*)," as Nathaniel Berman has duly noted, "is simply irrelevant when it comes to the applicability of the rules governing the conduct of the occupation." The apparent thinking through of this issue, whether in America or in Israel, is a misunderstanding of the categorical connection between the rules concerning the initiation of armed force (*jus ad bellum*) and rules concerning the conduct of armed conflict (*jus in bello* or as international humanitarian law). No matter that "the applicability to the Israeli occupation of the Geneva Conventions and other treaties and customary rules governing its conduct commands a near-universal consensus among international lawyers,"[56] the pro-Israel thinking is that somehow amidst an apparent occupation, such conventions of war do not apply.

Rather than face the real ethical issues at hand in a nation-state that chooses to remain unbound by any constitution, Gordis claims the real ostrich-like avoidance of painful questions revolves around whether Zionist Israelis can still live with those of opposing views, claiming that going forward, the true Israeli "will need to convince those who do not wish to be part of the future of the Jewish state not to live in it."[57] Fascism never sounded so fair! Despite Gordis' aversion to importing the American culture he hoped to leave behind upon emigrating to Israel, he smacks of imported McCarthyism as the solution to vital norms of at best, a severely limited democracy. This kind of intolerance is matched only by a poetic myopia of even a nursery rhyme by Israel's poet laureate.[58] This poetic myopia extends to an even more troubling cultural myopia, in that Gordis sees this generation of "Hebrew-speaking gentiles" so devoutly secular they had "no access to the richness of the very texts that made the Hebrew language eternal" as endemic of the current culture outside Jerusalem. This of course could not be farther from the truth, as generations later there is the proliferation of secular *yeshivot* like *Alma* and *Binah* that are fashioning creative hybrids of secularism within Israel's religious society to great effect. Just another example of more "complicated reasons" for not seeing the depth of truth even within the poetics of one's own culture, never mind of the other.

Finally, there is the "new Jew" that Gordis seeks to create in the future Israel he is saving through the auspices of the Shalem Institute and Project David. Again it appears that one may agree with Gordis that: "The time has come to honor the revolution that was Zionism by inventing the new Jew once again. For its newly reconceived vision of the Jew, no less than its military, is going to be a key to Israel's hope for a future."[59] Yet if reimagining the Israeli Jew is critical, why is Gordis so limited in looking to the precedent of creating a world-class fighting force, or the secular Jews so liberated from Jewish content they become "Hebrew gentiles"? Or conversely, can Israeli Jews ever evolve beyond being what Laor calls "a very special kind of *colonized colonizer*" whereby "we are part of you as long as we are here"?[60] Ultimately, the challenge of Boyarin and Elon stands, namely, if Zionism has replaced Greekness as the means to Jewish masculinity and assimilation, is it a sufficient construct for future longeviety?[61]

How Zion May Mark Out a Future: Overcoming Reification through a Poetics of Justice

What both Gordis and Laor fail to see is how the new Jew is already a part of a burgeoning Hebrew culture in Israel. Along with either a poetic myopia or a cultural one, the renaissance happening right under their noses is missed, especially in journals like *Dimui* or *Mashiv haRuah*. These journals are forums for the future direction of the love of Zion that are not fixed to the categories of religious Zionist or secular messianist. Rather as phenomena these journals are to be read as cultural hubs that are already creating a more creative discourse whereby the new Jew has more than ever to say about what Israel *is*, what it *should be*, and why it *matters*. Returning to honor that revolutionary call of Zionism is crucial, but needs guidance.

This brings us full circle to the need for overcoming self-reification on the personal, interpersonal, and communal levels. Although social criticism, as Honneth remarks, "has essentially limited itself to evaluating the normative order of societies according to whether they fulfill certain principles of justice," it is clear that "this approach has lost sight of the fact a society can demonstrate a moral deficit without violating generally valid principles of justice."[62] Social criticism no longer seems capable of discerning social pathologies when the dialectic of desire and justice is not resolved. This leads to an abrogation of the ethical or at the very least reserving it for "a sacrosanct interpretive authority."[63] Even more problematic, when social criticism is attempted, too often it is shut down by coercive ideologues that brandish the sword of anti-Zionism over any and all critique. If awareness of reification has the power to elicit a corrective tenet of Critical Theory again, then this dehumanizing tendency needs to be seen as forgetfulness of recognition.[64] The stakes are high for Honneth, as he points to the raîson d'être of his research on reification as stemming from "the difficulty in interpreting 'industrial' mass murder." The challenge remains before any Critical Theory, such that:

> Even today it is difficult to comprehend reports describing how young men could nonchalantly shoot hundreds of Jewish children and women in the back of the head. And elements of such horrifying practices can also be found in all the genocides that marked the end of the twentieth century. If we as humans relate to each other through antecedent recognition, . . . then these mass murders raise the question as to how we can explain the vanishing or "forgetting" of this previous recognition.[65]

This is precisely why it is important to return to Critical Theory, even amidst the exile on *Ben Yehudah Street* that encapsulates contemporary Israel. The pursuit of justice is always possible, even if not fully realized, but the more that this pursuit comes from an ingrained sense of recognition (or its reawakening), the more that such tragic forgetfulness of antecedent recognition can be seen as aberrant. Only then will cultural rebalancing come more rapidly and institutional self-reification become less prevalent. In Israel, however, there remains an urgent need to return to negative dialectical thinking. Such thinking can be witnessed in the poetic critiques of Yitzhak Laor[66] and Hannan Hever.[67] But such thinking may also be recovered in the neo-Hegelian dialectics of the first Chief Rabbi of Mandate Palestine, Rav Avraham Isaac Kook (1865–1935). Yet it takes a Diaspora thinker who has served in the IDF, like Shaul Magid, to begin that process of recovery, by outlining the contours of this process of return to negative dialectical thinking through a re-evaluation of spiritual aesthetics.[68]

Reconfiguring Critical Thinking and Zionism: Re-Membering Revelation from Artists to Lawmakers

The reconfiguration of Critical Thinking in a Judaism that has become so utterly artless needs to begin by what Magid reads in Rav Kook as the "distinctive assertion exhibiting a dialectical tolerance and affirmation of literary and visual art . . . as a vehicle for at least three things: (1) disclosing [a] messianic utopian vision; (2) curing the ossification of the rabbinic imagination, and (3) using art to extend a mystical critique of contemporary rabbinism."[69] It is aesthetics in general, and for Kook visual art in particular, that have the capacity to perform a negative dialectical function of undermining (and thus reconfiguring) a traditional Judaism that had become mired in the minutia of legal distinctions.[70]

If the law has enabled the freedom to change as it must to evolve, even in a theocracy, then the artist must be in a position to guide the rabbi through the limitations of their sacred vocation.[71] If the streets are affected by "beautifying Jerusalem (something he says has not existed since the destruction) and 'open[ing] the aesthetic sensibilities' that are innate, but concealed, in the nation of Israel,"[72] is an integral part of the culture and governance, then an awakening from self-reification is not only inevitable but ongoing. Already in Kook's pre-State consciousness there is an awareness that "both morality and righteousness are defined here as part of the beautification of Jerusalem, both literally and metaphorically."[73] What should be coursing through the veins of artists and singing through the streets of Judah is something more than the "symbols of a bourgeois effort to disengage from the large national narrative and legitimize concrete and particular interests."[74] The time for the concretion of a more diaphanous spirituality through diverse aesthetic modalities[75] is long overdue—only the artists have the capacity to show the lawmakers the way to such expansive consciousness.

What needs to be recovered then in contemporary Israeli discourse is Rav Kook's daring assumption that institutions like "the *Bezalel Art Institute* [exist] as a 'Jewish' art institute [with] one of its goals the creation of a genre of art that while not Jewish in any formal sense, expresses the pioneering spirit of the Jewish people and the Land of Israel."[76] The corrective to exilic consciousness, which even today permeates living in the Land of Israel, is found in all artistic expression. Whereas for Kook such artistry as "done for the sake of national renaissance is not only a legitimate practice,"[77] it is the artist who can envision the texture of an aesthetic for a just society. Yet it is "only the sage who is at once embedded *in* and transcendent *of* the rabbinic world, one who can facilitate the dialectic of subversion as fulfillment, [who] can carry through this project to its conclusion."[78]

That vision of the artist as prophet needs to be heard with greater clarity and urgency today in the existing ministries of culture and governance throughout Israel, so that the separation fences cutting off culture and power might become more porous, more just, and more beautified.[79] Harnessing the intellect in the service of negative dialectical thinking through the practice of what Magid calls "*halakhah* as art"[80] is a critical part of this revolutionary process. This truly revolutionary corrective in thinking would put to rest, once and for all, the current status quo of *halakhah* as coercive theocracy that rules the day in Israel. Only once the Bezalel Institutes and the Cinémathèques of Tel Aviv and Jerusalem have a seat around the table of the Knesset will any love of Zion be truly capable of revealing a new vision for a viable future. One can only wonder why it is then that a recent exhibit title at the Jewish Museum, called "Reinventing Ritual," happens to be taking place in New York with Israeli artists? Why is it that Israeli artists who have something significantly critical to express through their work must ultimately export it? If *halakhah* as art can once again be truly thought and practiced, then this kind of critical reinvention of ritual already underway needs to be taking place not only in its exported forms in America, but even amidst the exile within Israel. Only when theory and praxis reunite can Israel be redeemed from reification so that Zion can once again be authentically re-membered.

Chapter 5

Returning to Authenticity: From Jargon to Praxis of Critical Judaism

Spiritual freedom means: flattering no one,
neither *oneself* nor the *world*; not being subservient
to anyone, neither to the *self* nor to the *society*.

—A. J. Heschel[1]

Until further notice, *authenticity* and *inauthenticity* have as their criterion the decision in which the *individual subject* chooses itself as its own possession. The subject, the concept of which was once created in contrast to reification, thus becomes reified. Yet at the same time reification is scoffed at objectively in a *form of language* which simultaneously commits the same crime.

—Theodor W. Adorno[2]

For intellectuals, it is a matter of *correcting the perspective of public issues* within the descriptive system accepted by the democratic public sphere, whereas for social critics, it is a matter of *interrogating* that *descriptive system itself.*

—Axel Honneth[3]

Truth and Critical Theory: Gaps in *Eigentlichkeit* and *Emesdikeyt*

There is truth and then there is *truth*—authenticity is the integration of praxis and theory. Authenticity is the act of living and thinking within that deeper truth. Such integration requires interruption. To see the relative orders of truth and dismantle the very presuppositions upon which they rest is the task of every seeker of truth. Such a seeker is a social critic rather than an intellectual. Most, even many intellectuals, are content to live out existence in some version of a first-order truth. But to live an authentic life, one must ultimately seek a higher order of truth—a more authentic truth. Belonging to oneself and being beholden to a greater truth is crucial if Critical Theory is to have any persistence, durability, and efficacy in the lived life.[4] This is a paradoxical belonging that is both *in the world* but *not of it*. This is living from "an internal perspective that has been displaced to the outside" so as to "observe the whole of practices and convictions that have spread in their own culture of origin with a growing distance as a second nature."[5] It is from such margins that one is positioned, as third generation critical theorist, Axel Honneth remarks, to "see a unified mechanism in the multiplicity of public statements and events."[6] Getting the proper distance from "socially rehearsed interpretive models" can draw its spiritual source from exile or even "outsiderness."[7]

At the outset, within the term authenticity itself, there is already a profound distance separating *Emesdikeyt* from *Eigentlichkeit*. It is in this very chasm separating these two approaches that there arises a need for bringing theory and praxis into closer alignment so as to live out that authenticity. When meaning boils down to the sense of belonging to oneself, and oneself separate from society, then the self becomes the last, unlosable possession within *Eigentlichkeit*. If self becomes the ultimate measure of meaning, then such "metaphysics ends in a miserable consolation: after all, one still remains what one is."[8] If this very "selfness of the self, is to provide the ground . . . which the authentics possess and the inauthentics lack,"[9] then as Adorno warns, the danger is of transforming "a bad empirical reality into transcendence."[10] How can this trap of *Eigentlichkeit* be avoided while searching for truth?

The authenticity of *Emesdikeyt*, by contrast, is about living a uniquely subjective truth while remaining interconnected with other beings. Arbiters of how "authentic" authenticity *should be* are highly suspect, if not a complete threat to freedom. This is captured in a remarkable gathering that took place in the early 1920s; as Adorno describes it, "Their common ground was an emphasis on a newly acquired religion, and not the religion itself . . . they were less interested in the specific doctrine, the truth content of revelation, than in conviction."[11] He continues to recount how his friend, who was attracted to this group of seekers, was not invited. "He was—they intimated—not *authentic enough*."[12] This is partly where the danger of jargon begins, when it unites anti-intellectual intellectuals. Too often those who confirm their convictions on a higher plane by excluding an other unwilling to "pronounce the same credo"[13] are taken to be authentic. Yet even when this misperception is confirmed, the anxiety pulsates unabated.

Theory Split from Praxis: The Cracks within Everything

Not living up to what one can truly be, or what one is called to be, lies at the core of every subject's anxiety. When one is gripped by false consciousness, the release can take years away from life. That is the predicament of Ernst Simon (1885–1977)—of living a dichotomized life, separating discourse from prayer, and prayer from discourse that overflows with false consciousness. But it is a predicament familiar to too many for Simon to have stated his case in vain: *The people I can pray with, I can't talk to; and the people I can talk to, I can't pray with.*[14] But if so many succumb to this dichotomized way of living, why does it persist? Partly, it is a function of our atomized existence—no matter how integrated the culture industry makes us feel, there always remains a supreme sense of alienation. As the realities of one-dimensional society continue to take hold, the ideality of social change dissolves. It becomes more and more apparent that "in the absence of a decisive agent of social change,"[15] there is a feeling of radical aloneness. The Frankfurt School saw as its task the restoration of the actuality of critical rationality. What gives birth to so much pain in existence is the sense of a split between theory and praxis, between thinking and doing, and so authentic life is put on hold.

That split is sometimes a function of a kind of romantic thinking. This is the romanticism of returning to religion's *doing* while abdicating its *thinking*. That gesture of the romantic return to authentic religion more often than not leads to a bifurcated existence where one does religion *without thinking*. For the Frankfurt School this is also a kind of "reification" of the concepts embedded in religion and represents for them a kind of "forgetting" what experience actually belied those concepts to begin with.[16] As a result, it is urgent to follow in the wake of the Frankfurt School, whose work was "essentially a remembrance, from the historical setting of the mid-twentieth century, of the notion of critical reason."[17] One can only last so long in oppressing both natural drives and the need to question until this bifurcation leads to living an utterly compromised and thus compartmentalized life, pursuing critical study *here*, while praying *there*. Why is it then that religious existentialism always appears to veer away from any modicum of Critical Thinking?

Aura of Authenticity and the Dangers of Existentialism

Religious existentialism comes to give space to the voice of the individual seeking meaning. This shift is especially pronounced in postwar Germany and its existentialists, especially Martin Buber (1878–1965) and Martin Heidegger (1889–1976). Once the *Shoah* had destroys the fallacy of "objectivism" then existentialism, in part, serves as a retreat from the brutality of objectivity gone mad. Yet now in the ashes of Auschwitz, what Adorno could see most clearly is that the German existentialist perspective "became an ideological mystification of human domination—while pretending to be a critique of alienation."[18] This is where the jargon sets in, with the proliferation of magical expressions, what Walter Benjamin (1892–1940) called "aura."[19] It is this "aura of existentialism" and its apparent historical need for meaning, freedom, and equality that lead to the mystification of any relation between language and its objective content. What Adorno must critique is the jargon of authenticity's incapacity to express the relation between language and truth.[20] The ensuing false objectivism causes a loss of the reflection's intent necessary to maintain the thinking subject's self-consciousness. So the truth of an individual's path in thinking is effaced by a false objectivity masquerading with the aura of authenticity. The situation of romantic return to religion is a classic culprit of such false objectivity. The pure expressivity of ritual life and idealized forms devoid of any spiritual content has the alluring aura of authenticity. But integrity and truth are lost to fetishisms of the jargon[21] as human consciousness slips back into false objectivism and unawareness.

Despite the aura of authenticity that pervades Buber's normative mystical paradigm of subjectivity he referred to as *Ich und Du* or I and Thou,[22] religiosity becomes an end in itself. There is a shift taking place whereby subjectivity eclipses critical reason as an *in-it-selfness*. Nothing but the totality of one's own subjective experience becomes the marker of authenticity. This retreat into selfhood is rife with dangers. Lamentably, one need only recall Buber's encounter with his student, and that student's consequent suicide, to realize that complete retreat into subjectivity without any connection to critical reason is at its limit case, suicidal.

That fateful afternoon continued to haunt the master's thinking when a young student, unknown to Buber, came to his office in search of guidance upon his search for authenticity. Buber assumed his natural role as teacher: "I certainly did not fail to let the meeting be friendly, and I did not treat him any more remissly than all his contemporaries who were in the habit of seeking me out about this time of the day as an oracle that is ready to listen to reason."[23] Buber was attentive to the student's questions, as they conversed openly together. The conversation meandered until the young man left Buber's office. Not long after this meeting, Buber was informed that the young man had committed suicide. Buber was devastated.

Regarding the conversation with this young seeker, after having learned of the suicide Buber remarked that although he answered the student's questions, he "omitted to guess the questions which he did not put."[24] Buber then realized that the young man had come to him "not casually, but borne by destiny, not for a chat but for a decision."[25] The teacher understood this student was on a quest for authenticity, a yearning for meaning in his existence. From that moment on, Buber recollected, it was the everyday encounter that mattered to him the most, the concrete and ordinary everyday relationships between one human being and another, as he writes: "If that is religion then it is just *everything*, simply all that is lived in its possibility of dialogue . . . This moment is not extracted from it, it rests on what has been and beckons to the remainder that has still to be lived. You are not swallowed up in a fullness without obligation, you are willed for the life of communion."[26] Should one then be really surprised by this suicidal reaction to religiosity functioning as an end in itself? When subjectivity eclipses critical reason as an *in-it-selfness*, the subject before the other in the encounter becomes an object, all living encapsulated in the encounter universalizes the relationship without allowing for its singularity to shine through.

Struggling with Authenticity: Returning to Religious Existentialism

Another exemplar of that struggle within the confines of religious existentialism to seek out and live the truth is revealed in the recent recovery projects of a certain lost strand of Polish Hasidism known as Przysucha. This strain of religious thought, so preoccupied with authenticity, emanates only a few generations from the spiritual revolutionary of Hasidism, known as the Ba'al Shem Tov (BeSH"T). In the fourth through sixth generations of disciples from the revolutionary teachings during the early eighteenth century of the BeSH"T, one encounters a consistent focus on authenticity within the confines of religious existentialism through the teachings of Rabbi Yaacov Yitzhak, the Yehudi (d. 1814), Rabbi Simhah Bunim of Przysucha (d. 1827), and Rabbi Menahem Mendel of Kotsk, the Kotsker Rebbe (d. 1859).

One act of recovering Przysucha and translating it into contemporary idiom is marvelously captured in A. J. Heschel's *magnum opus* on the Kotsker Rebbe, originally titled, *In Gerangl far Emesdikeyt*, or *Struggling with Authenticity*.[27] Rendering the intimate struggle in this Yiddish title into a more universal and somewhat neutralized tone with *A Passion for Truth*,[28] Heschel's own authenticity is smelted through the dialectical lens of the Ba'al Shem Tov and the Kotsker Rebbe. While one's heart is in Mezbizh and one's mind is in Kotsk,[29] within this dialectic, Heschel points to the primacy and volatility of authenticity within the religious life of devotion. While a deeper refinement of the immediate is possible, there is the constant peril of forfeiting authenticity.[30] For an imbalanced authenticity without love can be damaging to oneself and to the other.[31]

In keeping with the themes of existentialism at large, part of what comes through in *A Passion for Truth* is the focus on free will and the empowerment in choosing and acting on one's own decisions.[32] But such a search for truth is delimited by Judaism; if indeed "Judaism is Truth, Truth is inwardness, inwardness is authenticity and authenticity is attained through intense, passionate inner action."[33] This focus on inner action as the path to authenticity is not limited to human life, rather "what he sought was the authenticity of transcending human nature in confronting and observing God's requirements."[34] It is the falsehood of self-regard and self-centeredness that creates the overwhelming sense of inauthenticity that pollutes the sphere of religion.[35] This leads to the understanding that "to be authentically human is to be able both to surpass oneself and to fulfill one's special relevant role *vis-à-vis* God."[36] Yet this quest for authenticity is singular and must be traversed alone which brings its own sense of agony and estrangement.[37] Must religious authenticity become a solitary quest divorced from disciples and community? Or does such a communal structure exist that could support this kind of quest? That question will be addressed in our sixth chapter, "From Jewish Radicals to Radical Jews: Truth of Testimony as Model for Community."

Despite moments of brilliance in Heschel's translation of the Kotsker into a contemporary and more universal path for Judaism, reading the Kotsker in comparison with Danish philosopher, theologian and cultural critic, Søren Aabye Kierkegaard (1813–1855) remains problematic. Adorno appears better equipped to think critically through Kierkegaard's nemesis of self-love.[38] By glossing over this difference, Heschel elides important differences between Jewish and Christian existentialism.

Refining the Gap: Between *Emesdikeyt* and *Eigentlichkeit*

The other act of recovering the *Emesdikeyt* in Przysucha Hasidism and translating it into contemporary idiom is found in the more recent *The Quest for Authenticity*.[39] In this systematic study, Michael Rosen attempts to delineate the elements of the search for authenticity that sets apart the quality of this search through the course of Przysucha Hasidism. The search for truth and the quest for authenticity are mediated by a passion and purity of motive as well as an intolerance of routine and external measures of accomplishment.[40] What Rosen manages to convey is the need for analyzing this body of received teachings in a more organic and contextual manner, namely that the seemingly idiosyncratic quest for authenticity that somehow appears in the Kotsker Rebbe's teachings actually follows a line of inquiry stemming from earlier generations.[41] The supreme value of personal authenticity within the soul searching that typifies the religious existentialism of Przysucha Hasidism (*Emesdikeyt*) differs dramatically from the philosophical existentialism so focused on the selfness of self,[42] which Adorno is so critical of in Heidegger (*Eigentlichkeit*). The contrast could not be starker in terms of delineating a point of entry into engagement with personal authenticity, whether it be through the doorway of *Emesdikeyt* as the doorway of the human soul in search of the divine or through the doorway of *Eigentlichkeit* as the self in search of the transcendent nature of selfness. It is the inviolable nature and deep intensity of such a piety based on personal authenticity that sets this prime focus of *Emesdikeyt* in Przysucha Hasidism apart from any of its precursors.[43]

What drives this quest for authenticity? While there is much passion for truth, as Heschel already portrays in his renowned Kotsk-mind and Mezbizh-heart dialectic,[44] Rosen translates this as a cognitive-affective dialectic.[45] What is lost in Heschel's often ambiguous existentialism of *A Passion for Truth* is what Rosen reiterates here as the nature of connection necessary for the search for *Emesdikeyt* in Przysucha—the inner core of the heart being uncovered is the real source of connection with ultimate meaning known as the divine.[46] Introspection is a method for serving with sincerity,[47] however, purity of motive becomes, what Rosen calls, "the umbilical cord to consciousness."[48] Seeing that introspection itself is never enough, lest it entrap one in seeking out the self-ness of self, this is why there is such an intensive focus on purifying the motive. By contrast, the necessary purification of motive that arises from introspection then leads to an intolerance of external expectations imposed upon the self. When a devotional regimen becomes a rote routine, it is devoid of passion and damaging to that integral connection between the human soul and the divine.[49]

Shifting from the particulars of the human-divine matrix to the more general existential situation, authenticity is no less challenging. The catastrophic potential of authenticity is seen to originate, according to Charles Taylor, in the confusion of *manner* and *matter*.[50] The shift of focus toward the subject as the center of the universe rather than some external reality leads to more autonomy and thus a greater responsibility for that very freedom:

> Modern freedom and autonomy centers us on ourselves, and the ideal of authenticity requires that we discover and articulate our own identity.
>
> But there are two importantly different facets to this movement, one concerning the *manner* and the other concerning the *matter* or content of action. . . . Authenticity is clearly *self-referential*: this has to be my orientation. But this doesn't mean that on another level the *content must be self-referential*; that my goals must express or fulfill my desire or aspirations, as against something that stands *beyond* these.[51]

The subtle distinction here that Taylor so aptly warns of revolves around the potential confusion of self-referential *manner* versus *matter*. The catastrophe of the contemporary moment is to live under the illusion that self-referentiality of *matter* is as inescapable as self-referentiality of *manner*. The contemporary culture industry cannot escape its manner of constantly referring to self, nevertheless the content of that referencing can transcend immediate desires that ultimately extend beyond the self.

Adorno's Critique of Heidegger: When *Eigentlichkeit* Elides into *Jemeinighkeit*

It is here that a necessary corrective to the catastrophic elision of Heidegger's *Eigentlichkeit*[52] is recovered through Adorno's critical thinking. Self as the locus of the universe or *always-being-my-own-being* [*Jemeinighkeit*][53] as embodied in Heidegger's *Da-sein* conflates this self-referentiality of *manner* with a lethal monolithic self-referentiality of *matter*. Despite the transparency that comes through self-knowledge,[54] Heidegger's *Eigentlichkeit* leads to an effacement of alterity and makes space for (even justifying) a completely subjective ethics. This stance typifies a nonrelational *being-toward-death*[55] that paves the way for thinking through to the Final Solution of the *Shoah.* Inauthenticity arises when one becomes too entangled in the busyness of the world to be awakened to authentic existence.[56] It is through the experience of angst that disclosure of truer self is possible and individualization takes place. Such individualization opens up the possibility of confronting authenticity or inauthenticity as a path for living.[57]

What Adorno is attempting with *The Jargon of Authenticity* is to transcend and include in the perspective of critical reason the truth of human subjectivity.[58] Despite the appearance of seeking fulfillment in life, Adorno criticizes Heidegger for advocating the unfulfillment of life by projecting existentialism from the beginning.[59] The authenticity being proffered perpetuates *want* over and against abundance. So the process that makes for transparency of the self requires a narrowing focus on *mineness*, to the point where *Da-sein* must choose itself as its *own possession* to be authentic.[60] Whatever attempt has been made by Heidegger to free the subject from reification for Adorno, has become utterly reified.[61] There appears then to be little in the way of true self-transformation, providing no consolation to the downfall of metaphysics, if "after all, one still remains what one *is.*"[62] By proffering a ground of being that has "no substratum but its own concept, the tautological *selfness* of the self," the path to authenticity is irreparably damaged in that "it transforms a bad empirical reality into transcendence."[63] What results is a contradictory subjectivity, whereby fact and reality are attributed to consciousness.[64] This presents a problem to the process of self-transparency since whatever is inauthentic for *Da-sein* becomes unidentical with itself and reinscribes the very identity-thinking of Idealism which Heidegger sought to escape.[65] The experience of consciousness then becomes reduced to *self-experience.*[66]

A Need for Subtler Languages: Adorno in light of Taylor

There is a need for subtler languages, and no one articulates this more succinctly than philosopher Charles Taylor. In his *Ethics of Authenticity,* Taylor invokes the clarion call for subtler languages whereby the poet at this hour must at once define, create, and manifest the authentic matter at hand.[67] This call to manifestation of authenticity is partly a function of disconnection from divine and secular history,[68] or existing in a time when as the poet Hölderlin once phrased it, "holy names are lacking [*es fehlen heilige Nahmen*]."[69] There is a perforation of the holy from within existence, seeing that the correspondence once intrinsic to living has been ruptured.[70] What Taylor is charging beings to realize is that authenticity is too important to relegate to unrefined language and inaction. Rather, "[i]f authenticity is being true to ourselves, . . . then perhaps we can only *achieve it integrally* if we recognize that this sentiment *connects us to a wider whole."*[71] That awareness of the wider whole of existence to which the individual is inextricably linked can be compensated, for Taylor, "by a stronger *inner* sense of *linkage.*"[72] And yet for authenticity to shine forth, that inner sense of linkage must be interlinked with an outer sense as well, one which appreciates the "shape of human life and its relation to the cosmos."[73] In contrast to Heidegger's polarities of angst and care, the task of an ethics of authenticity within modernity, for Taylor, is to embrace its polarities of grandeur and misery.[74] When collective existence becomes too instrumental or atomistic, the individual withdraws into hopelessness and alienation.[75] Rather than becoming swallowed up by a vicious circle of fragmentation resulting from a lack of identification and powerlessness, one strives to be uplifted within the virtuous circle of common action and empowerment.[76]

Experiential Philosophy Reconsidered: Adorno in light of Rosenzweig

Reb Zusha told his students:

When I reach Heaven and they ask me: "Why weren't you like Abraham our forefather?"

I will answer: "Because I wasn't Abraham."

If they inquire: "Why didn't you match the greatness of Moses?"

I can answer that I wasn't Moses. Even if they try to compare me to my brother Reb Elimelech, I can still say that I wasn't Elimelech.

However, if they ask me: "Why weren't you Zusha?"

. . . to that I have no answer.[77]

The resolution for a critical thinking and praxis of Judaism begins in returning to Zusha's anxiety over the perpetual call to be authentic, to be true to that core, both internally and externally. It is an experiential philosophy which opens one to the movement between ideas and reality, between concepts and experience. Already intuited early on by Franz Rosenzweig (1886–1929) even before 1925, there is that need to integrate theory and praxis since:

Experience, no matter how deeply it may probe, will discover again and again in man only what is human, in the world only what is worldly, in God only what is divine. . . . [I]t is at that point, where philosophy to be sure would come to the end of [its way of] thinking, that experiential philosophy [*erfahrende Philosophie*] can begin.[78]

That very same desire for a deeper integration of theory and praxis links Rosenzweig to Adorno. The willingness to challenge the reification of the concepts of humanity, the world, and God by Rosenzweig is carried forward in

Adorno's need for existence to be modulated by negative dialectics. Rosenzweig articulates this circle of mutual renewal between theory and praxis in the following manner:

> Such confidence in experience would be the teachable and transmittable aspect in new thinking, if, as I certainly feared, precisely this confidence itself is already an indication of a renewed thinking.[79]

The reciprocity of experience and knowledge is remarkable in this passage in that it points to the ongoing renewal of thinking. Living that truth as an experiential philosophy requires a flexibility that never fully succumbs to reifying authenticity as a concept. Rather one must live with enough flexibility to find ways onto the authentic path for as long as possible. And when inauthenticity sets in or takes over, as it inevitably does, there is always a greater sense of hope propelling one on in the journey. This journey is uplifted within the virtuous circle of common action and critical thinking constantly awaiting its reunification.

Chapter 6

From Jewish Radicals to Radical Jews: Truth of Testimony as Model for Community

Arbetn oif zich

—Kotsker Rebbe

Abrbeit macht frei

—Auschwitz

Anyone who pointed, for example, to the lack of any *spontaneous resistance* by the German *workers* was told in reply that things were so much in a *state of flux* that such judgments were impossible; anyone who was not on the spot, right among the poor German *victims* of aerial warfare—*victims*, however, who had few objections to air-raids as long as they were directed at the *other side*—had no right to open his mouth, and in any case agrarian reforms were imminent in Rumania and Yugoslavia.

—Adorno[1]

Nous sommes tous les juifs allemands
—Protestors for Daniel Cohn-Bendit, 22 mai, 1968

All German Jews? Come on now, we were all imaginary Jews
—Alain Finkelkraut[2]

Critical Theory after the Revolutions: From Germany to France

One of the greatest challenges facing Critical Theory is its process of translation into community. Is there a clarity of purpose and vision that Critical Theory can provide to those ready to act upon this work and create conscious community?

Moreover, when theory and praxis unite, what is the nature of the work that emerges for a given Jewish community to open to such a transformation? That is the question this chapter seeks to explore in the wake of Adorno through the lens of his Critical Theory. Amidst Adorno's exile from and return to Frankfurt, the only encounter with a real revolution[3] took place in Berkeley during its student uprising. As this student activism made its way into his classroom, Adorno's distrust and distance grew from the revolution in his midst.[4]

Rather than focus on the *near* revolutions that were never fully realized in Germany,[5] it is the recent history of the May 1968 revolution in Paris and its afterlife in Critical Theory that will serve as our present case study. What model of community emerged when the Sorbonne became a commune and poetry ruled the streets in May 1968? *A traditional community or an elective community? A negative community or a community of lovers? An undisclosable community or a community of testimony?* While members of the Institute for Social Research, primarily of assimilated Jewish descent (like Adorno), constituted a community of critical theorists unto themselves, their impact upon other communities was more theoretical than practical. By contrast, the scope of the May 1968 revolution starting in Paris, for example, was much broader and it had a unique influence upon the Jewish radicals who transformed into radical Jews in France. Further exploration is required into the distinction between "Jews who are radicals," as opposed to "radicals who happen to be Jews" and their ensuing forms of community.[6]

While our previous chapter presented Adorno's early and prescient critique of Heidegger, we will now extend this critique by comparing and considering how Lévinas' critique of Heidegger affects the work of transforming Jewish radicals into a conscious community of radical Jews. The Adorno-Lévinas correlation is a comparative construct contrasting German and French cultures that still both share a common desire to unite theory and praxis. What the Lévinasian critique of Heidegger points to is a shift in how the truth of testimony overcomes the truth of disclosure. What becomes clear is that the work of the May 1968 revolution shattered the social identity that allowed politics as usual to take place in France. In the revolution that shook the Gaullist regime to its foundations, France experienced a watershed moment when the dialectic of theory and praxis united. There was a new experience of living freedom and liberty that could be truly thought at the moment. There was a shift in how the truth of testimony could overcome the truth of disclosure.

Undisclosable Community or a Community of Testimony: Blanchot's Critical Legacy

By contrast to the American response to the student uprisings that integrated this radical spirit of innovation into Jewish communal models, like *Havurat Shalom* founded in 1968,[7] there remains a growing cultural reluctance to consider collective political agency in France, specifically among French Jewry. That is why these questions become critical. While these categories of community are suggested by a philosopher and critical theorist, like Maurice Blanchot (1907–2003) (whose pivotal moment of interrogation occurs in May 1968), specifically with *La Communauté Inavouable*, it is harder to pinpoint any notable influence upon Lévinas' thinking in the afterlife of 1968. Is Lévinas' thinking part of the discourse that includes Blanchot and others whose site of interrogation revolved around May 1968? Is Lévinas' shift to ethics as first philosophy part of the new discourse of ethical morality surrounding human rights produced by ex-gauchistes and the rise of New Philosophers distancing themselves from May 1968? Is Lévinas' discourse part of the post-1968 postmodern turn or is resisting that turn a sign of uninterrupted discourse from *Temps et L'Autre* (1946/1947)?

Considering that the French Jewish community is the primary focus of Lévinas' *Difficile Liberté*, the absence of any explicit, post-1968 article directly addressing the Jewish communal implications of the revolution beckons further investigation. Aside from Lévinas' terse comment during his *Lecture Talmudique: Judaïsme et Révolution* (b*Baba Metsia* 83a–83b) at the 1969 *Colloque des Intellectuels Juifs*, and some pre-1968 allusions sprinkled throughout *Difficile Liberté* supporting Judaism's tendency to neutralize the messianic impulse and remain suspect of Utopia, there is no cogent, post-1968 articulation of community for the work toward truth. In correlating Lévinas' "*Education et Prière*" (ca. 1963) with "*Vérité du dévoilement et vérité du témoignage*" (1972), I challenge Lévinas' Jewish writing and its form of community for the work of truth. By shifting priority away from the "Jew of the Psalms" (prayer/ecstasy) toward the "Jew of the Talmud" (learning/ethics), Lévinas' exoteric Jewish writings privilege rational ethics, while the esoteric philosophic writings privilege a more mystical ethics. There is a shift operating here from prayer as the provocation that comes from God as one's invocation, to the ambiguity of prophecy. From prayer to prophecy, there is a resounding in the Name of the God of all language that reveals a path to the truth. That path to truth is one which opens beyond the remoteness or absent otherness of *illeity* to the critical cluster of thirds in *tertiality*. It is this shift that is necessary to building community. In so translating Hebrew into Greek (or Judaism into philosophy), Lévinas alludes to a mode of undisclosable community wherein the truth of testimony discloses the glory of the Infinite.

Post-68 Pathway of Lévinas: From Undisclosable Community to the Truth of Testimony

In reflecting upon the background of the revolutionary generation that blossomed in France of 1968, it is evident that this younger generation did not have vast resources of Judaism to build upon for their community needs. Rather

the communal model of enlightened but radical Judaism that inspired them was
one of the greatest centers of Jewish culture in the world—Vilna (*Vilnus*). In
making this identification with the Jewish world of Vilna, this generation of
1968 "stumbled upon cultural and political models that suggested new ways for
them to live as Jews in present-day France."[8] Leading up to this identification
with revolutionary forms of culture, the Six Day War of 1967 in Israel also provoked an ideological crisis on the left. The rise of minority nationalism led to
the further realization of how insufficient and superficial[9] such identity was
becoming for French Jewry. While they could support "the right to be different"
(*le droit à la différence*) and work to maintain the diverse ethnic cultures in their
midst, the project itself began to ring hollow.[10]

Decades after the revolution, young militants of 1968 began to occupy
important positions in the French university system (*Centre Nationale de Recherce
Scientifique*), the media, as well as various publishing houses (*Éditions de Verdier*).[11]
The afterlife of the revolution could be felt influencing the direction of
the larger Jewish community in France, dominated by the following three
groupings:

1. **The Israélites**: the assimilated French bourgeois who promoted Jewish
   education in the universalist tradition in France and abroad primarily
   sponsored by *Alliance Israélite Universelle*.
2. **The Orthodox:** the petite bourgeois of North African immigrants and
   European Jews of Le Marais and Belleville who were part of non-Consistoire
   synagogues.
3. **The Yiddishists**: the Jewish immigrants from Eastern Europe who cherished
   secular Yiddish culture, belonging to *landsmanschaften* much like their
   Orthodox brethern.[12]

These categories will serve as an heuristic to analyze the strains of theory
and praxis within the French Jewish community. The broad scope of the May
1968 revolution's influence upon Jewish radicals who transformed into radical
Jews in France is critical for the purposes of the overall project at hand. Yet the
most radical thinking and praxis falls into the first two categories (Israélites
and Orthodox), even though the resonance of the Yiddishists echoes subcon-
sciously through much of secular French Jewry. Case in point will be explained
in relation to the latter two thinkers to be discussed who both engaged in the
Yiddishist cultural circles, but ultimately abandoned them in search of more
radical Judaism offered by the Israélites and the Orthodox. The distinction
then between "Jews who are radicals" (radical Jews) as opposed to "radicals who
happen to be Jews" (Jewish radicals) affects the ensuing forms of community
under investigation along with each of the following thinkers: (1) Emmanuel
Lévinas (1906–1995); (2) Benny Lévy (1945–2003); and (3) Shmuel Trigano
(b. 1948). All the while, the grounding question of what kind of community

emerges in relation to and catalyzed by these thinkers remains, namely: *A traditional community or an elective community? A negative community or a community of lovers? An undisclosable community or a community of testimony?*

Survivor-Turned-Philosopher: Daring to Disclose Undisclosable in Community

Emmanuel Lévinas, a survivor-turned-philosopher, dedicates a majority of his career working for the restoration of French Jewry as a community educator. This is manifest in a number of ways, including most prominently through his commitment to the communal cause of educating *"judaisme méditerranéen"* through the *École normale israélite oriéntale* (ENIO).[13] As director of the ENIO, Lévinas lives in the school with his family, teaching formally and informally (which includes his renowned Sabbath afternoon course on Rachi)[14] all in the hope of creating and "aiding a mediterranean Judaism to form elites."[15] Despite his cogent vision for forming an elite of teachers with rigorous intelligence, solid Hebrew studies and a fusion with the best of French thinking and culture,[16] Lévinas never fully realizes this Utopian community. "ENIO ceases to be a preparatory school for elite heads of institutions to become a secondary private Jewish establishment."[17] Yet Lévinas does not see this commitment to the formation of the *élites instituteurs* as the "culmination of an academic career."[18] Rather Lévinas' project is to translate Rosenzweig's German *Freies judisches Lehrhaus* from Frankfurt to his French ENIO in Paris; a symbiosis of radical communal culture.[19] Lévinas also contributes to the renewal of French Jewish intellectual life more broadly with his *Lecture Talmudique* at the *Colloque des Intellectuels Juifs*, which remained an annual gathering point for this peripatetic and thus decentered intellectual community. Of course his essays and columns for the Jewish community collected in *Difficile Liberté* show another facet of this calling to shape community.

Outside of Jacques Derrida's (1930–2004) important critique of Lévinas'[20] and a small group of philosophers, it is only more recently that the post-1968 generation has been influenced by his work. If there is one model of community that Lévinasian thinking brings into praxis, it would have to be called a community of testimony. Lévinasian community must overcome the "truth of disclosure," what Heidegger called *Erschlossenheit* or disclosedness.[21] If truth is singularly connected as the primordial self-manifestation of being,[22] then subjectivity is really only a means to an end. The discovery of meaning in existence is limited to those moments wherein one discovers authentic being. Granted part of what causes Heideggerian thinking to withdraw from community is that human tendency of falling prey to illusory community,[23] manifest in idle chatter. But Lévinasian community seeks "the exception to the rule of being,"[24] which is encountered in the testimony of the Infinite. It starts with a reorientation of language, no longer as merely "the house of being"[25] but "language, as a sign given to the other, is sincerity or veracity, according to which glory is glorified."[26] Testimony is linked to prophecy, whereby all of one's spiritual life is experienced as prophetic.[27] Testifying to the Infinite means living the *Saying* without the *Said*, embodying the "here I am/*me voici*" in the presence of others. Whereas Moses as prophet confronted the other side of the Infinite passing over him while hidden in the cleft of the rock, for the Lévinasian community "the Infinite is not before the witness but rather as though it were outside presence or on the "reverse side" of presence, already past, beyond grasp: an ulterior motive too elevated to thrust itself to the fore."[28] Living out this "reverse side of presence" happens through a primordial language, "a sign given to the other of this very giving of a sign, '*me voici*' signifies in the name of God, in the service of men, without having anything by which to identify myself, save the sound of my voice or the movement of my gestures—the saying itself."[29] Testimony is thus a glorifying of the dignity of beings in community, one that must be experienced, even if it remains undisclosed. Yet, through such communal concealment, there continues to be an oscillation of the prophetic impulse.

Revolutionary-Turned-Philosopher: Returning to Undisclosable Community

Benny Lévy (a.k.a. Pierre Victor), born in Cairo of 1946, as one of three boys, they each "inherited a love for *revolution*, not Judaism."[30] Family ties with the Egyptian Communist party imbued the young Lévy with a revolutionary foundation at an early age. With the Suez Crisis of 1956, his family relocated to Belgium and then France, where he eventually began studying philosophy at the esteemed École Normale in 1965. Lévy's passion for philosophy was matched by his passion for political activism, joining the Union des Étudiants Communistes (UEC), shifting into the Union des Jeunesses Communistes (marxistse-léninistes) (UJC [ml]), then transforming into La Gauche Prolétarienne (GP).[31] Amidst all these transformations in his activism, his final move is to renounce the world of theory, choosing rather to take his activism "out of the library and into the streets, abandoning books in the name of *direct*, violent action."[32] That hunger for uniting theory and praxis tips the scales in favor of the latter during this formative moment of the 1968 revolution. Lévy's Maoist cell within the publication arms of these activists leads him to work with Jean-Paul Sartre to create the first ever radical left paper called *Libération*. This intimate connection with Jean-Paul Sartre continues through the 1970s as Lévy becomes Sartre's secretary and study partner. With Sartre, Lévy begins his return to the philosophy he abandoned in his activist days. Through this study, he rediscovers Judaism through Lévinas' *Lectures Talmudiques*. A few weeks before Sartre dies, Lévy publishes three interviews with his mentor in *Libération*. These become Sartre's last words, wherein Lévy convinces the philosopher to revise his positions on a number of issues, including the Jewish question.[33]

Lévy's return to the study of Judaism's sacred texts through a rigorous philosophical lens meshed well with the overall Lithuanian approach to Talmud study. Thus many former leftist activists follow Lévy on his journey to *Yechiva de Étudiants* in Strausbourg headed by Rabbi Abitbol. This cohort of former leftist activists transforming into *ba'alai teshuvah* grows after Lévy extends a forbidden invitation for a rabbi to join their avowedly secular *Cercle de Gaston Crémieux*. Headed by Richard Marienstras, this circle traces the problems facing secular Jews both in defining themselves in contemporary France since the French Revolution, as well as exploring the political circumstances that led to the creation of the *Consistoire Centrale* by Napoleon.[34] What Marienstras realizes and empowers others in the circle to understand is that Jews sacrificed their national identity in order to gain their political emancipation. If they wanted to enjoy the rights of citizenship, Jews had to assimilate and become "Frenchmen of the faith of Moses," that is, culturally homogenous members of society who merely wanted to join a Jewish synagogue. The questions emerging from the secular *Cercle de Gaston Crémieux* were critical as regards the search for ideal community in asking each other: "What can we do today in France? What programs can we offer to enhance the cultural life of Jews beyond the ones that already exist at this time? What role should community institutions play?"[35] This is a model of community that seeks to serve the ethnic groups living in the Diaspora rather than looking to Zionism for answers to local questions. Lévy takes these questions to the next level, truly grappling with their implication, and in turn influences a group of former Maoists to live in a commune at the foot of the French Pyrenees of Lagrasse. In moving back to the land the intention of this microcommunity is to join the political struggle of the wine producers. Lévy convinces this commune that comes to head up *Éditions de Verdier* to translate and publish sacred writings of Lithuanian thinkers like Rabbi Hayyim of Volozhin (1749–1821), a disciple of the Gaon of Vilna (1720–1797).[36]

As a critical point of departure and return the Gaon serves their needs for a more unified theory of lived praxis for Lévy and the former Maoists. As the Gaon is taught through the lens of Moroccan Rabbi Eliahou Abitbol, a very different picture of Lithuanian Jewry is painted for Lévy than the one painted by Lévinas. What results in these divergent readings are models for different communities. The model of community Lévinas sought was a harmonization between the Talmudic tradition of the Vilna school and its affinity to Western European philosophy, ultimately drawing out shared universalistic themes. By contrast, the picture of community being evoked by Abitbol is diametrically opposed to any universalism inherent to the Talmudic tradition of the Vilna school, rather embracing "a viable alternative to the values of modernity and the West."[37] By the mid-1980s, Abitbol gathers more than one hundred families in his undisclosable community,[38] including the Lévy family. Their community stands in staunch opposition to the rising trend of Lubavitch Hasidism in

France, most notably in their unassuming dress as well as in their rational Talmudic tradition of the Vilna school as applied even to *mystical* texts.

Despite Lévy's ongoing radical transformation of self, his yearning for a communal life deeply dedicated to the union of theory and praxis is manifest, whether in his radical left activism or in his ultrareligious practice. Both extremes accommodate one seeking a commitment to radical ideology that is lived daily and manifest continuously in every aspect of communal structure. This expression of a radical community of lovers is firmly rooted in the union that Critical Theory aims to realize, or what Blanchot categorizes as a negative community becoming a community of lovers, an undisclosable community becoming a community of testimony. By seeking truth on both extremes of the pendulum, Lévy's transformative journey straddles each communal form seeking to unite theory and praxis.

Exiled Zionist-Turned-Philosopher: Re-Membering Undisclosable Community

Shmuel Trigano, born in Bilda, Algeria of 1948, like Lévy, received no formal Jewish education but was exposed to Jewish holiday observance at home. In leaving Bilda for Vichy and eventually for Paris, Trigano's exilic identity leads him to the *Colloque des Intellectuels Juifs* for a grounding in a sense of peoplehood. While Zionism has great appeal, he does not reach Israel until 1969. During the 1968 revolution in Paris, however, he refuses to participate, seeing the uprising as offering but "one more example of how Western solutions to humanity's problems were morally and ethically bankrupt."[39] Yet even while studying political science and Jewish philosophy at Jerusalem's Hebrew University for four years, Trigano becomes deeply disenchanted by the Western influence over politics and government, neglecting Jewish law in favor of a science of Judaism.[40] Ultimately, deeply troubled by Israel at large, Trigano "had to leave the country in order not to grow *cynical* and *lose faith* in Zionism."[41] Leaving Jerusalem one month before the Yom Kippur War of 1973, Trigano is convinced that unless Israel redefines the Zionist project outside of the Western nation-state, its future remained in question.[42]

Upon his return to Paris, Trigano joins the socialist Zioinist group, Le *Cercle Bernard Lazarre*. As fate would have it, in 1978 he meets up with another visionary radical in search of clarifying his identity, named, Benny Lévy. Both former activists were studying at Université de Paris II. Trigano defends his dissertation in 1981, founds a scholarly journal in Jewish Studies, called *Pardès*, and becomes director of a *Beit Hamidrash* at A.I.U. Trigano also agrees around this time to teach Hebrew to Benny Lévy and Arlette Elkaim-Sartre, ultimately leading to their first translations of classic Jewish texts into French through the former Maoists collective that becomes *Éditions de Verdier*.[43] These Hebrew courses by Trigano introduce the students to a philosophical universe antithetical to the Western civilization surrounding them. Trigano continues challenging the proposition of the nation-state, choosing rather to promote a nascent Jewish culture in France through *College des Études Juives* at A.I.U. The problem with the nation-state is that for Trigano, it leads to the spiritual disintegration of the Jews.[44] His political philosophy aligns more closely with the Yiddishists and Bundists in their demand for national and cultural autonomy,[45] all the while being an Sephardic Jew from Algeria. Reacting against the rise of minority nationalism or any other secular definition of Jewish culture in France, Trigano argues that Jews need to live in a state infused with Jewish values establishing a spiritual center in the Diaspora. His critical stance vis-à-vis Israel decenters the normative focus of Zionism, refocusing on a center without restrictions of Western European hegemonic culture. Rather Trigano searches for models of Diasporic community that come from his own Sephardic culture. What makes this stance even more unique than merely his decentering the symbiosis of cultures in the Zionism of *Ahad ha'Am* or Asher Ginsburg (1856–1927) is that Trigano transcends Ginsburg's agnosticism by living his life as guided by Jewish Law or *Halakhah*. Daringly Trigano recognizes how too often the development of secular traditions leads to the abandonment of cultural specificity which *Halakhah* preserves. Rather than end up conforming to values emanating from hegemonic culture of Western European nation-states,[46] Trigano exemplifies the search for an authentic truth of testimony in Diasporic community.

Radical Reprogramming: Talmudic Judaism Replacing Prayerful Judaism

The tentative turn toward prophetic prayer is of critical import. Despite its apparent supercession in the renowned quote from "*Éducation et Prière*" (1969) which decries its radical revisioning of the future focus of Judaism: "*Le juif du Talmud doit prendre le pas sur le Juif des Psaumes*,"[47] Lévinas cannot fully let go of the Psalms. Rather he rereads the Psalms as ecstatic prayers with a prophetic lens, as he remarks: "A psalm is after all not such a bad text on which to found justice for the toiling man."[48] The radical reprogramming necessary for Jewish communal life after the 1968 revolution is a return to a *Mitnaggdic* transcendence privileging intellectualism in study as prayer while transforming the *Hasidic* rapture privileging immanence in prayer into ethics. Yet the proposed building block of Lévinasian community is in the prophetic posture, where the "Infinite eludes objectification and dialogue signifies *illeity* in the third person, but according to a 'tertiality' different from that of the third man, from the third that interrupts the face-to-face of the welcome to the other man, and by which justice arises."[49] The betrayal of justice in community is a function of philosophy becoming too sophistic, and too disconnected from the ethics of an authentic prayer life. To redress that betrayal, or at least reduce it, we must continually turn to "the trace of sincerity that words themselves bear."[50] The Lévinasian praxis alluded to through the ambiguity of prophecy[51] is a deeper cultivation of "sincerity and testimony,"[52] which is "resounding in the name of God of all language"[53]—is this not the calling of a deeper prayer life? The model of the transcendent One interrupting the essence of being[54] (so much the focus of communal prayer) is the very power that "needs ambiguity—a frontier at once inevitable and finer than the outline (*le tracé*) of an ideal line."[55] Authentic prayer must therefore be radical enough to both embrace the other to interrupt the self within a communal structure.

Revolutionary Radicals from France to Germany: Why the French Model Matters to German Critical Theory

After these sketches of three influential and critical French Jewish thinkers, it is worth a contrast with Hebrew culture's reception of these very same personnae. In reflecting further on Yair Auron's *We are All German Jews: Jewish Radicals in France during the Sixties and Seventies*, we will briefly consider the reception of the May 1968 revolution and its thinkers/activists in the Hebrew culture of Israel.[56] In a context where radicalism is equated with the fight for religious equality, after Efrat Frankl is arrested for her public expression of devotion in a prayer shawl at the Western Wall, the divide between Jerusalem and Tel Aviv continues to grow. Writing from the divide between Jerusalem to Tel Aviv through the bridge of Paris,[57] Auron distinguishes between *radicals* and *radicalism*. There were those French Jews who emigrated to Israel after the 1968 revolution to be a part of Auron's *kibbutz*. But after a few years, these deeply committed Jews, like Trigano, took leave of the bastion of socialism. And Auron rightfully wonders—why? These French Jews are not *radical Jews*, or Jews who are fashioning and practicing a radical Judaism, but *Jewish radicals*, simply radicals who happen to be Jews.[58] This distinction is one tension between Judaism and Universalism, between the Zionist revolution and the Universal revolution, between particularistic Jewish identity and universalist human identity.[59]

There is a movement toward harmonizing these polarities into more Jewish communal involvement. The fourfold factors influencing these radical Jews to integrate into Jewish community include: (1) a foundational reorientation of the *Shoah*; (2) their struggle against fascism, racism, and anti-Semitism; (3) their ambivalence and restlessness in relation to the State of Israel; (4) their shared conviction of a communal ethics within Judaism.[60] The restlessness fluctuates, depending on the ethics of Israel's actions and policies as well as the relative danger it constantly is exposed to.[61] Even with over 30 years of hindsight, this tension between universalism and particularism continues unabated. The challenge is to find an appropriate equilibrium between these forces. Such an integration between the universal and the particular remains a challenge in

Israel, where the lessons gleaned from the *Shoah*, for example, tend to reinforce the need for a stronger more secure nation-state rather than a sobering call for human rights. Yet in an age where human rights suffer its own delusional myopia,[62] that search for balance is even more urgent. Real rebalancing is needed now on the side of the universal which appears to be eclipsing the particular rights of Jews to dwell in a democratic nation-state of Israel.

From Critical Praxis Back to Zionist Theory: Returning to Adorno's "Lyric Poetry and Society"

A shift is necessary from praxis back to theory, from the concrete reality of living in a nation-state. Operating with its own combination of pragmatism informed by corroding Zionist theory, the question of Critical Theory once again comes to the fore. What was so lacking during Adorno's tenure at the *Institut* was any critical engagement with Zionism. In order to reach that point of re-articulating the unsaid, it is necessary to reread an overlooked element of Adorno's view on the redemptive society. In this regard, returning to Adorno's often neglected 1957 essay, "Lyric Poetry and Society"[63] serves as an implicit critique of the social poetics of Zionism. When experience is reduced to reification and categorical subsumption, the poet turns inward, moving from expressing her alienation to rejecting collectivity altogether. Something of this alienation is felt so strongly in the silence that befalls two of the greatest Hebrew poets emigrating into pre-Mandate Palestine, namely, Hayyim Nahman Bialik (1873–1934) and Avraham ben Yizhak (1883–1950).

Although lyric poetry embodies a plethora of personal feelings and subjective experiences, as an art form it is too often dismissed as socially disconnected or irrelevant. Yet Adorno argues that it is precisely in the utter celebration of subjectivity that lyric poetry can point the way for navigating the given society and its engagement with the world. In keeping with the larger project of *Negative Dialectics*, Adorno is specifically searching for a universal social form that emerges from the particularity of the lyric poem itself. If the lyric poem has the capacity to serve as the "philosophical sundial of history,"[64] why then do two of the greatest Hebrew poets of all time fall silent in their writing of poetry once they have emigrated to Israel? The relation of the poet's subjectivity seems highly antithetical to its social reality. Only by way of the interpenetration of both formal and thematic elements "does the lyric poem actually capture the historic moment."[65] The kind of lyric poetry that is most constructive in this endeavor evokes "various levels of society's inner contradictory relationships"[66] within the poet's own voice and language. The challenge is for the poet to become "a vessel for the idea of pure language,"[67] that is, a way of resisting reification. Whereas the German language of lyric poetry to which Adorno turns is often alienated by virtue of its archaism, the Hebrew language that needs to be so read remains alive and spoken in Israeli society. What Adorno could not see in German lyric poetry was the reality that regarding Hebrew poetry, the language that is spoken is the very language that is imagined. Once the poet is freed from the bounds of self, then a "chimerical longing of language for the impossible is made into an expression of the [poet's] insatiable erotic longing"[68] in relation to the other. That encounter then becomes the dyadic building block of a group, ultimately leading to redemptive communal forms.

Communal Prayer as Critical Praxis

This has implications for communal prayer and its symbiotic influence or "recurrence" acting upon the lived life of ethics. In truth, a deeper symbiosis between ecstatic prayer and critical thinking is necessary for a vibrant community of testimony.[69] What appears to be lacking, however, is a language of the *said* that alludes to the ongoing *saying* of prophetic experience in community. Overcoming the model of the transcendent One that remains in need of ambiguity "finer than the outline (*le trace*) of an ideal line"[70] can only be found in poetry. This is not a new need; such a supererogatory devotional praxis that exceeds legal norms is, so common for mystics. Consider some past supererogatory prayer models[71] of Arousal or *Tokhakha* and Supplication or *Bakasha* that are integral to devotional study.[72] One example almost a millennium ago that continues to resound is Bahya ibn Paquda's *Hovot haLevavot*, which remains part of many Sephardi *mahzorim* for *Yom ha-Kippurim* (that would be commonly found in the non-*Consistoire* synagogues of the Maghrebian Jews Lévinas' Alliance work so benefited).[73] That Bahya's book of ethical refinement could become such a seamless part of so many devotional communities through the ages alludes to a model whose dualistic content may be outdated but whose integral form could serve as inspiration for deepening that testimony of truth.

Testimony of Truth through Communal Prayer

But it means expanding beyond God's need to be known through humankind's testimony, as the rabbinic *midrash* boldly articulates: "*If* 'you are my witnesses,' *then* I am God; but *if you are not* My witnesses, *then*, as it were, I am not God."[74] This potential death of God through lack of testimony in communal prayer is partially motivating Lévinas' radical claim. Lest we forget, however, the liturgical poetry of the *paytannim* and their willingness to expand traditional liturgy, especially in the *Yotzer piyyutim*, echoes as modernity's hollowmen, ringing with a whimper in community.[75] This hollow echo of prayer beckons a reconsideration of how prophetic experience can and must inspire new forms, crossing boundaries of self and other, of Jew and the world. Communities of testimony must integrate into their prayer lives the reality that not only is Judaism *in the world* but the world *is in Judaism*.[76] This is the work, the *avodah* of transforming "radicals who happen to be Jews" into "Jews who are radicals." For the *said* of communal prayer to resonate more vibrantly with a prophetic *saying* there needs to be the radiant touch of living poets embedded in community. This project has escaped most of French Jewry, while the *saying* of the Hebrew poet, as I have argued most recently in *Contemporary Hebrew Mystical Poetry: How Hebrew Poetry Redeems Jewish Thinking*,[77] continues to emanate from Israel. This is the next step in the project of translation that can be learned from Lévinas. Not only do we need to translate the Talmud into Greek (for a more ethical existence), but we also need to translate poetry back into prayer (to resuscitate devotional communities). It is a matter of reconnecting Diasporic poetics with Hebrew poetry. If indeed, "[t]he words of the poet open possibilities in the offing of a rebirthing of redemption as embodied in the deepest prayerful poetry"[78] then the testimony of community should empower all present to join together chanting:

Did you know—I am my prayer?

Part III

Genealogical Proviso

Chapter 7

Awakening to the Transpoetics of Physics and Metaphysics: Correlations in the Poetics of Science and Art

Science should not be "*aestheticized*," nor *art* made *scientific*. Instead, argued Adorno dialectically, it was precisely as *separate* activities, both true to their own *particularities*, that they converged.

—Susan Buck-Morss [1]

One finds oneself thus in the presence of two *antinomic cultures*: the one culture, like *quantum physics* with its focus on the absolute non-referent Object in the transcendental sense . . . is declared *exterior* to the human being and so *separated*; the other culture, with its focus on the absolute non-referent Subject also in the transcendental sense, namely an unknown Subject whose profane ego senses itself to be *exiled*.

—Michel Camus [2]

Gaps in *Gay Science* Bridging to *Melancholy Science*

"To be *in* the matter and *not always beyond it*"[3] remains critical for the possibility of what Adorno termed his *Melancholy Science*. This approach, by no means as willing as Nietzsche's *Gay Science* to embrace reality as is, informed the composition of *Minima Moralia*. Adorno's *Melancholy Science* required a "fidelity to one's own state of consciousness and experience" despite "the temptation of lapsing into infidelity."[4] Such infidelity was any affirmation and embrace of reality that was uncritical. The overall falseness of society is really part of a greater perspective of illusory existence. One way of overcoming such an illusion is by subjecting society to a critical perspective, requiring entry into subjectivity without becoming overwhelmed by excessive autonomy. "The subject still feels sure of its autonomy," as Adorno so aptly puts it, "but the nullity demonstrated to subjects by the concentration camp is already overtaking the form of subjectivity itself."[5] Thus what arises is a hesitation, an evasion, and a fragmentation, all of which mark the stance of the critic in relation to a society of illusory existence, entrapped in the culture industry. Despite the malaise inspiring this *Melancholy Science,* Adorno's preference for the (negative) dialectical mode implies something that remains a relatively unexplored aspect in the legacy of his thinking: namely, the relationship between art and science.

This dialectical tension, however, between art and science has already been noted in Susan Buck-Morss' landmark study, *The Origin of Negative Dialectics.*[6] The tension between subjective and objective perceptions of reality is one whereby: "[t]he cognitive value of art, which was by definition other than given reality, depended on the adequacy of aesthetic form to the content or idea which it expressed; the value of science, which gazed at reality head-on, depended on the adequacy of the theoretical concepts used to describe its objects."[7] The purpose of philosophy then is to act as a third way within this dialectic between the subjective and objective experiences of knowledge, such that speaking the truth happens "by the critical interpretation of both art and science, showing how their adequacy demonstrated the *in*adequacy of reality."[8] The realization then arises that within the dialectical process there is the need for a bridge. That bridge reaches between the antinomies and does not collapse or elide its critical tension through any kind of synthesis. The gift of effective philosophy then is to speak that truth by way of such a bridge, or more commonly referred to by Adorno as the "Gaps" [*Lücken*], between the dialectical poles of art and science.[9]

This third way between poetry and science, more recently termed *trans-poétique,* becomes the basis of an extended reflection by Michel Camus, with a subtle shift, however, taking place. The third way between poetry and science is transformed into the "third hand" or the "hidden hand" which is inseparable from "the third secretly included" [*le tiers secrètement inclus*].[10] To clarify what Camus is alluding to, it is necessary to first understand his perception of the current malaise affecting human consciousness. While the human being has always interrogated the universe for meaning, a distinct inability remains for any self-interrogation, any self-examination connected to the origins of the universe, or between observer and the observed.[11] To rectify this malaise, a call beckons out for a deeper transfiguration or transcendental subjectification that only happens in strong poetry,[12] but Camus is also careful to delimit this call. Advancing toward the research of the hidden unity of science and poetry is possible so long as one does not eclipse or collapse the other discipline. Specifically, science has no insight to gain from the Kabbalah's spheres of the Tree of Life, but a relation of complementarity can be seen between foundational science and traditional esotericism.[13] While Adorno would likely have been suspicious of such claims as lapsing into the occult, there remains a critical convergence in Camus' quest, namely: "The question that arises is to know how to unfold consciousness so that its own enigmatic essence can be revealed to itself."[14] The need for such a self-revelation of consciousness bespeaks a hunger for more of an immanent transcendence, the very possibility of convergence between art and science. Opening to the depths of such a deeper illumination requires self-realization. If there is a consciousness of one's double abysmal nature, absolutely conscious of the relativity of consciousness and knowledge, then the interior of infinity can be revealed.[15] That ongoing search for an "infinite identity" that escapes any existential or phenomenal identification needs what Camus calls a "translanguage where direct perception is streaming forth ideas and thoughts."[16] What poetic knowledge of the unknowable makes space for is the interiority of the infinitely open. If there is indeed an attempt to equate this formless vacuity with an intensified self-consciousness, whereby its very residue reveals its own empty fecundity, then according to Camus, immanent transcendence can be rediscovered at the heart of consciousness. That heart of consciousness, or *Ein Sof*, is what his *transpoésie* simply refers to as the Silence of the heart.[17] But this raises its own host of problems, especially if such "[a] metaphysic equation of the Awakening . . . is not meant to be resolved, but to be lived."[18]

The problem arises as to how to process consciousness of an infinite identity that escapes any existential or phenomenal identification.[19] This is then further complicated as our current perception of three-dimensional existence becomes more illusory and extra dimensions emerge as a more plausible way of seeing "a host of new possibilities for the fabric of spacetime."[20] What then would such a convergence between art and science, between metaphysics and physics, really look like? Is it simply a matter of importing one identity into the other? For example, with regard to Darwinian evolution, is it sufficient to "embrace it and uncover its sacred dimensions?"[21] Moreover after Adorno's vigilant warning against identity-thinking, is it possible to claim that "the evolution of species and the evolution of religious ideas, or of our understanding of reality, are continuous parts of a single evolutionary process?"[22] I have argued elsewhere that in the process of such transpoetic convergence, there is a need to remain vigilant regarding how language is translated and transferred from one field to another, and it is here that a nuanced poetics is so critical.[23] This then is an example where science has unfortunately been "aestheticized" rather than engaged in its own particularity in the dialectical process without succumbing to synthesis. In neglecting Adorno's negative dialectics, these separate realms of art and science, when synthesized cannot then both be true to their own particularities, and thus any convergence into a "single evolutionary process" is de facto flawed.[24]

That a trajectory for convergence opens in dialectical tension between the poetics of quantum physics and that of spiritual consciousness is, however, not a flawed thought. But if such convergence is meaningful, then the poetics of religion must truly read and absorb the particularities of quantum thinking and then respond to and reorient in relation to the following issues: Extra-dimensionality;[25] Warped Geometry and Duality;[26] T-Duality;[27] Mirror Symmetry;[28] Matrix Theory;[29] String Theory;[30] Braneworlds.[31] Harnessing the insights of extra-dimensionality from this critical scientific perspective into dialectical tension with religion will affect readings of the Jewish mystical canon, especially in a neo-Lurianic Kabbalah reading that would likely include the multiverses of Ellipses and Strings [*Igulim v'Yosher*]; Bands [*Akudim*]; Points [*Nekudim*], and so on. The proposed transpoetic convergence would then necessitate a rereading of the particularities of a neo-Lurianic Kabbalah in light of these extra-dimensional implications of quantum physics,[32] but it would not synthesize the findings into a single process. Rather this convergence of the poetics of religion and science must continue opening to that tension within the dialectical process which keeps creativity vibrant. Moreover, there remains a strong need to turn to contemporary mystical poets whose quill is deeply dipped in the residue of neo- Lurianic Kabbalah.[33] Such a convergence posed by transpoetics requires an openness to variability and a resistance to identity-thinking. That same experimental attitude which allowed Adorno to make his "radical interpretation of modernity as cultural modernity"[34] needs to flow into the transpoetic dance between metaphysics and physics, between the art of religion and science.

Chapter 8

Aesthetic Theory of *Halakhah*: How a Poet*h*ics of Theory and Praxis Enhances Existence

Halakhah is never *abandoned*; it is "*artist-ized.*" Just as *artists* submit to the *creative power within* themselves, truly *pious persons* submit to *ritual* because it gives form to the Divine in her own being.
—Shaul Magid[1]

[Artistic] *commitment* is a higher level of reflection than *tendency . . . Commitment* aims at the *transformation of the preconditions* of situations, not merely making recommendations; to this extent it inclines toward the *aesthetic category of essence.*
—Theodor Adorno[2]

This is the guide. This is why a constantly *changing process* is not a process of *confusion* but one of *growth.* This is the key. This is the *secret.* As you see, there are *no secrets.*
—Peter Brook[3]

A Lost Art Form: Recovering the Journey of *Halakhah*

If undertaking the journey of life through the lens of *halakhah* remains neglected as a function of its uncompelling appearance to most heterodoxical Jews, what then are the ways to return to the term without lapsing into living such identity-thinking? Namely, what would a way of walking through the world, or journey-making, also known as *halakhah*, look like as practiced in a more compelling and integral way?[4] Once *halakhah* is no longer the "will of God,"[5] is it sufficient to see *halakhah* as the human response of "filling in the spaces of the wordless divine call"?[6] Moreover, is it possible to respond to the implied content of an internalized call to action through a monist identity-thinking[7] that necessarily effaces any dialectical tension? Finally, is it possible for a vibrant and transformative *halakhah* to exist without that very dialectical tension between liberty and commandment,[8] between immanence and transcendence,[9] between autonomy and commitment?[10] In our time, unless the ongoing revelation of religion is mediated through aesthetics, it is doomed to stagnate amidst the irrelevance of its creation.[11]

Recent attempts at resuscitating this lost vibrancy of religion has led to several reorientations of *halakhah* toward the pole of legal lore, narrative,[12] or genre,[13] which at first blush strike one more often than not as ingenious. Yet once the pole of lore becomes the focal point of the practice, or the shift moves in the other direction exclusively toward legal positivism then a lapse into identity-thinking takes place. That tension between *halakhah* and *aggadah* is what once allowed for a vibrant dialectic of Jewish Thinking and praxis,[14] yet the uprooting of this dialectic causes anxiety for the lone prophetic poets.[15] In shifting the discussion over from this paradigm of *halakhah* and *aggadah*—a paradigm so broken it is questionable whether it is any longer fulfilling its purpose—there emerges another way to envision the landscape of life's journey. That third way is through aesthetics. Seeing *halakhah* as an art form,[16] as Magid boldly suggests, requires the aspirant to see religion as an art form and become a *practicing* artist:

> Painters, dancers, or musicians submit to two mutually inclusive models of obedience. First, they submit to some *internal mechanism* that enables inspiration to assume form. Second, they submit to an *external medium* that determines what that form will take. The contemplative must submit to the *inner nature* of their *creative instinct*, guided by a submission to the "still small voice" of the Divine. Creativity begins with listening.[17]

The nature of that listening that translates into praxis has changed through time. The way one's ancestors listened may not be the way that one can listen today.

> For the contemplative Jew in the past, *halachah* was a form of yoga, and the *halachic* life was a devotional "dance" that made concrete one's yearning for closeness to God.[18]

Aesthetic Commitment of the *Halakhic* Life

Despite the genius of recasting of *halakhic* life as a "devotional dance" by Magid, the challenge remains how to motivate individuals to follow the artist's path. Is it then possible to imagine that when legal commandedness fails, artistic commitment could then prevail? That is why Adorno's aesthetics is so crucial in understanding what is meant by "artistic commitment," which he begins to outline as follows:

> The element of objective praxis inherent in art is transformed into subjective intention when, as a result of society's objective tendency and of the critical

reflection of art, art's antithesis becomes irreconcilable. The accepted term for this *subjective intention* is *commitment.*[19]

Commitment also implies a passion for change. But Adorno remains measured in setting limits regarding the impact of such commitment, whereby it "aims at the transformation of the *preconditions of situations,* not merely making recommendations."[20] Despite the immanence of art works, however, an a priori distance becomes more and more apparent. Disaffection with the status quo is necessary for the cultivation of such commitment. Moreover, a tacit Utopia must always be seen or felt[21] for it to be authentically artistic. It is misguided to try to measure the impact of such praxis that stems from artistic commitment, rather it is always the hidden potential of their truth content that matters.

Inhalt of *Halakhah*: Artistic Commitment and Commandedness

Once artistic commitment is truly considered as a replacement for command-edness, a further aspect remains in need of addressing; namely how to bring the spiritual and the secular into deeper alignment. It has already been noted by Buck-Morss that: "Aesthetic creation itself was not subjective invention so much as the objective discovery of the new within the given, immanently, through a regrouping of its elements. What this means is that critical interpretation becomes a kind of secular revelation."[22] Recall that for Adorno, "even spiritual content [*Inhalt*] remains material and is consumed by the artworks, even when their self-consciousness insists that this subject matter is essence."[23] Yet in this very process of revealing what is concealed, of bringing forth what remains hidden beneath the surface, a subtle transformation has taken place—the *in-itself* is transformed into a *for-itself,* "[a]rtworks became for-themselves what they previously were in-themselves.[24] If it is through artistic commitment that "something that is sealed up in art becomes external by means of growing control and practicability,"[25] it is then this very vitality of art that inspires an existence enhanced by aesthetics.[26]

   Such a reality of existence enhanced by aesthetics is further addressed in Magid's reflections on *halakhah* as an art form ab initio in his prioritizing piety over ecstasy.[27] Further exploration is warranted, however, in fleshing out exactly what such an anomian path would look like, especially how to delineate the limits of and reinforce a threshold of the ethical within a devotional dance of artistic commitment.

Beyond Aesthetic Commitment: A Need for Poet*h*ics

Aesthetics, however, is ultimately not enough. Preliminary reflections on poet*h*ics—that correlation between aesthetics and poetics—make clear some ugly truths along this desired path. Adorno's thinking would thus demand a testing of the limit case of an aesthetics utterly devoid of ethics, as with Nazism vis-à-vis degenerate Jewish art, whereby: "Hitler's empire put this theorem to the test . . . [t]he more torture went on in the basement, the more insistently they made sure that the roof rested on columns."[28] By setting up aesthetics as the measure of the beautiful while purging it of all ugliness leads to a kind of resignation to living a depraved life.[29] This is why Adorno can pronounce that "the element of the ugly is bound up with art's spiritualization.[30] Where Adorno's need for the ugly in tension with the beautiful misses the mark is in finding the iconoclastic tendency of art to resist the "authority of their success" within Hellenistic art. While a need for tension always exists, given the history of aesthetics leading up to its depravity within Nazism's aesthetics utterly devoid of ethics, a reorientation is required. I have argued elsewhere for the need to shift away from the Greek mind, toward the nuances of the Hebraic imaginality.[31] In that realm of the interworld between reality and imagination, the Hebraic imaginality has the capacity for transforming a "radiance that is dark, where the 'beautiful permeates negativity.'[32]

More recent reflections on poet*h*ics by Fox[33] challenge the neo-Kantian strain,[34] nascent even in Adorno's aesthetics of "redemptive ugliness."[35] Granted Adorno is quick to acknowledge the weakness in the Kantian predisposition to ultimately allow for the "aesthetic condemnation of the ugly [as] dependent on the inclination, verified by social psychology, to equate, justly, the ugly with the expression of suffering and, by projecting it, to despise it."[36] Ingeniously, Fox calls for a more Humean perspective that is avowedly anti-Kantian, "insofar as ethnocentrism and gender bias have informed taste in ways only recently recognized."[37] Ultimately, the ethical corrective that emerges from the lacuna in Kantian aesthetics is that "[j]udgement concerning what is good and what is beautiful requires wisdom."[38] Going one step further, Fox dares to emphasize that until a poet*h*ics fusing poetics and ethics comes to the fore, aesthetics will remain forever trapped in a vacuum, in that:

[T]he guidelines of such judgment are ethical; an evil person is not to be judged as beautiful in the eyes of God. A Poet*h*ics does not allow for positive aesthetic judgment to be made on racist films or racist poetry.[39]

Poet*h*ic Redemption of *Halakhah*

It is possible, as I have been arguing after Adorno, for a vibrant and transformative *halakhah* to exist by way of a dialectical tension. That tension is one that oscillates between liberty and commandment, between autonomous inspiration and artistic commitment. It is this artistic commitment to the ongoing revelation of religion as mediated through aesthetics that one can redeem *halakhah* as a compelling path to enhance existence once again. Poet*h*ic redemption of *halakhah*, then, is a clarion call unto both artist and scholar, as Bruckstein remarks, to become "the new guardian[s] of a particularism that knows how to safeguard the dignity, the integrity and the inviolability of any body-surface (whether text, artwork, or skin) without giving up the universal gestures of humanity,"[40] all the while ritually rebirthing god anew from the ashes of Auschwitz.[41] Recognizing artistic commitment as a higher level of reflection is crucial to this process of revitalizing *halakhah*. Once this sense of commitment is rekindled, individuals might enter into community to transform suffering and its preconditions toward redemption. To truly "artist-ize" *halakhah* is to craft a living form from the glimmering inner divine presence along creaturely bypaths.

Chapter 9

Sprachspiel and *Halakhah*: Necessary
Incompleteness in Ethics

The barbaric *success-religion* of today is consequently not simply contrary to morality: it is the *homecoming* of the West to the *venerable morals* of our ancestors. All *morality* has been modeled on *immorality* and to this day has reinstated it at *every level*.

—Theodor Adorno[1]

One can . . . even give examples of propositions . . . which are really contextually [materially] *true* but *unprovable* in the formal system of classical mathematics.

—Kurt Gödel[2]

The only *philosophy* which can be *responsibly practised* in the face of despair is the attempt to *contemplate* all things as they *would present* themselves from the standpoint of *redemption*.

—Theodor Adorno[3]

You can't *hear* God *speak* to someone else.
You can *hear* him only if you are *being addressed*.
That is a grammatical remark.

—Ludwig Wittgenstein[4]

The Trouble with Jewish Thinking and Praxis Today

Religion—bereft of ethics;[5] spirituality—masquerading as occultism;[6] thinking—a neglected past-time troubling no one.[7] Judaism is by no means immune to this broken state of affairs. The trouble with Jewish Thinking today is that its critical tools of thought are no longer part of the discourse. To be unwilling to speak the *unspeakable* truths, knowing that they exist but fearing their *saying*, is irresponsible, if not unethical. Recent critiques of *Wissenschaft des Judentums*, the critical study of Judaism as having lost its way, are a symptom of the larger malaise affecting Judaism.[8]

The courage to speak critically is only outlining the foothills of wisdom. The real work, however, is entwined in the intricacy of both *saying* and *showing* another way for Jewish Thinking. If overcoming the near irrelevance of the neo-Hegelian philosophical tenets of *Wissenschaft des Judentums* is possible, then fostering an openness to those faculties of mind that engender critical thinking becomes crucial. What began as the promise of a "genuine message of the hermeneutic-linguistic philosophy of our century,"[9] namely not to overlook context, has led to a situation where Jewish Thinking wallows in the mire of a myopic positive-historicism. While it is critical to be aware of the historical point of view being observed, one must also be attuned to the ways in which its symbolic order is described. Without a deeper appreciation of the "intricate interconnection of thought and life-form in the language-game,"[10] an unexamined life of apathy becomes the new norm. If it is still possible to talk about ethics after Theodor W. Adorno (1903–1969), Ludwig Wittgenstein (1889–1951), and Kurt Gödel (1906–1978), then how incomplete should ethics remain in order for a critical thinking to still matter?

At the outset, it should be noted that Adorno critically revises an aspect of Wittgenstein's thinking for the purposes of his own aesthetics, which in turn has implications for ethics. Recall Wittgenstein's masterful concluding note to the *Tractatus Logico-Philosophicus*:[11]

7. Of that which one cannot know, it is best to remain silent[12]

Whether this is an allusion to the mystical or the ethical domain of life, Wittgenstein's thinking leaves it all to what is *unsaid*. By contrast, Adorno sees a need to transfer Wittgenstein's dictum of ineffability to aesthetics, whereby it is then possible to redress "the ontological asceticism of language [a]s the only way to say the unutterable."[13] It is the very paradox of art—being at once opaque and particular—that provides Adorno a way of seeing beyond Wittgenstein's apparent impasse. In contrast to Wittgenstein's *unsaid* ethics, Adorno sees aesthetics as having the unique ability to bridge the universal and the particular, seeing that "[i]n art, universals are strongest where art most closely approaches language: that is, when something speaks, that, by speaking, goes beyond the here and now. Art succeeds at such transcendence, however, only by virtue of its tendency toward radical particularization; that is, only in that it says nothing but what it says by virtue of its own elaboration, through its immanent process."[14] Whereas for Wittgenstein, it is the feeling of the world as a limited whole that evokes the *mystical*,[15] for Adorno, it is the knowing of the world through aesthetics that evokes the *ethical*.[16]

It is this very tension between ethics and aesthetics, between the *saying* and the *unsaid* that beckons the current correlation of Wittgenstein and Adorno. Notwithstanding Adorno's critique of Wittgenstein's inability to "grasp the constitutive relation of language to the extralinguistic,"[17] further reflection is still warranted on how the "language-game" of life reveals glimmers of the ethical without necessarily turning to aesthetics. Whichever route is taken, what becomes clear is that by continuing under the illusion that history is the only tool within the shed of critical modes of thinking, any meaningful convergence in the dialectic of Jewish Thinking and practice, of theory and praxis is utterly lost. Such a loss results in a religion without ethics, or *halakhah* that is unethical.

Coming to terms with cultivating insight into problems of our age is a function of our symbiosis between the Zeitgeist (the spirit of a generation's thinking) and *hitmassrut hanefesh* (passionate commitment).[18] Indeed our task after Ludwig Wittgenstein (1889–1951) is to clarify our modalities of hearing to see how God is speaking to us in our critical devotional lives. From this particular hearing of that inner calling, one opens to the responsibility of Jewish Thinking. As thinking deepens, the rift becomes all the more real between *saying* and *showing*. This is where the communal element of ethics becomes crucial. What remains unsayable for the particular becomes a necessity as a general communal order. The order of communal ethics should then direct a national *saying* and *showing* that is redemptive. When Adorno decries the final task of philosophy "to *contemplate* all things . . . from the standpoint of *redemption*,"[19] there is an immediate relevancy to the clarion call. That immediacy breeds a yearning for redemption. But to live toward such a redemptive bypath, there is a critical requirement—incompleteness.[20] To appreciate this insight, a brief exposition of the *Incompleteness Theorem* is required.

Seeing the Meta-System

In showing how propositions that are really contextually true but unprovable in the formal system, an insight for (meta)mathematics was brought forth that changed the world. When this revolutionary insight of Kurt Gödel (1906–1978)—known as his *Sternstunde*, or his shining hour—was revealed on the final day of the Königsberg conference on "Epistemology of the Exact Sciences" (1930),[21] a single sentence changed the course of all thinking. Philosopher Rebecca Goldstein speculates on the response that remained *unsaid* that fateful day of the Königsberg conference:

> Excuse me, *Herr Gödel*, but I somehow thought you just said that you'd proved the existence of unprovable arithmetical truths. Of course, you couldn't have been saying that because, besides flying in the face of all of our views on the nature of mathematical truth, that sounds like a contradiction in terms. How could you prove that there are arithmetical propositions that are both *unprovable* and *true*? Wouldn't that proof, in showing them to be true, constitute a proof of them, thus contradicting your claim that the proof proves them unprovable? Logician that you are, you couldn't be asserting a blatant contradiction like that. So what did you really say?[22]

Philosophy as a Turn to Narrative

It is no accident that as a philosopher who wants to think critically through her Judaism, Goldstein has to escape to another genre altogether—namely, fiction. Jewish Thinking today appears to make no room for her kind of thinking. Her break with orthodoxy toward heterodoxy begins with Spinoza[23] but cannot end there. Yet her foray into fiction is in no way an abandonment of philosophy. Outside of philosophy and fiction, somewhere between the objective and subjective truth, she brings forth interrogative traces of Jewish Thinking that can hope to still be a symbiosis between the Zeitgeist and *hitmassrut hanefesh*, between thinking and passionate commitment.

To rediscover this lost symbiosis in Judaism requires a newfound understanding of the implications of incompleteness. By extrapolating the core of the *Incompleteness Theorem* as indicated in intersections of thought in Ludwig Wittgenstein and Kurt Gödel, a critically minded Jewish Thinking might re-emerge. This application is then intended to explore the impeccably "freeze-dried" foundations of *Wissenschaft des Judentums*, and defrost them back into a critical thinking Judaism. The focus of our exercise will be applied to three distinct domains:

(A) Particular, (B) Communal, (C) National,

which correlate to three real situational experiences:

(1) Ritual, (2) Law, (3) Zionism.

Incompleteness suggests ambiguity. But how ambiguous can existence really be? Life is revealed through its language. It is next to impossible to escape language, even in silence. Words create our reality. This leads to moments where language and experience appear to be dissonant. "This is not appropriate!" could be the exclamation of the jury when one of its members enters the court in a bathing suit. None of the pieces themselves are inappropriate but the *situation* is dissonant. "Look at that!" when pointing to a scantily clad woman receiving an honor at the Torah. Is this exclamation aimed at the color or the shape of the garment? What happens when this kind of ambiguity enters into the language of our experience?

Seeing the Name and the Thing Named

For the Austrian (Jew)[24] exiled to Cambridge, Ludwig Wittgenstein, this dissonance was said to be a "language-game" [*Sprachspiel*].[25] A key enigma Wittgenstein was relentlessly seeking to clarify through his investigations was the following: "What is the relation between name and thing named?"[26] In posing this problem confronted in any language-game, Wittgenstein is demanding a greater consistency between language and reality. The interrelationship in need of clarification is "in the fact that hearing a name calls before our mind the picture of what is named; and it also consists, among other things, in the name's being written on the thing named or being pronounced when that thing is pointed at."[27] This quandary leads Wittgenstein to the distinction between *ostensible* and *demonstrative* usages of language. There are three levels of argument that need to be worked through to apply the differences between *ostensible* and *demonstrative* usages of language.

The nuances inherent in the *Sprachspiel* reflect the greater flow of an ongoing critique proffered by Ludwig Wittgenstein.[28] As that "arresting combination of monk, mystic and mechanic,"[29] this Viennese *émigré* to Cambridge carried on a paradoxical, concealed Jewish life.[30] On the one hand, he had three Jewish grandparents yet remained outside the boundary of what is *halakhically* Jewish. On the other hand, the confession he made about his Jewishness implies a concern to affirm the Jewishness of his lifework's thinking. He remained committed to a project of (Jewish) thinking while doing nothing to prevent the misapprehension about his (Jewish) identity.[31] Wittgenstein's contribution to Jewish Thinking is just beginning to be explored, while any real application to Judaism remains in the offing. Directions for future Jewish Thinking can be discovered and bolstered in applying Wittgenstein's critical approach to a variety of problems that inhere within Judaism through language. Rather than "presenting the results of thought but illustrating a way of thinking," Wittgenstein's concern is not as much to *say* things as it is the possibility of *saying*.[32]

Recall Wittgenstein's masterful concluding note to the *Tractatus Logico-Philosophicus*, sometimes referred to as the "logical poem":[33]

7. Of that which one cannot know, it is best to remain silent[34]

Wittgenstein I's central project in the *Tractatus Logico-Philosophicus* is to reflect upon the connection between language, thought, and world.[35] Yet here, at its closing note, the "positivist and mystic"[36] philosopher accedes to the possibility of a mystical experience, so long as it remains beyond language and the world. In bold distinction to German Jewish thinker, Franz Rosenzweig (1886–1929), whose correlations written in the front lines of the war sought to overcome the limitations intimately linking *Gott—Mensche—Welt* [God—Human—World] with *Schöpfung—Offenbarung—Erlösung* [Creation—Revelation—Redemption],[37] already in 1918 Wittgenstein is forcing that very question: what kind of experience is really being described in language through its limitation? It is an experience of opposing ineffability and transcendence to what can actually be articulated in language,[38] which is precious little (even though Wittgenstein's notebooks are so prolific in explicating this reality). Yet ironically, like the mystics who decry the impossibility of using finite language to praise the Infinite

One, Wittgenstein admits there is, at the very least, a domain of the ineffable. This domain in turn is less concerned with theology than in pointing to the need for the ethical.

This need for the ethical in thinking is spelt out as the point of the *Tractatus* in a letter to an editor, wherein Wittgenstein remarks that—

> [M]y work consists of two parts: the one *presented here* plus all that I have *not written*. And it is precisely this *second part* that is the important one.[39]

Much of this thinking strives to show the possibility of *saying* the *unsayable,* what transcends the limits of the world through knowledge while containing that insight in ethics. The *unsaid,* ineffable realm for Wittgenstein—ethics—is crucial as it shows more effectively what language struggles to say awkwardly or incoherently.

Starting with those slippery linguistic moments of *Sprachspiel* or that playfulness of the language-game[40] is what limits his exploration to the empirically demonstrable. Wittgenstein's battle cry was always against any "bewitchment of language."[41] That tended to be his way of epitomizing analytical philosophy and linguistics. To illustrate another way of thinking through problems, however, one must momentarily take leave of both language and the world. Some of Wittgenstein's critics at Cambridge saw his behavior as a confirmation of his becoming "a mystic whose asceticism cuts him off from the common pleasures of life—someone who looks to a secret source for knowledge of the world."[42] Wittgenstein notes this need for transcending the empirically demonstrable toward the ethically mystical at several other points in the *Tractatus,* as he limits language by limiting the world:

> 6.44 Not how the world is, is the mystical, but that it is.
> 6.45 The contemplation of the world *sub specie aeterni* is its contemplation as
>   a limited whole.
> The feeling of the world as a limited whole is the mystical feeling.[43]

While contemplating the limits of the world that constitute the holiness of its very wholeness, Wittgenstein realizes how all thinking is irreducible to the very *saying* that cannot be fully *said* in language. While the supra-rational experience may not be sayable, it nonetheless can be experienced as the limitation that makes for a wholly delimiting experience of existence. Rather than seeing language as proscribing the ineffable, language's limitations for Wittgenstein are what open this very possibility for the ineffable to exist.[44] While this delimitation forces the speaker to utilize a language that may be logically inexact, that represents no-thing or comes to nonsense, nonetheless this is a language that evokes something else, something beyond, qualifying as supra-rational or mystical and thus possible. This delimitation of the ineffable as real but often eluding language should be the starting point of Jewish Thinking concerned with legislating the ethical today.

It is at this juncture that poetry is proffered to be the most evocative of languages, in Hadot's reading of Wittgenstein, one that gives birth to the world before the individual. Truly seeing the world, for Wittgenstein, through *saying* and *showing* as an imprint of the primordial poem draws closer into proximity the Ineffable Poem—*Torah.* Prior to the primordial, however, it is through this very *indicative* and *evocative* capacity of language that Wittgenstein shows through *ostensible* language that:

> 6.522 There is indeed the *ineffable.* This *shows itself,* it is the *mystical.*[45]

It is in the very self-disclosure of the ineffable that philosophy discovers the impossibility of its own project—*to show the insurmountable limits of language.* This is precisely where the *mystical becomes possible* and *the ethical necessary.* Once this impossibility for philosophy is apparent, what remains possible about the necessity of mystical experience is as Wittgenstein notes:

> 4.1212 What can be *shown* cannot be *said.*[46]

The determination to bridge this paradox of showing the *unsayable* through writing brings us to reflect on the *possibility of ethics within Jewish mysticism.* It is here that the symbiosis between the Zeitgeist and *hitmassrut hanefesh* in Judaism requires incompleteness. As Goldstein so aptly notes:

> Just as Gödel demonstrated that our formal systems cannot exhaust all that there is to mathematical reality, so the early Wittgenstein argued that our linguistic systems cannot exhaust all that there is to non-mathematical reality. All that can be said can be said clearly, according to the *Tractatus,* but we cannot say the most important things. *We cannot speak the unspeakable truths, but they exist.*[47]

If indeed such unspeakable truths exist, this leads to moments where language and experience once again appear to be dissonant. What follows are reflections through three levels of such dissonance operative as *Sprachspiel* within Judaism, and how reading them in this way opens up new pathways for thinking, showing, and meaning Judaism.

I. PARTICULAR—Ritual

1. *Matzah zu—This* unleaven bread that we eat . . .
2. *Mah ha'Avodah ha'zot—*What is *that* work's purpose to you?
   . . . *ba'avur ze—* . . . because of *this*

1. *Ostensive* definition of *matzah:* The clarion call of the Passover *seder* is encapsulated in the words of Rabban Gamliel who used to say: "Whoever does not say these three things on Passover has not fulfilled one's duty." What is the nature of the ritual taking place at that moment? Why is it necessary to both *say* and *point* in order to fulfill the ritual obligation of the Passover experience?

The ritual moment of *matzah* can only take place by the simultaneous act of *pointing* and *saying*. This is a peculiar ritual moment which necessitates a simultaneous *pointing* and *saying*. When both of these acts are realized together a manifestation of the ineffable is possible—*why?* This moment frames a revelatory encounter between beings round the table. This confraternal framing is necessary for the ethical encounter to take place and the *symposium* to be complete. There is no philosophizing alone, disconnected from others. Wittgenstein duly notes the distinction being worked on presently as follows:

> It is quite true that, in giving an *ostensive* definition for instance, we often *point* to the object named and *say* the name. And similarly, in giving an *ostensive* definition for instance, we *say* the word "this" while pointing to a thing. And also the word "this" and a name often occupy the same position in a sentence. But it is precisely characteristic of a name that is defined by means of the *demonstrative* expression "That is N" (or "That is called 'N'"). But do we also give the definitions: "That is called 'this'," or "This is called 'this'"?[48]

2. *Demonstrative* expression of exclusion: When the wicked child asks this question, a demonstrative expression is taking place by distancing him/herself from the community. No longer a part of the shared experience of redemption, this child remains at a distance from the experience itself. Language becomes this alienated child's lifeline to an otherwise irrelevant and insignificant ritual experience. The answer that "smashes this child's teeth" reorienting his/her worldview of language returns to "this." *Ba'avur ze* (Exodus 13.8), that is, "because of this," what is here and close to you, that redemption was and remains possible. Not just redemption, but ongoing revelation in confraternal moments like these. Despite the distance of *demonstrative* expression, this child connects from the outside to the inside of this ritual moment by transforming the language of "that" back to "this."

After *Yahatz*, the breaking of the middle *matzah*, is the act of *saying* and *pointing* to the *matzah* still possible? When Wittgenstein asks whether the sword *Excalibur* is still *Excalibur* when found in fragments,[49] he echoes the same challenge posed earlier by Menahem Mendel of Kotsk's (1787–1859) embrace of this very paradox: "There is nothing as whole as a broken heart."[50] If it is broken, how is it still whole? If it is whole, how can it be broken? Has language gone on holiday here? The insight about *Excalibur* can be applied to the heart or the *matzah*. Both are experienced—in their *telling*—more wholly through their incompleteness.

II. COMMUNITY—Revelation

> 3. *Zeh 'eli v'anveihu*—"*This* is my God and I shall adorn this One"
> 4. *Zot ha'torah*—"*This* is the *Torah*"
> 5. *Kavod haTorah*—Dignity due to *Torah*

3. *Ostensive* definition of Revelation: To taste that fantastical moment of eternity erupting into temporality, of the *time-that-is-coming* converging into the *time-that-is-now*, is troped as a circular dance whereby language is no longer on holiday. Those who are immersed in the primordial poem of *Torah* in their lives gather in this circle to *point* and *say*: *Zeh 'eli v'anveihu*, "This is my God and so shall I adorn this One" (Exod. 15.3). The process of adorning and enshrining requires a simultaneous *pointing* and *saying* as scholars revel in the delight of the Indwelling Presence. In that moment of eternality erupting into temporality, the divine presence transforms into a diadem for the head of each and every righteous person. The immersion or integration in this act of *devekut* as seen by medieval kabbalists,[51] in our extrapolated Wittgensteinian mode, becomes an opportunity for making manifest the ineffable through community. Revelation is this simultaneous *pointing* and *saying*, which allows those imbued with a deep aesthetic sense,[52] normally excluded to be included.

4. *Demonstrative* expression of Revelation: Any appeals to embody the revealed Law through commitment tend to fall upon deaf ears. Is this a function of merely lacking a simultaneous *saying* without *pointing*? Or is it a function of merely *pointing* to something that remains outside the realm of deeper devotion of our leaders? The clarion call of Deuteronomy 4:44, recited each time the *Torah* is lifted before community is a *demonstrative* expression of revelation. The language has become hackneyed in our age, leading to its content, for all intents and purposes, to take leave on vacation: *V'zot hatorah asher sam Moseh lifnai bnai Yisrael* "*This* is the Teaching that Moses set before the Israelites." I would argue this instance of *zot* is actually perceived as "that," distant and removed from our daily lives. Recalling the answer to the wicked child in the *seder*, namely, that appealing to outer observance without inner devotion is an exercise in futility. The need for transforming outer observance by revealing inner devotion within community is paramount for ongoing revelation. Despite the distance of *demonstrative* expression, community can once again make this shift from the outside to the inside of this ritual moment by transforming the language of "that" back to "this."

5. The glory of *incomplete* revelation: How Law is revealed presents a paradox. There seems to be dichotomy of experience by way of its proximity and distance—so is language once again on holiday? In the Reed Sea Poem, proximate revelation takes place by *pointing* and *saying*, "This is my God and so shall I adorn the One." Whereas everyone assembled at a reading of the *Torah* after Sinai points and says, "*This* is the *Torah* which Moses placed before the People of Israel by way of the hand of God." The communal ritual of reading can still be revelatory, but remains at a distance in many ways. Language has gone on holiday because most gathered no longer connect intimately to it. Whereas in the Yemenite community to this day, for example, Saadia's Arabic translation antiphonally accompanies each Hebrew line being recited to actively *point* and *say* this is being revealed, the English world remains bereft.

Bereft, however, is not the same as incomplete. True incompleteness finds the pinnacle of its manifestation in the scholar or *talmid hakham*. The glory of Torah is only revealed by a *talmid hakham* through his/her concealed revealment.[53] The ultimate glory of Torah is made manifest in allowing it to remain incomplete, in resisting the temptation to totalize by scholarship. By letting go, we take hold of Torah.

III. NATION—Zionism

   6. *Ostensive* definition and *demonstrative* expression of Zionism
   7. Returning to an *ostensive* definition of Zionism

6. *Ostensive* definition and *demonstrative* expression of Zionism: Everyone knows the case of two people who come upon something lost—a prayer shawl—and argue over its true ownership. Dealing with the experience of lost and found sets the scene for seeing a more nuanced reading of Zionism through *ostensive* definition and *demonstrative* expression. That *mishnah*[54] reads:

> Two are tugging at a prayer shawl.
> This one is saying: "I found it [first],"
> and that one saying: "I found it [first]."
> This one is saying: "It's all mine,"
> and that one saying: "It's all mine."
> —[the law is] this one must swear that he owns no less than half of it,
> and that one must swear that she owns no less than half of it,
>   And then they can tear it in half.

If the *tallit* can be physically divided into halves, in the first case, such that each half still retains half the original value, then a tearing apart takes place. If no such division can take place, then the *tallit* is sold and the litigants divide the proceeds.[55] The *mishnah* in question, however, seems to be dealing with a *tallit* found under circumstances that do not obligate the finder to return it to the one who lost it.[56]

> This one is saying: "It's mine,"
> and that one saying: "Half is mine."
> —this one saying: "It's all mine,"

assuring that he has no less than a third
and that one saying: "Half is mine"
assures that she has no less than a quarter
So this one takes three quarters
And that one takes one quarter.

A variation on the first case is another situation of lost and found where things are more entrenched. If we already agree that half the *tallit* belongs to the first litigant then their dispute is really focused on the second half. By taking an oath, as in the first case, each substantiates his/her claim to the disputed article and then they must divide what remains. The first litigant takes three quarters of the cloak while the second litigant takes only one quarter, which is half of the disputed second half. Here is where I propose an application of this *mishnah*'s thinking to Zionism. Much of the history of Zionism has been the same story of litigants and their claims on land, perhaps with less exacting results. Israel [this one] and Palestine [that one] each know that merely looking upon their lost land is not enough to lay claim to it. *Kula sheli* "it is all mine" means physically *taking hold* of the object is necessary;[57] *seeing* is not enough. Renaissance and occupation, rebirthing and stillbirthing, the tugging continues.

Two peoples tugging at a piece of land
This one is saying: "I found it [first],"
and that one saying: "I found it [first]."
This one is saying: "It's all mine,"
and that one saying: "It's all mine."
—[the law is] this one must swear that he owns no less than half of it,
and that one must swear that she owns no less than half of it,
        And then they can tear it in half.

This tug-of-war moves into a tearing with no seeming solution in sight. But *seeing* is not enough, there must be some way of *marking* physical connection. For some, the annexing of Gaza and the West Bank is that very returning of the missing half or quarter to its rightful owner. But the ethical solution that could be made manifest still remains unsayable rather than ineffable. There has to date been no simultaneous *saying* and *pointing* to Israel [this one] and Palestine [that one] for a just solution. A key to the problem remains that the language in these negotiations has become *Sprachspiel* or the most duplicitous of language-games, described so playfully by Wittgenstein. *Pointing* without *saying*, *saying* without *pointing*, in this context words and gestures have become void of meaning, of commitment, of trust. Is it still possible to imagine a time, a place, and a circumstance where the ineffable is possible, where the ethical can be realized, and where *pointing* and *saying* lead to a harmonized, democratic Jewish state?

7. Returning to an *ostensive* definition of Zionism: If language were not to go on holiday, as it always seems to during such negotiations, then it would be possible to reach that ethical manifestation of the mystical Wittgenstein yearned for and that Scholem long abandoned. If we were to further extrapolate this yearning for the ineffable rather than settling with the unsayable, it would mean that the contours of the *tallit* need to be changed.

As evinced above, the sword Excalibur or the *yahatz matzah* both retain their identities, even when broken or divided through the *demonstrative* expression of exclusion. Rather through their brokenness, wholeness emerges. Despite the distance of *demonstrative* expression, a connection from the outside to the inside is possible by transforming the language of "that" back to "this."

Tugging at an infinite *tallit* must now take the place of a tug-of-war over a finite plot of land. Any simultaneous *saying* and *pointing* to Israel [this one] and Palestine [that one] for a just solution calls into question either one's ownership over the land, as it is conditional for both to remain on the land. Conditional upon ethical living. If not (as the Deuteronomist says clearly time and again), the land will vomit up its inhabitants. Unless there is a reversal of behavior, the land will remain intertwined in a destructive compartmental-ization of *seeing*, separated from *pointing*, disconnected from *saying*.

It is precisely here at this impasse where Wittgensteinian thinking has so much to offer, revealing another way to realize the elusive ethical reality through *saying* and *pointing*. This reality is confronted immediately in returning to reread m*Baba Metzia* 1: 1. This tug-of-war so lucidly described in the *mishnah* reveals a new reality. The whole tension between *this* one and *that* one, between *ostensive* definition and *demonstrative* expression, takes place in that open *point-ing* and *saying*—

"I found it [first]"
"It's all mine."

What is lost is found by *this* one, as he says [*ze 'omer*], "I merit clarifying monetary matters. What I have found are the lost sparks from the roots of your soul. They were lost as soon as you were born into the world." And what is lost is found by *that* one as she says [*ze 'omer*], "I've found what is lost, in clarifying the lost sparks from the roots of your soul." That same tug-of-war is now being read over an infinite *tallit* of the soul. That *tallit* is no mere "prayer shawl"; it is the *levush hanefesh* or "soul shawl."[58] Making manifest that ethical reality that Wittgenstein understood to be ineffable remains possible when the embodied soul before us is seen in all its divine glory.

This crucial *mis*reading of the *mishnah* relocates the locus of that tension. That tension between *this* one and *that* one, between *ostensive* definition and *demonstrative* expression, between masculine and feminine, relocates the possi-ble when there is a shifting of the site of that tug-of-war within the singular. By realizing the site of particular revelation is the community, and that of the community through the nation, and that of the nation through the singularity of interdependence, each existent comes to better understand its greater responsibility. It is not enough to remain in the tug-of-war between *definition* and *expression* as merely an exterior experience.[59] Rather what is being *said* and *pointed* to, through this final Hasidic *mis*reading of the *mishnah* (seen through the lens of Wittgenstein), is that each and every creature is already responsible for hearing the true other.

Hearing God speaking as Other to the one addressed is a simultaneous *pointing* and *saying* that I care for my fellow (whether her monetary matters or his land). For indeed, the ethical grammar of life[60] necessitates this movement through a series of concentric circles—particular, communal, national. This demands that each existent not be spared the trouble of thinking, but take the time to stimulate thoughts of one's own.[61] Such stimulation is revelatory when the trouble of thinking grows from critical roots into passionate knowing.

Chapter 10

Listening as Redemption, Suspicions of Utopia: Can Musical Thinking Redeem Religion's *Imago Templi?*

Each artwork is *utopia* insofar as through its form it *anticipates* what would finally be itself, and this *converges* with the demand for the abrogation of the spell of *self-identity* cast by the subject.

—Theodor Adorno[1]

The two images, of the *destruction* and of the *rebuilding* of the Temple, are inseparable from one another, and they configurate a *vision* of the world which in both its *horizontal* and *vertical* dimension is dominated by the Image of the Temple, Imago Templi.

—Henri Corbin[2]

Aesthetic experience is that of something that *spirit* may find neither in the world nor in itself; it is possibility promised by its *impossibility*. Art is the *ever broken promise* of happiness.

—Theodor Adorno[3]

Preliminary Reflections on Adorno's Musical Thinking

In turning his final years of reflection to the question of an aesthetic theory, Theodor W. Adorno's thinking unites many of the recurrent thematic fragments of redemption so far explored throughout his writings. For just as "genuinely modern art is *experimental, fragmented, shattered*—and irreconcilably opposes false consciousness," so too does Adorno's musical thinking aspire to a "direct-ness given intellectual form and *fragmented by reflection*."[4] While it seems to be a tautological turn, given Adorno's ceaseless invocation of the *Bilderverbot* or interdiction of graven imaging, still in aesthetics he finds a matrix for experiencing the possibility of redemption. It is a nuanced aesthetic matrix. The nuance is twofold: first, there is a freedom from objectivity as limitation through listening, and secondly, there is a need to experience the sublime as opposed to its imitation.

Regarding the former nuance, it is music rather than painting which offers the way into thinking, since "[m]usic, however, lacks any bond to the objective world from the outset: the ear does not perceive objects. Therefore, it neither needs to dissolve objectivity, as something heteronomous, nor to withdraw its control over objects."[5] Regarding the latter nuance, Adorno is always drawing a distinction between *Bilder* and *Abbilder*, namely, between an "image" and its "copy." The sublime, however, is only experienced in the image, not in its duplication. Thus "[a]uthentic art (as well as an authentic individual life), Adorno argues, should try to avoid being a copy."[6] For a thinker who ceaselessly decries any reification into categories or slippage into identity-thinking, Adorno remains relentless in his search for this impossible possibility of redemption intrinsic to a singular modality of aesthetic experience. That modality is embodied in the critical listening of the speculative ear.

It is in these aesthetic moments of existence—most profoundly in music—that such a vision of the invisible Utopia is experienced. This experience never exhausts the artwork, rather its truth hides what is visible and is thus hidden by being visible.[7] Such a concealed disclosure—a hearing of the ineffable rather than seeing it—complicates the ability to convey such synesthesia to any theory about aesthetics in general, and music in particular. Moreover, how such an aesthetics of redemption correlates to society remains a salient concern for Adorno. The intention in what follows then is to focus on the correlation between this aesthetics of redemption within musical thinking as well as its societal impulse and implications. In returning to music as the particular within the more theoretical paradigm of Adorno's aesthetic theory, implications arise in applying Critical Theory to the study of the form containing this "spiritualization"—namely, religion, in general, and Judaism, in particular.

From the outset, one must admit it is unlikely that Adorno is ever directly addressing religion per se as even resembling a form that could house this recurrent neo-Hegelian "spiritualization." Philosophy for Adorno, much like religion, has lost its relevance after Auschwitz. Rather in this fragmented world only through the unrealized trace of redemption is there hope for the task at hand:

> Philosophy, which once seemed obsolete, *lives on* because the moment to realize it was *missed*. The summary judgment that it had merely interpreted the world, that resignation in the face of reality had crippled it in itself, becomes defeatism of reason after the attempt to *change the world* miscarried.[8]

All the while remaining critical of any tendency toward totality in the Hegelian model of spirit [*Geist*], Adorno seeks to trace the aesthetic experience within the fragmentation of particulars, within the ashen remains of any aesthetic subject. This tendency to focus upon fragments as a path toward an experience of a unified whole composed of monads, like society, is well-attested in Adorno. This is precisely where Adorno weighs in on the debate over the methods of sociological theory, namely, between Critical Theory and Critical Rationalism. Whereas empirical methodology fails in its taking "the social atom at its face value"[9] leading to an interpretation of nothing more than a totality of facts, Adorno proffers the vision of society as a totality, whereby each subjective element is determined by its objective mediation within that totality.[10] Only by way of the individual monad can the fragments of subjective experience be brought together toward any sense of whole, albeit ruptured. Balancing this broken wholeness, ultimately a paradoxical mode of thinking remains integral for realizing what is at stake in such an aesthetics of redemption.

Adorno rarely, if ever, refers to "religion" as a concept in his thinking. Any exoteric or explicit reference to "religion" by Adorno would de facto follow the Marxist view of religion as an opiate of the masses. The opiate quality of religion lies in it masking of reality, thus being seen as delusional and remaining an obstacle to redemption *via* objective mediation of disempowered subjects within society. It is, however, Adorno's post-Marxist thinking that translates the condition of disempowerment here more as opiates into irrational stimulus and calculations in the following way:

> *Religion* is on sale, as it were. It is cheaply marketed in order to provide one more so-called *irrational stimulus* among many others by which the members of a calculating society are calculatingly made to *forget* the calculation under which they *suffer*.[11]

But what happens to this reified category of religion once such forgetfulness is forgotten and there is an interruption of redemptive consciousness? Is not this reified category then caused to rupture and make itself known again in its tautological truth to the thinker or to the group of thinkers constituting a thinking society? It is such a redemptive component, so salient to Adorno's thinking on aesthetics, that invites an extrapolated "what if" from the realm of the spiritualized, specifically in his reflections on music. Moreover, Adorno's Critical Theory may prove a necessary bypath [*Umwege*] in elucidating the redemptive potential of religion in general and Judaism in particular.[12]

Redemptive thinking might begin with such a turn to language, but Adorno is always in search of that fleeting moment which "points beyond itself by reminding us of something, contrasting itself with something or arousing our expectations."[13] The difference between the Frankfurt and Frieburg schools, between Adorno and Heidegger was the focus on time and temporality. Although it is by way of such a turn to language that an injection of a temporal locus within reflective thought is revealed, for Adorno music remains the "beyond" that language as a conceptual system will never achieve. Both language and music take place within time and need temporality. However,

Adorno's musical thinking remains vigilant in decrying how "language cannot be raised to the position of an absolute voice of existence."[14] Conceptual thinking—to which Heidegger's ruminations on the poetics of *Da-sein* [Being-there] may fall prey—remains antithetical to musical thinking. While the recurrent primordial concepts of language that undergird Heidegger's epistemology and ontology may resemble ciphers established by tonality and their lexical items in chords,[15] music remains beyond the limitations of a semiotic system such as language.

Dialectics of Musical Thinking

Despite the paralysis of metaphysical experience, Adorno soldiers on with a most "desperate and negative recuperation."[16] Most intriguing about Adorno's seemingly hopeless gesture is that the "negative recuperation" of metaphysics itself then "turns into something else—namely theology."[17] The inexorable correlation between the metaphysical and the theological remains by and large unsaid. Adorno's movement toward this linkage, however, is most explicit in his more sustained philosophical and aesthetic reflections on music. Why is it that the language of philosophy is muted to these metaphysical sounds, while the language of music is able to delimit a fuller revelation? Recollection of what has already passed over—the revelation of metaphysical experience—is anticipated in the presencing of music. Any such revelation would then unveil both a linguistic and acoustic experience. This then marks a return to the earlier quandary of synesthesia, namely an overflow of one sense into the other.

The convergence of these realms through synesthesia is investigated in further detail by philosopher of aesthetics Mikel Dufrenne (1910–1995) who dedicates an entire study to this need for recovering the primacy of acoustic perception in aesthetics. Hearing, for Dufrenne, is an interiorization of sound. The source of sound cannot be determined, per se, rather it exceeds its categorical envelope, as Dufrenne indicates: "There is more: I am myself a sonorous being."[18] This overflowing of the boundaries of the external and the internal is evident in how subjectivity is constituted by way of sound: "I resonate in it as it resonates in me, I vibrate."[19] Sound is no stranger to revelation of the metaphysical experience, for instance, within reflections on the Sinaitic revelation: "And the Name spoke to you from within the fire, the sound of things did you hear, seeing no similitude; nothing but a voice" (Deut. 4.33). The acoustic, as matrix for revelation of the metaphysical experience, then finds deep resonance in Adorno's reflections on music. Adorno is punctilious in his writings on music to differentiate music from language as such:

> Music resembles a language in the sense that it is a temporal sequence of articulated sounds which are *more than just sounds* . . . But what has been said cannot be detached from the music. Music creates no semiotic system.[20]

The inherent mediation of any semiotic system, in its web of composed signifiers and signifieds, cannot be overcome. Linguistic conceptualization, since Ferdinand de Saussure (1857–1913), of denotation (*signifier*) and connotation (*signified*), in and of itself cannot be extricated from its conceptual foundations. Adorno, however, proffers that extrication from the concept begins by its very elusion, namely, by engaging in a self-reflection that turns the concepts of the system against themselves. In this self-reflexive turning, a parallel process is reiterated by Adorno *vers une musique informelle* that should be a "music whose end cannot be foreseen in the course of production . . . the re-presentation [*Vorstellung*] of something not fully imagined [*vorgestellt*]."[21] Fulfilling the imagination by transcending it shines forth as a unique power intrinsic to music. Imagining the unimaginable or ineffable is a paradoxical movement toward the immediacy of the metaphysical experience of music which will remain "as yet undreamt of"[22] and which must always "leave possibilities unused [*Möglichkeiten ungenützt*]."[23] Within this movement, the very intentionality framing the idea as it re-presents itself is under self-reflection. The groundwork for this self-reflection is already evident in Walter Benjamin's iteration in *Ursprüng des deutschen Trauerspiels* that: "Truth is the death of intention."[24] Is it possible that this death of intentionality indicates a shift toward a *philosophie informelle*, a veritable "open thinking"[25] of sorts?

It is in the theological core negatively recuperated within the husk of the paralyzed metaphysical experience that Adorno makes a case for music. Then there is the possibility of music as a vessel for this very experience. Distinct from the deadening language of intentionality, rather the experience of music:

> contains a theological dimension. What it has to say is simultaneously revealed and concealed. Its Idea is the divine Name which has been given shape. It is demythologized prayer, rid of efficacious magic. It is the human attempt, doomed as ever, to name the Name, not to communicate meanings.[26]

The immediacy of experience intrinsic to naming the Name itself (as opposed to the mediacy of communicating meaning in names) moves toward the recollection of the primordial act of naming. That time, place, and circumstance of such naming—which according to Adorno is "doomed as ever"—is a function of the rupture caused by exilic existence. However, for Adorno the mystery of the Name becomes more audible despite its ultimate ineffability. This is precisely what provides another layer within the dialectic of musical thinking:

> Music aspires to be a language without intention. But the demarcation line between itself and the language of intentions is not absolute; we are not confronted by two wholly separate realms. There is a dialectic at work.[27]

In its ability to "find the absolute immediately"[28] music seems to be the way out of that albatross of metaphysical experience. Yet "at the moment of discovery it becomes obscured, just as too powerful a light dazzles the eyes, preventing one from seeing things which are perfectly visible."[29] It is the need to move beyond intentionality which is so crucial to this turn in Adorno's thinking, for: "[w]ith music intentions are broken and scattered out of their own force and reassembled in the configuration of the Name."[30] Such a reunification indelibly links the shattering of the metaphysical vessel with the possibility of redemptive thinking in reconfiguring the fragmented Name. This link is possible only through the revelation of this hidden temporality by which music is continuously nourished. This nourishment is experienced through:

> the congealed time contained in musical texts [that] can be actualized in every performance or reading, and hence is not identical with empirical time . . . As soon as the notation is actualized—that is to say, the piece is played— it merges with empirical time and possesses chronological duration, even while appearing simultaneously to belong to another order of time, namely that of the work which is immortalized, as it were, by being written down.[31]

Indeed, this zone between temporalities, both empirical and immortal, is where the power of music dwells. This nexus of such dwelling, between the immanent and the transcendent, is what allows for any possibility of synesthetic gesturing toward Utopia:

> What the musician longs for, because it would be the fulfillment of music, has not yet proved capable of achievement. . . . The aim of every artistic utopia today is to make things in ignorance of what they are.[32]

Yearning for the fulfillment of what remains unfulfilled, forever beyond grasp, in musical thinking is the artistic Utopia to which we must now turn our attention.

Nowhere are the sociological models of Utopia more explicitly confronted than in Adorno's musical thinking. The yearning for the fulfillment of the unfulfilled in music finds its diverse expression most prominently in both the polarities of Utopias and dystopic apocalypses present in varying degrees, as we have seen earlier in the third chapter, within the three composers of Wagner, Mahler, and Schoenberg.[33] The perspective of musical thinking nuances the possibilities and dangers of redemption, respectively as Phantasmagoric, Near, and Negative. Adorno's reflections on each of the three composers have already suggested a most lucid articulation of the possibilities and concomitant dangers of a Redeemer and an ensuing event of Redemption.

Returning Time for Redemption: Rectifying Time after Stravinsky

Any society willing to find the time to idealize death inevitably becomes an oppressive totality. Death—the salvational nexus upon which Wagner's Redeemer and Redemption turns—is laid bare for what it truly is by Adorno. Such redemption must, at once, address the time of the individual's cry as well as that of the collectivity surrounding it. In its epic status, what Wagner's phantasmagoric temporality of redemption, misses is the cry of the individual. This leads to an effacement of the individual within a total and reified whole. If death is the ultimate salvation, it enters into the realm of the ideal, only to be reified. Falling prey to such a reification of the concept is phantasmagoric, especially with an experience so intrinsic to communal life—this is utterly anathema to Adorno.

By contrast, as has already been seen in the Near Redemption of Mahler's "disintegration of the sound by a certain caustic sharpness," a mediating emanation is experienced in *Gevura*'s acoustic power. Through this point of mediation, the subjective interweaves with the objective, such that the needed tension remains extant between the fragment and the whole, between the individual and the community. It is in the reflexivity of mediation itself that a realization of the loss of time inherent to existence becomes apparent. That realization of loss opens to the ensuing irruption of the redemptive into mundane temporality. But in relation to this loss of temporality, there is more to reconsider vis-à-vis the models of time Adorno is working through.

If the true experience of time is often lost, how then can it be rectified toward redemption? Conjuring away time happens, in terms of Adorno's musical temporality, when Igor Stravinksy (1882–1971) is "playing the *temps espace* against the *temps durée*."[34] If indeed Stravinksy's music leads us to "forget lived time and to surrender ourselves to spatialization,"[35] then in Adorno's estimation a problematic dualism inheres. That temporal dualism, inherited from Henri Bergson (1859–1941), means that Adorno then "opposes lived time to clock time, yet music is concerned with more than these two temporal forms."[36] The loss of time's texture happens when it is limited to the dichotomy of inner versus outer time, of qualitative versus automatic time, of tempo versus the metronome. Something more is clearly going on, and shockingly, Adorno is missing it. While he yearns to return time to its redemptive source, Adorno is unable to rectify this reified dualism of the concept in question.

To return time to redemption requires a rectification of temporality. That something more, so absent, is timelessness as advanced by autodidactic conductor Hermann Scherchen (18911–1966) and philosopher Jean Gebser (1905–1973).[37] The temporal dichotomy of forms, for Scherchen, hovers between metrum and rhythm. The former, metrum, is "the capacity of order that can resist time," while the latter, rhythm, is "a life process lost in time."[38] Furthering Scherchen's return to time, Gebser notes the need for attunement to the timelessness of what he calls "magic time" as evident in primordial music.[39] Unique about this musical temporality within the magic time of primordial music are "manifestations without beginning and end, a chance intrusion of the voice and a chance ending: a sleep that has, as it were, become sound."[40] What Adorno takes note of throughout his philosophy of new music[41] (despite the Bergsonian reified dualism) is a unique moment in the perception of musical temporality. Both Adorno and Gebser would agree that this new music *un*defines and may very well abolish previous time-forms.[42] A corrective to Adorno's inner versus outer time is found in Gebser's reading of this new musical temporality as one approaching timelessness.[43] In consciously surpassing timelessness there is a certain "time-freedom" that then emerges. In affirming the instability of its temporal condition, new musical temporality reveals a structural change. And it is this very "structural change which has irrupted through the new valuation of time in music."[44]

To return time to redemption, moreover, requires a rectification of the "perspectival rational modes of realization"[45] within the human subject. There exists a kind of "arationality" in the new music that the present subjective constitution is not equipped to fully perceive or absorb. What Adorno would see as a gap between the subjective and the objective, Gebser sees as a necessary evolution. "To a certain extent this music presupposes the 'new,' the aperspectival and integral man."[46] This is an evolution of spiritual consciousness toward a more integral form of existence. Such a shift then takes us back to Stravinsky so as to move forward.

How then does Adorno read Stravinsky's musical temporality[47] vis-à-vis redemption? Taking on the task of critical thinking here, Adorno is quick to launch into a critique of Stravinsky for his having "dreamed of a 'distantiated' [*verfremdet*] sort of music that might have given that similarity to [backward-looking traditionalist musical] language the slip."[48] The illusion of order versus appearance [*Schein*] is what leads Adorno to critique Stravinsky as having the sincerity of a "trickster."[49] By contrast, Schoenberg "was the real radical" in his sincerity which thus allowed him to transcend whereas Stravinsky writes "music *about* music" which for Adorno devolves into "music *against* music."[50] This new objectivity evident in Stravinsky,[51] however, is what allows for rhythmic dissonance[52] and phonological dissonance[53] to be heard. What emerges in the wake of Stravinsky, in both music and poetry, is the "ultimate ambiguity. Living and partly living. Rooted and partly rooted."[54] It is this ambiguity that gives rise to the necessary tension Adorno seeks throughout existence.

It is evident, however, that as a composer, Stravinsky's intention about the new music is to necessarily bring about a unification of the senses, the intellect, and the psyche of the listener, as he comments:

> For myself, I cannot begin to take an interest in the phenomenon of music except insofar as it emanates from the integral man. I mean from a man armed with the resources of his senses, his psychological faculties, and his intellectual equipment. Only the integral man is capable of the effort of a higher speculation that must now occupy our attention.[55]

Rather than seeing the whole human of integral consciousness as a sum of earlier structurations, in reading Stravinsky, Gebser discovers something unique. It is a window into integral consciousness that is new, insofar as it "overdetermines these structures by the version of 'time' through which the past that co-constitutes us gains conscious efficacy."[56] The very plentitude of contrasts within this new musical form and the human desire to perceive it points to a supercessionism of subjectivity. Beyond the binarism of subjectivity/objectivity that demarcates Adorno's temporality, what Gebser's corrective temporality attempts is an opening to the evolving intuition of "subsequent man [*sic*] and his reality."[57]

Notwithstanding its iconoclasm, Gebser's integral temporality cannot be read responsibly without the critical lens of Adorno, who warns of the "myth-making sacrificial victim which then acts as a secret law governing all [Stravinsky's] work."[58] Adorno is deeply concerned about how any uncritical return to myth through hopeless repetitiveness creates a musical temporality that can be limiting. If "[f]reedom is an intrinsic necessity for music,"[59] then that protest against myth, against death, means that musical thinking must never give up the hope of an alternative. Otherwise musical thinking capitulates to identifying with the aggressor, and impinging on the imaginal realm itself.[60] When critical thinking and its matrix of "absolute negativity is deformed,"[61] then the negative truth unveiled in this dialectical process remains an illusion [*Schein*].[62] To become freed of such entanglement within the dialectical process itself is the greatest challenge, considering that once inside the process there is less likelihood of feeling the need to remain self-critical. Yet this is precisely the moment of greatest challenge when vigilance is critical. With such self-critical reflection then is it possible to surpass timelessness into the time-freedom of redemption.

Toward a Sociology of Musical Thinking

Music is under the same obligation as *theory* to reach out *beyond* the current consciousness of the masses.[63]

The importance of Adorno's contribution to the method of sociological research intertwines with his thinking toward a sociology of musical thinking, evinced in his insightful essay, "Some Ideas on the Sociology of Music" (1978). In recalling the renowned debate between the two dominant sociological theories in the late 1950s—between Critical Theory and Critical Rationalism as exemplified by Theodor W. Adorno and Karl Popper—it was Adorno's interpolation of Critical Theory, which provided the graver criticism. This critical moment is what made possible an opening for sociological insight, as Adorno noted early on in "Sociology and Empirical Research," (1957). The fall into fetishizing the object of sociological investigation, becomes apparent once the method's "reified nature" [*Dinghaftigkeit*][64] is imposed upon the objects themselves. Adorno proposes that sociology cannot progress from the partial assertion about society to the general; rather it is a question of relating the general to the particular in its historical concretion,[65] as a monad[66] unto itself. Becoming more attuned to the spontaneity of individuals that comprise a societal body would set "the petrified antitheses of its organization in motion," so as to "come to its senses."[67] Attunement as already evinced[68] then is a key factor in this approach to society's redemption.

Unsurprisingly then these bypaths are reiterated in Adorno's writings on music as well as in his writings on sociology. Society is experienced as a process, such that: "[t]he only knowledge of society worthy of the name is one that would grasp both that totality and its parts through the process of critical analysis."[69] This is the motivation for Adorno to then enumerate his sociology of music, which advocates, ab initio, abandoning "the separation of method from subject matter."[70] A fascinating link reveals itself regarding the question of method, namely that it "is not something to be applied to an object in a fixed, unvarying manner. Instead, *method* should adapt itself to its object and legitimate itself by *the light it sheds upon it*."[71] The radical dynamism of method being proffered in many ways mirrors the relation of musician to music. Once there is enough of a foundational depth in the discipline, the particular composition begins revealing its hidden objective nature to the subject. The dual relationship that a sociology of music plays to its object encompasses both an internal and external dimension.[72] "Any social meaning inherent in music is not identical with the music's place and function in society. The two do not even need to be in harmony with each other, and indeed nowadays are often in conflict."[73] It is by way of attunement and response to this conflict that the truth of musical thinking for society comes to light.

There is, however, the danger that music will be usurped from its pristine role into ideology through its commodification in society; yet music remains "essentially social in itself."[74] What is so unique about Adorno's approach, however, is that the self-reflexive component of critique is implied in the social theory of music. Such a critique addresses music as more than ideological—at its core, music is societal. Given the nonconceptual nature of music, Adorno reiterates his claim that mediation can take place through "a technical and physiognomical analysis that describes formal features as elements of organized musical meaning (or that points to the absence of such meaning) and goes on to infer social significance from those features."[75] Sociology of music, in Adorno's eyes, then "will depend essentially on the refinement and reflexive powers of the methods of analyzing music itself and their relation to the intellectual substance that can be realized in art only by virtue of the technical categories at work in it."[76]

As the subjective impulse for the objective composition, the composer does not make rules, yet by following them what is revealed is the dawning awareness of this truth within the composition. The composer acts as executor of the music itself, in many ways serving "as someone who complies with what the work requires of him."[77] In becoming attuned to the truth of the concealed melody, the composer's revelation is primarily a social one. Adorno acknowledges that even though this most subjective of achievements is a "synthesis of his own nature,"[78] the compositional subject does not remain an individual thing, but a collective one. Regardless of how individual music may sound in terms of its style, it always possesses an "inalienable collective substance: every sound says 'we'."[79] Moreover, when music seeks the idea of a dynamic unity, this is "nothing but the idea of society itself."[80]

This transcendent ideal of the redemptive society—always beyond imaging in keeping with the *Bilderverbot*—continues to be an integral concern for Adorno. The redemption of a "real humanism" that permeates music, for example, in Beethoven, remains at a distance from the "reality which has not yet caught up with his music."[81] While there is forever a gap, it is more than merely acknowledging that music evokes the "beyond." It is more than seeing the conceptual nature of language as a system of semiotic signs incapable of reaching such enactment. The power of music dwells in its ability to transcend society by enabling a formal shape to be given to the contradiction of the general and the particular. Music enables this "contradiction to find expression and at the same time by reconciling the irreconcilable in an anticipatory image."[82] Resistance to synthesizing this dialectal relationship is a crucial quality of music for Adorno. While music may be said to develop in accordance with its own internal laws, such development is anything but self-contained.

It is the very interiority of music as society's grounding that gives Adorno hope for redemption. This would explain why these laws can "also be moved and deflected directly by social forces,"[83] given that at its deepest core music's grounding is social. The paradoxical, albeit fragmentary analysis of Beethoven by Adorno regarding this ultimately transcendent interiority, posits: "it is conceivable that Beethoven actually wanted to go deaf—because he had already had a taste of the sensuous side of music."[84] Adorno further dwells on Bahle's theory of a deeper inner link to be drawn "between Beethoven's deafness and his immense inner concentration, his incessant auditory seeking and grasping."[85] By delving so deeply into this interiority, Beethoven stands as the ultimate musician, sacrificing himself on the altar of deafness "to draw nearer than others to God, and from that vantage point to spread the divine radiance among mankind."[86] More than merely reaching the origin of silence, music can transcend time, as in the case of Beethoven, in becoming immanently manifest through its transcendent trace. In line with the asceticism of the Schoenbergian *Bilderverbot*, Adorno also notices that:

> Beethoven's apparent *asceticism* towards subjective, spontaneous inspiration is precisely the way to *elude reification*. Beethoven, the master of positive negation: discard, that you may acquire.[87]

It is here that Adorno's nuanced contribution to the sociology of music in particular and to social theory in general, calls for a deeper appreciation. Finally an antidote to the plaguing dangers of reification. Music provides the model for this antidote most clearly for Adorno. It is this quasi-ascetic approach to the sociology of music that opens the correlation of an integral bypath in sociological research. There is a layer of the intentionless within experience that is integral to self-reflective critique. But what is now becoming more evident is that this level of refined experience is only accessible through music, as evinced earlier, that:

> [t]he layer of un-premeditatedness [*Vorgedachten*], freedom from intentions, on which alone intentions flourish, seems consumed.[88]

Regarding the dangers of such a depleting consumption, Adorno evokes the aforementioned phantasmagoric [*phantasmagorisch*][89] redemptivity of Wagner,[90] in its exemplification of this perverted quest for newness. Once the "veil of temporal succession" [*der Schleier der zeitlichen Sukzession*] is rent, the newness reveals "the archetypes of perpetual sameness" [*der Immergleichkeit*].[91] Such damnation interposes a linear time of a truly temporal redemption. Such interposition seems to recur with this "wish for survival" [*den Wunsch des Überlebens*], leading to the unconscious projection into "the chimera of the thing never known [*die Schimäre des nie gekannten Dinges*]—but this resembles death."[92] The difference in such proximity now comes to the fore. It is "the element of wish" [*das Element des Wunsches*][93] that constitutes the illusory chimera, whereas only "yearning" [*Sehnsucht*][94] can act as sound guidance toward the path of redemptive thinking—a taking hold that is its own release.

Hope is for more than the hopeless. Hope is, for Adorno, the freedom to move between Thinking and Thought. This freedom for dialectical movement is most aptly captured in a question recently posed by novelist China Miéville, when he asks: "What happens if *two apocalypses* are scheduled to happen at the *same time*? How cosmologically embarrassing."[95] However, the answer to such a question is likely to be found in musical thinking, specifically in Adorno's comments on Hungarian composer, György Sándor Ligeti (1923–2006): "who is as perceptive as he is truly original and significant, [who] observed correctly that in their effect the extremes of absolute *determination* and absolute *chance* coincide."[96] So the twofold nuance needs both a freedom from objectivity as limitation through listening as well as the discernment to experience the sublime. To encircle the wall separating Thinking from Thought—the veil between need and action—is to dance[97] through Thought toward the light of redemptive thinking. If society would only listen long enough to differentiate its barbaric conformity[98] so as to embody the liberating aesthetics of musical thinking, the world may just take one step closer to listening for a redemption beyond yearning where temporal extremes unite.[99]

Afterword

Liberation Through Reason: Retracing Residuals of Childhood in Revisioning the Future

Whoever walks on his head, ladies and gentlemen, whoever walks on his head has heaven as an abyss beneath him.

—Celan, *Das Meridian*

all that singing at the fingers

—Celan, *Atemwende*

The ensuing comments are offered as a modest way of thanking Aubrey L. Glazer for the opportunity to think together with him in the fecundity of his thinking on display in *A New Physiognomy of Jewish Thinking: Critical Theory after Adorno as Applied to Jewish Thought.* Writing an afterword—literally, the word that comes after the word that has come before—instantiates in a particularly significant way the dialogic art of *Sprachdenken,* insofar as it is a form of retracing, that is, writing in the shadow of what has already been written. But in some sense what is brought into view belatedly must have been envisaged previously—the anticipation of a rejoinder, writing for the response of the other, is unquestionably what inspires most authors to compose their essays and monographs. Here the lines of temporality and hermeneutics converge: just as the text is as much shaped by the interpretation as the interpretation is shaped by the text, so the past is as much determined by the future as the future is determined by the past.

Let me initiate my remarks by taking note of the conclusion of the passage from Adorno that serves as the opening epigraph to this volume. A distinction is made between those "who write a book in order to write a book" and those "who have something to say." On the face of it, this distinction makes little sense. Can we seriously entertain the possibility of someone writing a book without having something to say? Sadly, as incredulous as it seems, Adorno knew of what he spoke. It would be frivolous to assume that everyone who writes a book actually has something to say. Lamentably, this extends to the scholarly community as well. Particularly in an age of overproduction, inspired by the academic credo "publish or perish," and facilitated by the digital revolution that has occasioned a monumental change in the nature of textuality, too many academicians write books simply for the sake of writing books. Inverting the motto coined by Robert Browning that less is more, we can surmise that the glut of material available on any given topic has led to the realization that sometimes more can indeed be less. With the onslaught of publications, it has become even more necessary that the politics of reading modulates the select number of voices that dominate the landscape, while the vast majority, at least in the span of their lifetime, go virtually unnoticed. Abraham Isaac Kook perceptively wrote that in every kind of wisdom there are those who disseminate widely and those who plumb deeply. The former concentrate on the quantitative proliferation of concepts and thus they tend to exert an influence on the superficial ideas that permeate the masses; the latter, by contrast, penetrate into the depth of the truth that is in each concept and hence their influence is gauged not quantitatively but qualitatively. Seekers of truth do not write books simply for the sake of writing books; they write because they have something to say. Aubrey L. Glazer can be counted among those who belong to this group. Indeed, *A New Physiognomy of Jewish Thinking* has much to say and its readers, no doubt, will have much to contemplate in their attempts to grapple with the full implications of the path he has laid out, a path that can be traversed only by those with the courage to venture beyond the comforts of convention and the insipidity of platitudes. As T. S. Eliot insightfully remarked, "Only those who will risk going too far can possibly find out how far one can go."

Like all timely thinking that is timeless, Glazer's offerings are carefully calibrated to the unique resonance of the moment, even as they are rooted in the archaic wellsprings of the Jewish and philosophical traditions. Beyond the specifics of his argument, Glazer is to be given credit for producing a monograph that takes seriously the juxtaposition of Judaism and philosophy as a creative act of cultural formation. He is not interested in writing about philosophy from the perspective of Jewish history or about Judaism from the perspective of Western philosophy. Rather, his intent is to compose a constructive philosophical meditation on Judaism that is, concomitantly, a Jewish meditation on philosophy. In this conceptual space, the universal and particular need not be set in binary opposition: what is universal is thought from the standpoint of the particular and what is particular from the standpoint of the universal. There is no generality that is not idiomatically singular and no singularity that is not systemically generic. I am reminded of Rosenzweig's depiction of his own thought in *The Star of Redemption* as a "theological rationalism" that would produce a "new type of philosopher or theologian, situated between theology and philosophy."[1] Theological creeds must be philosophically sober, philosophical axioms theologically vibrant. Glazer's project, it seems to me, is a faithful execution of this mandate. The manner of the implementation, however, cannot

follow the lead of Rosenzweig uncritically; the exigencies of the current epoch
demand an approach that diverges from Rosenzweig, something the latter
would have well appreciated, insofar as the new thinking he articulated is, first
and foremost, a mode of understanding that occurs always in the present, "time
in the most temporal sense."[2] Speech-thinking necessitates a response attuned
to the moment, a response, consequently, that could not have been foreseen or
calculated.

In accord with this direction, Glazer seeks to delineate the contours of "new
constellations of Jewish thinking." He is driven to do so out of the conviction
that without a sustained philosophical reflection in the present the past runs
the risk of being for Jews nothing more than a memory that fades into nostalgia
and the future nothing more than an expectation that reverberates simply as
titillation. To be sure, nostalgia and titillation have the ability to distract the
mind by offering ephemeral and chimerical gratification, but neither has the
power to engender a durable and sustainable hope. Glazer aspires to unveil
truth by reclaiming an authenticity that will not be diluted into mere jargon.
To articulate the nature of that truth and to provide others with the tools necessary for such a retrieval, the author avails himself of Critical Theory, especially
of Adorno. To be more precise, Glazer constructs a Critical Theory *after* Adorno
to develop the supra-rational insight that will provide a justification for belonging to the collective form that is the Jewish community in its sociological diversity. Building on Adorno's claim that the possibility of liberation through reason
rests on the fact that the residuals of childhood, in which our thinking develops
through love, have a continued existence as "trace memories through the
socially compelled instrumentalization of our minds," Glazer asserts that "childhood residue of empathy and caring flows forth from the larger font of the
supra-rational," which he identifies further as the "imaginal realm." It is through
the internal tension of Adorno's negative dialectic that Glazer proffers the
"possibility of encountering the sparks of the imagination nesting in the *noumenal* realm."

What this book attempts, therefore, is nothing short of a new modality of
Jewish Thinking that will serve as the ground for a new modality of being Jewish
in the world. The dual emphasis on thought and being is the meaning intended
by the crucial word "physiognomy" culled from Adorno's lexicon. Needless to
say, the correlation of thought and being lies at the heart of Western philosophy, attested most poignantly by the dictum of Parmenides in his celebrated
hexametrical poem, "for the same thing can be thought as can be" [*to gar auto
noein estin te kai einai*]. For Adorno, however, the correlation of what-is and the
act of thinking no longer intends that real being is idealistically constituted
or even phenomenologically disclosed by theoretical apprehension. Closer in
spirit to the Heideggerian interpretation of the Parmenidean teaching, Adorno
accepts that the correlation, or belonging-together, of thought and being is
still the rudimentary insight of the philosophical mentality; thought bestows
on being the "figure of a life lived where theory and praxis are meant to be

unified." The configuration of reality is no mere exercise in abstract thought; it is rather the internal form of reflection, the constellation (a term that Adorno borrowed from Benjamin) that engenders a gestural expression of the fully embodied manner that one communally inhabits the spatiotemporal domain. The physiognomic nature of philosophy underscores the extent to which concepts may be employed to enunciate what is not, strictly speaking, explicitly stated through them; the constellation of thought, in a word, is a hermeneutical process that allows one to recover through the interpretive gesture the dimensions of sociohistorical experience—encompassing propositions of belief and patterns of practice—that surpass the horizon of conceptual cognition and linguistic demarcation.

The surpassing, however, is an act that preserves the very limit that is surpassed. In thinking the unthinkable, we are still thinking; in speaking the unspeakable, we are still speaking. Previously, I have explored this matter in a study on mysticism and the aesthetic impulse as the lawful venturing beyond the law.[3] Inter alia, I invoked Rilke's description in *Duino Elegies* of Orpheus, *Und er gehorcht, indem er überschreitet*, "And he obeys, even as he oversteps the bounds."[4] The poetic inspiration that proceeds from playing the lyre necessitates trespassing the bounds of language on the part of the bard even as he obeys the laws of rhythmic structure and metrical cadence. Significantly, Rilke's depiction of the "father of songs" may be indebted to the statement of Heraclitus, "They do not comprehend how a thing agrees at variance with itself: <it is> an attunement turning back <on itself>, like that of the bow and the lyre."[5] Attunement—a critical term in Glazer's own thinking—is here portrayed as a turning back on itself, an image that conveys the Heraclitean notion of harmony as the oscillation between agreement and disagreement, consonance and dissonance, the periodic coming-together and coming-apart. As Rilke himself formulates the axiom of transgression, *Kundiger böge die Zweige der Weiden, wer die Wurzeln der Weiden erfuhr*, "Whoever's known the roots of the willow is better trained to bend the willow's limbs."[6] Reversing the order of Rilke's maxim, it might be said that only by bending the limb does one truly know the root, which is a perfectly apt way to convey the idea that the law most fully expresses its potentiality as law at the point when it exceeds the limits of its prescriptions; the law is affirmed in the negation of its restrictiveness.

In the *Principle of Hope*, Ernst Bloch similarly referred to the "poetic venturing beyond the limits,"[7] which he also relates specifically to music—*all venturers beyond the limits to the absolute moment are also tonal characters*.[8] Music provides the means through which one advances past the confines of the moral sphere to a realm that transcends language understood as a form of communication that is based on a semiosis determined by an organized coherence of evocative sounds. The "latent expressive power" of music that "goes far beyond all known words" encapsulates the Utopian striving to exceed all limitation. The "most characteristic aspiration of music," therefore, is for it "to be, to find, to become, language sui generis. Indeed because the expressive power of music lies beyond all known names, in the end expression in music is no longer under discussion at all but *music itself as expression.*" Insofar as music goes toward its own language, which is a poiesis that moves away from the limits of verbal expression, it follows that it is one of the most appropriate aesthetic forms to capture the stimulus of mystical proclivity. Music embodies an irreducibly transgressive quality, which is expressed by Bloch in the statement that the "tension of sound passes from being physical to being psychical," for the "most characteristic feature of melody" is that "in each one of its tones the next one is latently audible, lies in the anticipating person, therefore in the expression, which is here above all a humanized expression."⁹ The transgressive character of music is related inextricably to the transcendence of a linear mode of communicative speech by an even more elemental rhythmic and sequential discourse.

From the rhetoric of music, then, we can adduce the operative principle that exemption from law is not only part of the law, but its bud and flower, its origin and destination. This insight was expressed in slightly different terms by Adorno, who viewed the aesthetic form in general, and music in particular, as an expression of the negative dialectic that tradition is preserved through its being rejected. In a remarkable aphorism in his unfinished work on Beethoven, which is titled "On the Metaphysics of Musical Time," Adorno describes the constructive power of music in terms of its destructive tendencies; music thus expresses the fundamental rhythm of time for it persists in its passing. Adorno links this idea to an ancient rabbinic teaching regarding the group of angels that are created afresh each day to utter a new song before God and immediately perish after their task has been accomplished,¹⁰ which he attributes to the lore of Jewish mysticism:

> Relate the end of my study to the teaching of Jewish mysticism about the grass angels, who are created for an instant only to perish in the sacred fire.¹¹ Music—modeled on the glorification of God, even, and especially, when it opposes the world—resembles these angels. Their very transience, their ephemerality, is glorification. That is, the incessant destruction of nature. Beethoven raised this figure to musical self-consciousness. His truth is the destruction of the particular. He composed to its end the absolute transience of music. The fire which, according to his stricture against weeping, is to be struck from a man's soul, is the "fire which consumes [nature]."¹²

The issue of the law and its being trespassed is perfectly analogous to the problem of language and its transcendence. In a passage from another essay, "Sacred Fragment: Schoenberg's *Moses und Aaron*," Adorno relates that Opus 27 of the composer's work expresses the view that music facilitates envisioning what cannot be envisioned: "If the text creates the theological scandal of speaking of the One God as the idea [*Gedanken*], then this is a scandal that is duplicated in the texture of the music, though rendered almost unrecognizable by the power of the art. The absolute which this music sets out to make real, without any sleight of hand, it achieves as its own idea of itself: it is itself an image of something without images."[13] Schoenberg establishes a unique relationship between Judaism and music on the grounds that the latter is an "imageless art" and it is thus excluded from the prohibition on making images (Exod. 20.4).

The experience of the ineffable marks the limit of human language, but the only way to approach that limit is through language; the unsayable cannot be (un)said except by way of what is spoken, albeit spoken as that which cannot be said. In the fragment on "Music and Language," Adorno contrasted the "language of intentionality" [*meinende Sprache*] and the "linguistic character" [*Sprachähnlichkeit*] of music: the former is a language predicated on signification, whereas the latter is a "language without intention," and thus it "points to true language in the sense that content is apparent in it." However, Adorno also observes that what musical language has to say is "simultaneously revealed and concealed." It is precisely in virtue of this concomitant concealment and disclosure that we can speak of the theological aspect of music: "Its idea is the divine name of God which has been given shape. It is demythologized prayer, rid of efficacious magic. It is the human attempt, doomed as ever, to name the Name, not to communicate meanings."[14] Glazer is correct to discern here an allusion to the Kabbalistic tradition where the ascription of the name YHWH to the nameless Ein-Sof is a kind of mystical language marked by the esoteric dialectic of concealment and disclosure: every act of disclosure of the infinite is a form of concealment, since the infinite cannot be disclosed except as that which is concealed. The teaching of truth, like truth itself, is characterized by this hide-and-seek drama, and hence the dissimilitude of the secret is predicated on letting that which is hidden appear as what is hidden and that which appears remain hidden as what appears, an orientation that revolves about the paradox that what is most visible is the invisible. The form that is seen, the imaginal configuration, preserves the invisibility of the unseen, just as the liturgical tradition to vocalize the Tetragrammaton as Adonai secures the ineffability of the name. The most sacred of God's names, YHWH, is simultaneously hidden and revealed, indeed hidden in its revelation and revealed in its hiddenness. Kabbalists have long noted that the philosophical implication of the liturgical custom that the Tetragrammaton is never uttered as it is written is that language (of which the name is representative) is always paired with the silence that transcends it. The esoteric nature of the secret is predicated, therefore, on the ultimate ineffability to which the secret refers, but the ineffability itself is the measure of what is spoken. That mystics in certain traditions (Judaism, Islam, Hinduism come to mind) bestow a positive valence on language as the medium by which the enlightened can participate in the creative process (especially through scriptural exegesis) does not mean that they oppose in principle the restraint on speech that is often associated with mystical experience and the strict code of esotericism. On the contrary, the avowal of language as inherently symbolic facilitates the acceptance of that which inevitably exceeds the boundary of language.

Adorno has adroitly applied the Kabbalistic worldview to the language of music, which he identifies as the vehicle for metaphysical experience, and the signifying language. On the one hand, intentional language desires "to mediate the absolute," but "the absolute escapes language for every specific intention," since it is limited; on the other hand, music "finds the absolute immediately, but at the moment of discovery it becomes obscured, just as too powerful a light dazzles the eyes."[15] Just as the language of music is dialectically related to the intentional language, so the hypernomian element, the lawful venturing beyond the law, cannot be separated from the nomian foundation of the tradition. The redemptive thinking to which Glazer appeals—the reclamation of halakhah as an artistic process (what he enigmatically calls a "poethics" of theory and praxis) by which the formless is endowed with form, since there is no form that can be completely detached from the formless and no access to the formless except through the garment of the form—revolves about this dialectic. Glazer's speculative meanderings inspire us to pierce through the veil to see the veil, to apprehend that the truth behind the veil consists of seeing the veil unveiled as the veil of truth. Therein lies the possibility of revision and a renewal of what is yet to come.

Elliot R. Wolfson
Judge Abraham Lieberman Professor of Hebrew Studies
New York University, New York
16th *Tevet* 5771

Notes

Preface

1 Yirmiyahu Yovel, *The Other Within: Split Identity and Emerging Modernity*, Princeton University Press, New Jersey, 2009.

Prelude

1 Theodor W. Adorno, "Criteria for New Music," *SF*, 1999, 179–180 [my italics].
2 Yonadav Kaploun, "Scent of Darkness," *You are Still Writing* [Hebrew], Keter, Jerusalem, 2004, 30 [my italics].
3 Adorno, "Criteria for New Music," *SF*, 167 [my italics].
4 Adorno, "Criteria for New Music," *SF*, 145–197.
5 Axel Honneth, "A Social Pathology of Reason: On the Intellectual Legacy of Critical Theory," *Pathologies of Reason: On the Legacy of Critical Theory*, trans. James Ingram, Columbia University Press, New York, 2009, 21.
6 Honneth, "A Social Pathology of Reason," 21.
7 Honneth, "A Social Pathology of Reason," 21.
8 Honneth, "A Social Pathology of Reason," 21.
9 Martin Jay, *The Dialectical Imagination: A History of the Frankfurt School and the Institute of Social Research, 1923–1950*, University of California Press, Berkeley, 1996, 34.
10 Jay, *The Dialectical Imagination*, 34, 56. See also, Jurgen Habermas, "Der deutsche Idealismus der judischen Philosophen," *Philosophisch-politische Profile*, Suhrkamp Verlag, Frankfurt, 1971, 41.
11 Habermas, "Der deutsche Idealismus der judischen Philosophen," 41.
12 Honneth, "A Social Pathology of Reason," 19.
13 Axel Honneth, "Reconstructive Social Criticism with a Genealogical Proviso: On the Idea of 'Critique' in the Frankfurt School," *Pathologies of Reason*, 45.
14 Honneth, "Reconstructive Social Criticism with a Genealogical Proviso," 45.
15 Honneth, "A Social Pathology of Reason," 28 [my italics].
16 Honneth, "A Social Pathology of Reason," 28.
17 Honneth, "Reconstructive Social Criticism with a Genealogical Proviso," 45.
18 Adorno, "Difficulties," *EM*, 674.
19 Adorno, "On the Fetish-Character in Music and the Regression of Listening," *EM*, 288–315.
20 Adorno, "Difficulties," *EM*, 675.
21 Adorno, "Little Heresy," *EM*, 318–324.
22 Adorno, "Little Heresy," *EM*, 318.

23 Adorno, "Little Heresy," *EM*, 318.

24 Adorno, "Little Heresy," *EM*, 321–322.

25 Michael Fishbane, *Sacred Attunement: A Jewish Theology*, University of Chicago Press, Chicago, 2008.

26 Martin Heidegger, *Being and Time*, trans. J. Stambaugh, no. 134, SUNY Press, New York, 1996, 126.

27 From the Greek *phusiognomonia*, from *phusis* "nature" + *gnomon* "judge or interpreter."

28 Axel Honneth, "A Physiognomy of the Capitalist Form of Life: A Sketch of Adorno's Social Theory," *Pathologies of Reason*, 55.

29 Honneth, "A Physiognomy of the Capitalist Form of Life," 55.

30 Honneth, "A Physiognomy of the Capitalist Form of Life," 63.

31 Honneth, "A Physiognomy of the Capitalist Form of Life," 83.

32 Honneth, "A Physiognomy of the Capitalist Form of Life," 83–84.

33 Honneth, "A Physiognomy of the Capitalist Form of Life," 56.

34 Honneth, "A Physiognomy of the Capitalist Form of Life," 69; Adorno, *ND*, 40 [203].

35 Honneth, "A Physiognomy of the Capitalist Form of Life," 70.

36 Honneth, "A Physiognomy of the Capitalist Form of Life," 70.

37 Honneth, "A Physiognomy of the Capitalist Form of Life," 70.

38 See for example, Elliot R. Wolfson, *Through a Speculum That Shines*, Princeton University Press, New Jersey, 1994, esp. 58–73. It is thanks to Wolfson's pioneering correlation of Islamicist Henri Corbin's *mundus imaginalis* that Jewish studies will now begin to delve further into the poetics of the imaginal.

39 Adorno, *EM*, "Little Heresy," 322.

40 Jay, *The Dialectical Imagination*, 56.

41 In a recent article called, "A Philosopher with New Disciples (in Music, Not Philosophy)," by Edward Rothstein in the *New York Times* (September 14, 2002), the continued influence of Adorno is sensed, in an oeuvre extending over:

> 23 German volumes and 10,000 pages, encompass[ing] critical theory, aesthetics and political theory. But his writings on music have had the greatest impact. In fact, no other figure has influenced American musicology more during the last 20 years.

The attempt of this present study is to correlate the insights of Adorno's musical thinking with Jewish Thinking.

42 Franz Rosenzweig, *The Star of Redemption*, trans. Barbara E. Galli, University of Wisconsin Press, Wisconsin, 2005.

43 Aaron W. Hughes and Elliot R. Wolfson, "Charting an Alternative Course for the Study of Jewish Philosophy," *New Directions in Jewish Philosophy*, Indiana University Press, Bloomington, 2010, 1. Despite the appearance of recent landmark philosophical studies, like Schwarzschild's *The Pursuit of an Ideal* and Kellner's *Must a Jew Believe Anything*, the territory remains remarkably neutered from strong thinking. See Steven Schwarzschild, *The Pursuit of an Ideal: Jewish Writings of Steven Schwarzschild*, SUNY Press, New York, 1990; Menahem Kellner, *Must a Jew Believe Anything*, Littman Library of Jewish Civilization, London, 2006.

44 Hughes and Wolfson, "Charting an Alternative Course for the Study of Jewish Philosophy," 2. One notable exception is the willingness of Fishbane to explore

how his own Jewish Theology as a way of life (despite its apologetic lapses), see Fishbane, *Sacred Attunement: A Jewish Theology*.

⁴⁵ Hughes and Wolfson, "Charting an Alternative Course for the Study of Jewish Philosophy," 13.

⁴⁶ Hughes and Wolfson, "Charting an Alternative Course for the Study of Jewish Philosophy," 14–15.

⁴⁷ Hughes and Wolfson, "Charting an Alternative Course for the Study of Jewish Philosophy," 8.

⁴⁸ Elliot R. Wolfson, *Alef, Mem, Tau: Kabbalistic Musings on Time, Truth, and Death*, University of California Press, Berkeley, 2006.

⁴⁹ Elliot R. Wolfson, "Light Does Not Talk but Shines: Apophasis and Vision in Rosenzweig's Theopoetic Temporality," *New Directions in Jewish Philosophy*, 146 n. 211.

⁵⁰ Wolfson, "Light Does Not Talk but Shines," 123.

⁵¹ Hughes and Wolfson, "Charting an Alternative Course for the Study of Jewish Philosophy," 10–11.

⁵² Hughes and Wolfson, "Charting an Alternative Course for the Study of Jewish Philosophy," 12.

⁵³ Hughes and Wolfson, "Charting an Alternative Course for the Study of Jewish Philosophy," 13.

⁵⁴ Hughes and Wolfson, "Charting an Alternative Course for the Study of Jewish Philosophy," 3.

⁵⁵ Gersonides, *The Wars of the Lord*, 2 vols., trans. Seymour Feldman, JPS, Pennsylvania, 1984.

⁵⁶ Immanuel Kant, *Critique of Pure Reason*, trans. Norman Kemp Smith, St. Martin's Press, New York, 1929; see Norman Kemp Smith, *A Commentary to Kant's "Critique of Pure Reason,"* second edition, Humanities Press International, Inc., New Jersey, 1992.

⁵⁷ Kant, *Critique of Pure Reason*, A115–118, 141–143; Kemp Smith, *A Commentary to Kant's "Critique of Pure Reason,"* 263–266.

⁵⁸ Despite its wondrous poetics, Heschel's *A Passion for Truth* is devoid of any kind of systematic thinking, epistemology or overall guiding philosophy, thus it often resorts to existentialist arguments to buttress highly subjective claims, see Abraham Joshua Heschel, *A Passion for Truth*, Jewish Lights, Vermont, 1995. The same problems exist in the important works of constructive theology by Arthur Green, *Eheyeh: A Kabbalah for Tomorrow*, Jewish Lights, Vermont, 2003.

⁵⁹ Adorno, "Criteria for New Music," *SF*, 179.

⁶⁰ David Novak, *The Election of Israel: The Idea of the Chosen People*, Cambridge University Press, Cambridge, 2007; David Novak, *Natural Law in Judaism*, Cambridge University Press, Cambridge, 2008.

⁶¹ Rabbi Zalman Schachter-Shalomi and Rabbi Daniel Siegel, *Integral Halachah: Transcending and Including*, Trafford Publishing, New York, 2007.

⁶² Arthur Green, *Radical Judaism*, Yale University Press, New Haven, 2010.

⁶³ Rabbi Elliot J. Cosgrove, ed., *Jewish Theology in Our Time: A New Generation Explores the Foundations & Future of Jewish Belief*, Jewish Lights, Vermont, 2010.

⁶⁴ Schachter-Shalomi and Siegel, *Integral Halachah*.

⁶⁵ Shaul Magid, "Post-Monotheism and American Judaism: Jan Assmann's 'Mosaic Distinction,' Zalman Schachter-Shalomi's 'Paradigm Shift,' and Arthur Green's 'Radical Judaism,'" *Jews and Judaism in Post-Ethnic America: New Particularism,*

Ethnic Identity, and the Struggle to Become an American Religion, Indiana University Press, Indiana (forthcoming 2011). Compare with, Shaul Magid, "Jewish Renewal, American Spirituality, and Post-Monotheistic Theology," *Tikkun,* San Francisco, May/June 2006, 62–66.

66 Magid, "Post-Monotheism and American Judaism," especially in the conclusion of the seventh chapter, referring to these radical theologians as pioneering "the first non-elective Jewish metaphysics."

67 Magid astutely notes the negative turn that is present in both theologians, namely that "Shalomi offers a critique of pantheism using the language of pantheism" and "Green disavows pantheism for mystical pantheism," see Shaul Magid, *Jews and Judaism in Post-Ethnic America: New Particularism, Ethnic Identity, and the Struggle to Become an American Religion,* Indiana University Press, Indiana (forthcoming 2011), 51.

68 Magid, "Post-Monotheism and American Judaism," 47.

69 Wolfson's recent study on the correlation of mysticism and ethics is welcomed in its scholarly rigor and willingness to reveal what layers of textuality have for too long concealed, see Elliot R. Wolfson, *Venturing Beyond: Law and Morality in Kabbalistic Mysticism,* Oxford University Press, New York, 2006. Compare with Magid, "Post-Monotheism and American Judaism," especially in the conclusion of the seventh chapter, n. 179.

70 Adorno, "Criteria for New Music," *SF,* 196.

71 Paul Celan, *Der Meridian,* folio 32a, Suhrkamp Verlag, Darmstadt, 1999, 8/409 [henceforth, Celan, *DM*].

72 Yonadav Kaploun, *You are Still Writing,* [Hebrew] Keter, Jerusalem, 2004, 5 [my italics].

Chapter 1

1 Adorno, *ND,* 25–26/41 [my italics].

2 Adorno, *ND,* 35/57 [my italics].

3 Axel Honneth, "Performing Justice," *Pathologies of Reason,* 71.

4 Eliezer Berkovits, "What is Jewish Philosophy?" *Tradition* 3, 1961, 127.

5 Julius Guttman, *Philosophies of Judaism,* Rinehart and Winston, New York, 1964, 4.

6 Hughes and Wolfson, "Charting an Alternative Course for the Study of Jewish Philosophy," *New Directions in Jewish Philosophy,* 3.

7 Regarding the essentialist tendencies of Emil Fackenheim's thinking, especially when it relates to Zionism, see Aubrey L. Glazer, "*Tikkun* in Fackenheim's *Leben-Denken* as a Trace of Lurianic Kabbalah," *Emil L. Fackenheim: Philosopher, Theologian, Jew.* Supplements to the *Journal of Jewish Thought and Philosophy,* vol. 5, ed. S. Portnoff, J. A. Diamond, and M. D. Yaffe, Brill, Leiden, 2008, 235–249.

8 Hughes and Wolfson, "Charting an Alternative Course for the Study of Jewish Philosophy," 3.

9 Guttmann, *Philosophies of Judaism,* viii–ix.

10 Guttmann, *Philosophies of Judaism,* viii–ix.

11 Alexander Altmann "Judaism and World Philosophy," ed. L. Finkelstein, *The Jews: Their History, Culture and Religion* 2, 1949, 954.

12 Colette Sirat, *A History of Jewish Philosophy in the Middle Ages,* Cambridge University Press, Cambridge, 1990, 5.

13 Maimonides, *Guide of the Perplexed*, 1: 71.

14 Berkovits, "What is Jewish Philosophy?," 127.

15 Hughes and Wolfson, "Charting an Alternative Course for the Study of Jewish Philosophy," 4.

16 Hughes and Wolfson, "Charting an Alternative Course for the Study of Jewish Philosophy," 5.

17 For more on the embarrassment and re-embracement of Jewish mysticism, see Glazer, "*Durée, Devekuth* & Re-embracing the Godlover," *Vixens Disturbing Vineyards*, Academic Studies Press, Boston 2010, 506–510.

18 Robert Gibbs, "Seven Rubrics for Jewish Philosophy," *Correlations in Emanuel Lévinas and Rosenzweig*, Princeton University Press, New Jersey, 1992, 255–259.

19 Zachary Braiterman, *The Shape of Revelation: Aesthetics and Modern Jewish Thought*, Stanford University Press, Stanford, 2007, 261: "While these rubrics remain essential building blocks for contemporary religious thought, they are not postmodern topoi. They belong to early German modernism to Hermann Cohen and Walter Benjamin, not to American postmodernism. In actual fact, a robust postmodern aesthetic of copies and fakes, semblance and artifice, has barely begun to make an impact on contemporary Jewish thought." Braiterman goes further to boldly claim at the conclusion of his remarkable study, that "If something continues to happen in contemporary culture that looks and sounds like revelation, it does so as an image-mediated form, not as a voice, but rather as the daughter of a voice (*bat kol*). In distinct contrast to Buber and Rosenzweig's heavy reliance on Scripture, contemporary religious thought that builds off their effort will come to resemble the Talmud." What his Talmudic aesthetics sounds like and looks like remains open for further exploration.

20 Neil Gillman, *Doing Jewish Theology: God, Torah & Israel in Modern Judaism*, Jewish Lights, Vermont, 2008.

21 J. Z. Smith, *Imagining Religion: From Babylon to Jonestown*, University of Chicago Press, Chicago 1982, xi.

22 Rabbi Daniel Wolf, "*Machshevet Yisrael*—Survival or Endurance?" *ATID*, 2008, 7.

23 Wolf, "*Machshevet Yisrael*—Survival or Endurance?," 3.

24 Wolf, "*Machshevet Yisrael*—Survival or Endurance?," 24.

25 Green, *Radical Judaism: Rethinking God and Tradition*.

26 Shaul Magid, "Is 'Radical Theology' Radical?" *Tikkun*, March/April 2010, 52.

27 For one of the earliest iterations of this conceptual triad of *God-Torah-Israel*, see Zohar III, 73a.

28 Wolfson, *Alef, Mem, Tau*.

29 Wolfson, *Alef, Mem, Tau*, 175.

30 Wolfson, *Alef, Mem, Tau*, 175.

31 Wolfson, *Alef, Mem, Tau*, 175–176.

32 Wolfson, *Alef, Mem, Tau*, xi.

33 Wolfson, *Alef, Mem, Tau*, 175.

34 Wolfson, *Alef, Mem, Tau*, xii.

35 Wolfson, *Alef, Mem, Tau*, xii.

36 Wolfson, *Alef, Mem, Tau*, xii.

37 Wolfson, *Alef, Mem, Tau*, xiii.

38 Adorno, *ND*, "Introduction," 3–37 [3–57].

39 Honneth, "Performing Justice," 72.

[40] Adorno, *ND*, "Introduction, 3 [3].

[41] Honneth, 77.

[42] Honneth, *Performing Justice*, 77.

[43] Honneth, *Performing Justice*, 78.

[44] Honneth, *Performing Justice*, 85.

[45] Honneth, *Performing Justice*, 85.

[46] Honneth, *Performing Justice*, 86–87.

[47] Honneth, *Performing Justice*, 76–84.

[48] Honneth, *Performing Justice*, 75.

[49] Honneth, *Performing Justice*, 75.

[50] Honneth, *Performing Justice*, 75.

[51] Adorno, *ND*, 35 [57].

[52] Honneth, *Performing Justice*, 78.

[53] Hauke Brunkhorst, *Adorno and Critical Theory*, University of Wales Press, Cardiff, 1999, 51.

[54] Honneth, *Performing Justice*, 81.

[55] Honneth, *Performing Justice*, 81.

[56] Honneth, *Performing Justice*, 82.

[57] On *involution*, see Glazer, "*Durée, Devekuth* and Re-Embracing the Godlover," *Vixens*, 505, n.1.

[58] See n. 38 of Prelude.

[59] Cornelius Castoriadis, "The Discovery of the Imagination," *World in Fragments: Writings on Politics, Society, Psychoanalysis and the Imagination*, Stanford University Press, Stanford, 1997, 213–245. Despite the prolific reflections on *poiesis* by Wolfson he does not address the contemporary contributions of Castoriadis to the imagination and his critique of Heidegger, see Elliot R. Wolfson, *Language, Eros, Being: Kabbalistic Hermeneutics and Poetic Imagination*, Fordham University Press, New York, 2004, xi–xxxi.

[60] Glazer, *Contemporary Hebrew Mystical Poetry: How it Redeems Jewish Thinking*, Edwin Mellen Press, New York, 2009, 246.

[61] Castoriadis, "The Discovery of the Imagination," 245.

[62] Glazer, *Contemporary Hebrew Mystical Poetry: How it Redeems Jewish Thinking*, 247.

[63] Brunkhorst, *Adorno and Critical Theory*, 59.

[64] Brunkhorst, *Adorno and Critical Theory*, 34.

[65] Castoriadis, "The Discovery of the Imagination," 245.

[66] Glazer, *Contemporary Hebrew Mystical Poetry*, 250–254.

[67] Brunkhorst, *Adorno and Critical Theory*, 36.

[68] Glazer, *Contemporary Hebrew Mystical Poetry*, 254–257.

[69] *Zohar Hadash, Bereishith*, 5d.

[70] Rav Kook, *'Orot haQodesh* vol. 3, 106–107. The ecstatic moment of song, *Shir 'El*, is what makes creative thinking possible Isra'El. Compare with Moshe Idel, "Music and Prophetic Kabbalah," *Yuval* 4, 1982, 150–169; Moshe Idel, "Music in sixteenth-century Kabbalah in Northern Africa," *Yuval* 7, 2002, 154–170. Glazer, *Contemporary Hebrew Mystical Poetry*, 257–260.

[71] Adorno, *BTPM*, 176–177:

> Relate the end of my study to the teaching of Jewish mysticism about the grass angels, who are created for an instance only to perish in the sacred fire.

Music—modeled on the glorification of God, even and especially, when it opposes the world—resembles these angels. Their very transience, their ephemerality, is glorification. That is, the incessant destruction of nature. Beethoven raised this figure to musical self-consciousness. His truth is the destruction of the particular. He composed to its end the absolute transcience of music. The fire, which according to his stricture against weeping, is to be struck from a man's soul, is the fire which consumes [nature].

The metaphysics of musical time reveals the transience of these angels created on the second day of Creation as a flaming fire, as well as grass, according to the Zoharic passage Adorno received from Scholem. That original passage does not speak of grass angels, per se, rather it vacillates between the possibility and impossibility of such a tenuous symbolic register. That register is what connects the transience of angels to the growing grass being eaten in the Psalm itself as expressed in Zohar III, 217a—

R. Hiyya opened [the discourse thus]: (Psalm 104: 16) "The trees of the Lord are satiated, the cedars of Lebanon which he has planted," why is it written in the verse prior (Psalm 104: 15) . . . Yet the verse "Who causes the grass to sprout for the beast" (Psalm 104: 14)—these are two thousand ten thousands angels sent as emissaries from the day of creation (Gen. R. 81). These are grass, but why "grass"? [The angels] grow like grass in a world where each day the [blades of] grass is cut every day, and then grow again as in the beginning. And so it is written, "Who causes the grass to grow for the cattle" (Psalm 104: 14).

[72] Paul Ricoeur refers to a "second naïveté" wherein scripture and religious concepts are read as symbols (i.e. metaphorical constructs), to be interpreted "in the full responsibility of autonomous thought." See Paul Ricoeur, *The Symbolism of Evil*, Beacon Press, Boston, 1967, 349, 350.

[73] Brunkhorst, *Adorno and Critical Theory*, 15.

[74] Brunkhorst, *Adorno and Critical Theory*, 18.

[75] Adorno, *ND*, 35 [57].

[76] For a preliminary attempt at addressing the interworld of colors in Jewish Thinking, see Aubrey L. Glazer, *Contemporary Hebrew Mystical Poetry: How It Redeems Jewish Thinking*, Edwin Mellen Press, New York, 2009, 243–290.

Chapter 2

[1] Friedrich Nietzsche, "*Der tolle Mensche* [the Madman]," Book III: no. 125 of *Die Fröhliche Wissenschaft* [*The Gay Science*] in *The Portable Nietzsche*, ed. Walter Kaufmann, Viking Press, New York, 1954, 95–96:

Have you not heard of that madman who lit a lantern in the bright morning hours, ran to the market place, and cried incessantly, "I seek God [*ich suche Gott*]! I seek God [*Gott*]!" As many of those who do not believe in God [*an Gott glaubten*] were standing around just then, he provoked much laughter. Why, did he get lost? said one. Did he lose his way like a child? said another. Or is he hiding? Is he afraid of us? Has he gone on a voyage? Or emigrated? Thus they yelled and laughed. The madman jumped into their midst and pierced them with his eyes. "Whither is God?" [*Wohin ist Gott*]? he cried. "I will tell you. *We have killed him*—you and I [*Wir haben ihn getödtet—ihr und ich!*]. All of us are his murderers. But how did we do this? How could we drink up the sea? Who gave us the sponge to wipe away the entire horizon? What were we doing when we unchained this earth from its sun? Whither is it moving now? Whither are we moving? Away from all suns? Are we not plunging continually? Backward, sideward, forward, in all directions? Is there still any up or down? Are we not straying as through an infinite nothing? Do we not feel the breath of empty space? Has it not become colder? Is not night continually closing in on us? Do we not need to light lanterns in the morning? Do we not hear nothing as yet of the noise of the gravediggers who are burying God [*Gott*]? Do we smell nothing as yet of the divine [*göttlichen*] decomposition? Gods, too, decompose [*auch Götter verwesen*]. God is dead [*Gott ist todt*]! God remains dead *Gott bleibt todt*]! And we have killed him [*Und wir haben ihn getödtet*]!

2   Adorno, *ND*, 401–402/Redmond trans. 25 [my italics].

Wer an Gott glaubt, kann deshalb an ihn nicht glauben. Die Moglichkeit, fur welche der gottliche name steht, wird fesgehalten von dem, der nicht glaubt.

3   Hent de Vries, *Minimal Theologies: Critiques of Secular Reason in Adorno and Levinas*, trans. G. Hale, Johns Hopkins University Press, Baltimore, 2005, 300.

4   On the distinction between faith and conviction, see Peter Berger, *In Praise of Doubt: How to Have Convictions without Becoming a Fanatic*, Harper Collins, New York, 2009. Compare with David Wolpe, *Why Faith Matters*, HarperOne, New York, 2009. The foundational problem separating faith from conviction is that for Wolpe faith is an act of grace, whereas for Berger conviction is attained through human effort and reason. See also, Rabbi Elliot J. Cosgrove, "A Quest-Driven Faith," *Jewish Theology in Our Time: A New Generation Explores the Foundations & Future of Jewish Belief*, Jewish Lights, Vermont, 2010, 123–128.

5   Rabbi Or N. Rose, "Spiritual Mappings: A Jewish Understanding of Religious Diversity," *Jewish Theology in Our Time: A New Generation Explores the Foundations & Future of Jewish Belief*, ed. Rabbi Elliot J. Cosgrove, Jewish Lights, Vermont, 2010, 70. An inspiring look at what is needed to move forward that is mired in looking too far backward to the pioneering (albeit unrealized) insights of Rabbi Zalman Schachter-Shalomi.

6   Rabbi Jeremy Gordon, "More *Theos*, Less *Ology*," *Jewish Theology in Our Time: A New Generation Explores the Foundations & Future of Jewish Belief*, ed. Rabbi Elliot J. Cosgrove, Jewish Lights, Vermont, 2010, 55.

7   Adorno, *AT*, 82.

8   Richard Leppert, "Introduction," Adorno, *EM*, 81.

9   Adorno, *AT*, 35.

10   Challenging the triadic theological cluster of a Great, Valiant, Awesome God [*ha'El ha'Gadol, ha'Gibor ve'ha'Norah*] in the *Amidah* liturgy, the Sages justify historical limitations in light of living through catastrophe. So Jeremiah can only

invoke a Great, Valiant God, in light of the destruction of the Jerusalem Temple, whereas Daniel can only invoke a Great, Awesome God in light of the Babylonian exile, see b*Yomah* 69b. Whereas the Sages dare delimit the adjectival attributes of God, a "theology of our time" would challenge the usage of "God" as noun altogether.

[11] For a preliminary attempt at this very challenge, see Aubrey L. Glazer, *Living the Death of God: Delimiting the Limitless in Edmond Jabés*, Lambert Academic Publisher, Germany, 2010.

[12] Vries, *Minimal Theologies*, 300.

[13] Vries, *Minimal Theologies*, 300.

[14] Emmanuel Lévinas, "Les Dommages Causés par le Feu," *Lectures Talmudiques*, Éditions de Minuit, Paris, 1977, 156. Emmanuel Lévinas, *Talmudic Readings*, trans. A. Aronowicz, Indiana University Press, Indianapolis, 1994, 182.

[15] Hayyim Vital, "*BeOlam ha-Aqudim*," *Derush* no. 2, *Sha'ar ha-Haqdamot, Qol Qitvai ha-Ari*, n.p., Jerusalem, 1988, 56a–60b. Hayyim Vital, "*B'Olam ha-Nequdim b'Tikkun Rishon*," *Derush* no. 2, *Sha'ar ha-Haqdamot, Qol Qitvai ha-Ari*, n.p., Jerusalem, 1988, 76a–78a.

[16] Lévinas, *DCF*, 156/182.

[17] Lévinas, *DCF*, 156/182.

[18] Alain Rey, s.v. *dériver*. *Le Robert Dictionnaire Historique de la Langue Française*, Tome 1, Paris, 1992, 1047b: "*detourner un cours d'eau de son lit*" (to divert the course or flow of water from the riverbed).

[19] See above n. 2.

[20] Martin Heidegger, *Contributions to Philosophy (From Enowning)*, trans. P. Emad and K. Maly, Indiana University Press, Indianapolis, 1999, 138 [henceforth, Heidegger, *CPFE*].

[21] Heidegger, *CPFE*, 139.

[22] Heidegger, *CPFE*, 139.

[23] Heidegger, *CPFE*, 139.

[24] Heidegger, *CPFE*, 139.

[25] Heidegger, *CPFE*, 142–143.

[26] Heidegger, *CPFE*, 12.

[27] Heidegger, *CPFE*, 143.

[28] Heidegger, *Elucidations of Hölderlin's Poetry*, trans. K. Hoeller, Humanity Books, New York, 2000, 30–31. Therein Hölderlin's poem, "*Heimkunft/an die Verwandten*" [Homecoming/To Kindred Ones] is reproduced in full.

[29] Heidegger, *CPFE*, 285.

[30] Heidegger, *CPFE*, 293.

[31] Heidegger, *CPFE*, 299.

[32] Heidegger, *CPFE*, 143.

[33] Heidegger, *CPFE*, 293.

[34] Heidegger, *CPFE*, 293.

[35] Heidegger, *CPFE*, 293.

[36] Heidegger, *CPFE*, 293.

[37] Heidegger, "Building Dwelling Thinking," *Poetry, Language, Thought*, trans. A. Hofstadter, Perennial Library, New York, 1971, 158–159 [henceforth, Heidegger, BDT].

[38] Heidegger, *CPFE*, 143.

[39] Heidegger, "What are Poets For," *Poetry, Language, Thought,* trans. A. Hofstadter, Perennial Library, New York, 1971, 94 [henceforth, Heidegger, WAPF].

[40] Heidegger, WAPF, 95.

[41] Heidegger, *Aus der Erfahrung des Denkens,* Pfullingen, Neske, 1947, 22–23; Heidegger, "The Thinker as Poet," *Poetry, Language, Thought,* trans. A. Hofstadter, Perennial Library, New York, 1971, 12 [henceforth, Heidegger, TTAP].

[42] Heidegger contrasts the lapses in and out of inauthenticity as regards both *being-toward-the-end* and *being-toward-death.* In *Sein und Zeit,* the thinker attempts to recover through its everyday evasion the existential reality of being-toward-death. "Factically, *Da-sein* maintains itself initially and for the most part in an inauthentic being-toward-death. How is the ontological possibility of an authentic being-toward-death to be characterized "objectively," if, in the end, *Da-sein* is never authentically related to its end, or if this authentic being must remain concealed from others in accordance with its meaning? Is not the project of the existential possibility of such a questionable existential potentiality-of-being a fantastical undertaking? What is needed for such a project to get beyond a merely poetizing, arbitrary construction? Does *Da-sein* itself provide directives for this project? Can the grounds for its phenomenal justification be taken from *Da-sein* itself? Can our analysis of *Da-sein* up to now give us any prescriptions for the ontological task we have now formulated, so that what we have before us can be kept on a secure path?" See Heidegger, *Being and Time,* II: 1. ∫∫ 53, 240.

[43] Heidegger, *CPFE,* 285.

[44] Heidegger, *CPFE,* 285.

[45] Heidegger, *CPFE,* xx.

[46] Heidegger, "*Einleitung in die Phänomenologie des Religiösen* (lectures 1920–21)," *Gesamtausgabe,* vol. 60: *Phänomenologie des Religiösen Lebens,* ed. Jung, trans. Graeme Nicholson, Regehly and Strube, Frankfurt A. M Klostermann, Verlag, 1995, 11 [henceforth, Heidegger, *EPR*] (I am grateful to Nicholson for sharing this draft translation of his with me).

[47] Heidegger, *EPR,* 11.

[48] Heidegger, *EPR,* 12.

[49] Heidegger, *EPR,* 15.

[50] Heidegger, *CPFE,* 285.

[51] Based on a lecture in Tübingen from March 9, 1927 and Marburg to February 14, 1928.

[52] Heidegger, "Phenomenology and Theology (1927)," *Pathmarks,* ed. W. McNeill, Cambridge University Press, United Kingdom, 1998, 53 [henceforth, Heidegger, P&T].

[53] Heidegger, P&T, 53.

[54] Heidegger, P&T, 52.

[55] Heidegger, P&T, 53.

[56] Heidegger, P&T, 61.

[57] Heidegger, TTAP, 6–7/4.

[58] Heidegger, TTAP, 6–7/4.

[59] Paul Celan, "Todtnauberg," *Selected Poems and Prose of Paul Celan,* trans. J. Felstiner, W. W. Norton, New York, 2001, 314–315 [henceforth, Celan, *SPP*].

[60] Such is the speculative elucidation proffered by Gadamer, who recognizes this star-shaped ornament as a good omen for the cast of fate, see H. G. Gadamer,

"Under the Shadow of Nihilism," *Hans-Georg Gadamer on Education, Poetry, and History: Applied Hermeneutics*, ed. D. Misgeld and G. Nicholson; trans. L. Schmidt and M. Reuss, SUNY Press, New York, 1992, 122 [henceforth, Gadamer, *EPHAH*].

[61] "Solely constellations represent, from without, what the concept has cut away from within, the 'more,' which the former wishes to be, so very much as it cannot be the latter. By gathering around the thing to be cognized, the concepts potentially determine its innermost core, thinking to attain what thinking necessarily stamped out of itself." Adorno, *ND*, 16 [162].

[62] Mieke Bal, "*Réfléchir la réflexion*," *Femmes Imaginaires: L'Ancien Testament au risque d'une narratologie critique*, Brèches, Québec, 1985, 199.

[63] Gadamer, *EPHAH*, 122.

[64] Heidegger, TTAP, 24–25/6–7.

[65] W. Boericke, *Pocket Manual of Homeopathic Materia Medica and Repertory*, B. Jain Publishing, India, 1927, 77 [henceforth, Boericke, *HMMP*].

[66] Boericke, *HMMP*, 279–280.

[67] Boericke, *HMMP*, 279.

[68] Zohar II, 95a. See Daniel C. Matt, "The Old Man and the Ravishing Maiden," *The Essential Kabbalah: The Heart of Jewish Mysticism*, HarperCollins, New York, 1995, 138.

[69] Celan, *SPP*, 314–315.

[70] Celan, *DM*, 12: 50b–c/413.

[71] R. Smith and K. Woodward, s.v. "meridian" *Derby & District Astronomical Society*, England, 2002, www.derbyastronomy.org/.

[72] "In the gift of the outpouring, earth and sky, divinities and mortals dwell together at once. These four, at one because of what they are, belong together. Preceding everything that is present, they are enfolded into a single fourfold." Heidegger, "The Thing," *Poetry, Language, Thought*, trans. A. Hofstadter, Perennial Library, New York, 1971, 73.

[73] Celan, *DM*, 11: 46/412.

[74] Celan, *DM*, 11: 45–46; 12: 49b–d/412–413.

[75] Hayyim Vital, *Sha'ar Ma'amarai Rash"Bi, Qol Qitvai ha-Ari*, n.p., Jerusalem, 1988, 105a–111a.

[76] Emmanuel Lévinas, "Envers L'Autre," *Lectures Talmudiques*, Éditions de Minuit, Paris, 1977, 39. Emmanuel Lévinas, "Towards the Other," *Talmudic Readings*, trans. A. Aronowicz, Indiana University Press, Indianapolis, 1994, 17 [French/English pagination].

[77] Lévinas, "Towards the Other," 17/39.

[78] Celan, *DM*, 11: 45–46; 12: 49b–d/410. I have made minor revisions to Felstiner's translation here for the sake of clarification.

[79] This sphere of *Binah* (Discernment) is the source of supernal judgment on *Yom ha-Qippurim* (Day of At-onement), alluded to in the exegesis of the verse "From all your sins before the Tetragram you shall be cleansed" (Lev. 16.30). To immediately precede is revealed in the words "*before* the Tetragram," so experience of the emanation of *Tifereth* (Splendor) is possible once *re-turn* to the words of dialogue within system of language has taken place. See Zohar III, 67a.

[80] Zohar III, 69a.

[81] Traditionally referred to as '*Asseret y'mai teshuva* or the ten days of re-turn, marking the time between the Year's Incipience [*Rosh ha-Shanah*] and At-onement Day [*Yom ha-Kippurim*].

[82] Hayyim Vital, *Sha'ar ha-Kavvanot*, *derush* no. 4, *Inyan Yom ha-Kippurim*, *Sha'ar ha-Haqdamot*, *Qol Qitvai ha-Ari*, n.p., Jerusalem, 1988, 288b.

[83] Wittgenstein, *TL-P*, 188–189: "*Wovon man nicht sprechen kann, darüber muss man schweigen.*"

[84] Adorno, *ND* (III: 1), 362/353.

[85] Adorno, *ND* (III: 1), 354–358.

[86] Notwithstanding the pioneering work of secular Israeli poets and activists like Yitzhak Laor, the lapse being referred to is found in Halbertal's thinking which displays an unwillingness to challenge the hegemonic rabbinic Judaism of the Chief Rabbinate of Israel, rather replaying it like an eternal basketball game. See Moshe Halbertal, "The Limits of Prayer: Two Talmudic Discussions," *Jewish Review of Books* 2, Summer 2010, 43–44. One near exception in the otherwise disappointing recent collection of new voices in Jewish Theology is a lone voice willing to consider a revision of Heschel's theology of divine pathos as the role of a "broken deity who is in search of man," see Rabbi Jeremy Gordon, "More *Theos*, Less *Ology*," 55. Unfortunately, Gordon too succumbs to the tendency prevalent in this entire volume that seems unwilling to commit to any deeper form of speculative listening, as sadly conveyed in the title of his essay.

[87] Vries, *Minimal Theologies*, 300.

[88] Halbertal, "The Limits of Prayer: Two Talmudic Discussions," 43–44.

[89] On the necessity of metaphysical atheism in Jewish Thinking compare Adorno here with Wolfson's brilliant reading of Franz Rosenzweig, see Wolfson, "Light Does Not Talk but Shines," 87–149.

[90] Namely, the theology that undergirds the fundamentalism of Israel's Chief Rabbinate and the Judaism in praxis that it regulates and perpetuates.

[91] Cosgrove, *Jewish Theology in Our Time.*

[92] Vries, *Minimal Theologies*, 300–347.

[93] Like the Rotem bill which was being proposed in mid-July 2010 to be passed in the *Knesset*, whereby in a Jewish nation-state it is possible to encounter a situation wherein one is no longer Jewish until proven so. When identity-thinking infiltrates institutions, especially the government, the consequences are devastating.

[94] Elie Wiesel, *The Trial of God*, Schocken Books, 1995.

Chapter 3

[1] Franz Kafka, "The Coming of the Messiah," Parables and Paradoxes, bilingual ed., Schocken Books, New York 1958, 80–81 [my italics].

[2] Gershom Scholem, "Toward and Understanding of the Messianic Idea," The Messianic Idea in Judaism and Other Essays on Jewish Spirituality, Schocken Book, New York 1971, 35 [my italics].

[3] No. 23, SEE BELOW, Adorno, *AT*, 358 [my italics].

[4] Adorno, *ND*, 15–16.

⁵ Franz Rosenzweig, *Franz Rosenzweig's "The New Thinking,"* ed. and trans. A. Udoff and B. E. Galli, Syracuse University Press, Syracuse, 1999, 87.

⁶ Rosenzweig, *Franz Rosenzweig's "The New Thinking,"* 87:

> All this is unthinkable to the thinking thinker, while it alone suits [*entspricht*] the speech-thinker. Speech-thinker—for of course the new, speaking-thinking is also thinking, just as the old, the thinking thinking did not come about without inner speaking; the difference between the old and the new, logical and grammatical thinking, does not lie in sound and silence, but in the need of an other and, what is the same thing, in the taking of time seriously.

⁷ Gershom Scholem, "Towards an Understanding of the Messianic Idea," *The Messianic Idea in Judaism,* trans. M. E. Meyer, Schocken Books, New York, 1971, 35 [henceforth, Scholem, TUMI].

⁸ Fred Dallmayr, "Adorno and Heidegger," *Life-World, Modernity and Critique: Paths between Heidegger and the Frankfurt School,* Polity Press, Cambridge, 1991, 51 [henceforth, Dallmayr, *LMC*]. Dallmayr's study draws heavily on the watershed comparative work by Mörchen, where the discourse and communication between Adorno and Heidegger is problematized, in spite of their meeting in January of 1929 after a lecture presented by Heidegger (*LMC*, 68 no. 3). See Hermann Mörchen, *Adorno und Heidegger: Untersuchung einer philosophischen Kommunikationisverweigerun,* Klett-Cotta, Stuttgart, 1981.

⁹ Martin Heidegger, *What is Called Thinking?*, trans. J. Glenn Gray, Perennial Library, New York, 1968. Martin Heidegger, *Was Heisst Denken?*, Max Niemeyer Verlag Tübingen, Germany, 1971, 3/6 [henceforth, Heidegger, *WHD*].

¹⁰ Heidegger, *WHD*, 3/6. Upon consultation with Graeme Nicholson, it is apparent that Gray's translation "of what desires to be thought" is a misleading locution. I thank Graeme for pointing this out, offering his own translation, as well as his generous gift of time.

¹¹ Heidegger, *WHD*, 5/9.

¹² Heidegger, *WHD*, 6/10.

¹³ Heidegger, *WHD*, 7/11.

¹⁴ Heidegger, *WHD*, 7/11.

¹⁵ I agree with Wolfson that a reconsideration of the notes on the lectures Heidegger delivered on Nietzsche's "will to power" are warranted, given the deeply problematic adaptation of this thinking into National Socialism. Is it possible this thinking constitutes Heidegger's unheard critique as a thinker of the tragedies unfolding in the name of truth by the hands of the Nazis? See Martin Heidegger, Nietzsche: The Will to Power as Knowledge and Metaphysics, vol. 3, ed. David Farrel Krell, HarperOne, New York 1991, 25: ". . . truth is both expressly and tacitly demanded, valued, and honored. Thus one could formulate the metaphysical essence of man in the following statement: Man is the one who honors, and consequently also the one who denies, truth? . . . Nothing less than that truth itself is an "illusion,"a mirage; for only if that is true can honoring truth be the consequence of "illusion."

¹⁶ Moreover, a veiled critique of the "will to power" continues to hover amidst the ashes, in that: "Will to power" is the essence of power . . . Consequently a *horror vacui* reigns in the essence of willing. Vacuity consists in the obliteration of

willing, that is, not-willing . . . To will "nothingness" here means to will diminution, negation, nullification, and desolation. In such volition power still secures for itself the possibility of command. In this way, negation of the world is itself merely a surreptitious will to power." ibid, *Nietzsche: The Will to Power as Knowledge and Metaphysics*, vol. 3, 196.

[17] P. Emad and K. Maly, "Translator's Foreword," *Contributions to Philosophy (From Enowning)*, Indiana University Press, Bloomington, 1999, xxii.

[18] Heidegger, *CPFE*, no. 257. Be-ing, 297.

[19] Dallmayr, *LMC*, 56. Dallmayr brings forth Adorno's threefold critique of Heidegger via Mörchen, to hinge on the following three misinterpretations of ontologization: "a misreading of the ontic-ontological difference; imputation of an atemporal meaning of being; and subsumption of ontic beings under atemporal essences." As the focus of our present investigation revolves around temporality, it is important to consider how much weight is to be given to such critiques and how affective they are in eliciting difference on key markings along the path of thought, rather than to eradicate one thought or another.

[20] Dallmayr, *LMC*, 59, esp. 70, no. 21, which lists extensive comparisons in Heidegger's oeuvre.

[21] Adorno, *ND* (III: 12), 398. My gratitude to Graeme Nicholson for sharing this more exacting translation.

[22] Heidegger, *WHD*, 3/6.

[23] Heidegger, *WHD*, 3/6.

[24] Adorno, *ND*, "Introduction," 16–18.

[25] Heidegger, *WHD*, 3/6.

[26] Adorno, *ND* (III: 12), 397/408.

[27] Adorno, *AT*, "Draft Introduction," 358.

[28] Adorno, *AT*, 358.

[29] Adorno, *AT*, 358.

[30] Adorno, *ND* (III: 1), 354–358. For Adorno's more sustained analysis of Beckett's *Fin de Partie*, see Adorno, "Trying to Understand *Endgame*," *NL*, 1991, 241–275.

[31] Emile Fackenheim, "The 614th Commandment," *The Jewish Thought of Emile Fackenheim: A Reader*, ed. Michael L. Morgan, Wayne State University Press, Detroit, 1987, 157–161.

[32] Adorno, *ND* (III: 2), 356/365.

[33] Adorno, *ND* (III: 12), 397–400. Also compare with the following passage, Adorno, *ND*, 204–205/207:

> Representational thinking would be without reflection [*Abbildendes Denken wäre reflexionslos*]—an undialectical contradiction, for without reflection there is no theory.

[34] Adorno, *ND* (III: 1), 354–358.

[35] Adorno, *ND* (III: 1), 362/353.

[36] Adorno, *ND* (III: 2), 356/365.

[37] Adorno, *ND* (III: 1), 354–358 [my italics].

[38] I am indebted to Jameson for this language of "negative recuperation," see Fredric Jameson, "Baleful Enchantments of the Concept," *Late Marxism: Adorno, or, the Persistence of the Dialectic*, Verso, London, 1990, 118 [henceforth, Jameson, *LM*].

[39] Jameson, *LM*, 118.

[40] Mikel Dufrenne, *L'Oeil et L'Oreille*, L'Hexagone, Montréal, 1987, 92: "Il y a plus: je suis moi-même un être sonore . . ." [my translation]. For further reflections on Dufrenne's application to the contemporary study of aesthetics, see Marie-Anne Lescourret, *Introduction à l'esthèthique*, Champs Université/Flammarion, Paris, 2002, 50, 94.

[41] Dufrenne, *L'Oeil et L'Oreille*, 91: ". . . je résonne en lui comme il résonne en moi, je vibre."

[42] Gershom Scholem, "The Name of God and the Linguistic Theory of the Kabbalah," trans. S. Pleasance, *Diogenes* 80, 1971, 59 [henceforth, Scholem, NGLTK].

[43] Deut. 4.12 [my translation].

[44] Hans-Joachim Kraus, "Psalm 29: The Powerful Appearance of Yahweh in a Thunderstorm," *Psalms 1–59*, Fortress Press, New York, 1993, 344–345. I have retranslated both the Tetragram as "Name" as well as *kol* by "sound" instead of Kraus' "voice."

[45] Shalom R. Sharabi, *Siddur ha'RaShaSh, Yeshitvath ha'Hayyim v'ha-Shalom*, n.p., Jerusalem, 1990, 1b–6b.

[46] Zohar III, 36a. Also compare with other definitions correlating Torah and Name in Zohar II, 87b, Zohar III, 80b, Zohar III, 176a, etc.

[47] Adorno, *QUF*, "Music and Language: A Fragment," 1.

[48] Adorno, *QUF*, "Vers une musique informelle," 303.

[49] Adorno, *QUF*, 322.

[50] Adorno, *MM*, 156/297.

[51] Walter Benjamin, "Epistemo-Critical Prologue," *The Origin of German Tragic Drama*, trans. J. Osborne, Verso, London, 1998, 36.

[52] Jameson, *LM*, 247. Jameson challenges such a postmodern reading as espoused by Richard Rorty. What concerns the present investigation, however, is that both thinkers are turning to Adorno's reflections on music as the pathmarks of a different type of thinking.

[53] Adorno, *QUF*, 2.

[54] Adorno, *BTPM*, 244 n. 305.

[55] One example of many occurs in another passage reiterating the potential correlation of recovering the metaphysical experience within Kabbalah:

> Is it still possible to have a metaphysical experience? That experience was never located so far beyond the temporal as the academic use of the word metaphysics suggests. It has been observed that mysticism—whose very name expresses the hope that institutionalization may save the immediacy of the metaphysical experience from being lost altogether—establishes social traditions and comes from tradition, across the lines of demarcation drawn by religions that regard each other as heretical. [K]abbalah, the name of the body of Jewish mysticism, means tradition. In its farthest ventures, metaphysical immediacy did not deny how much of it is not immediate.

Adorno, *ND* (III: 3), 363/372. For some reason, Ashton has chosen mistakenly to retransliterate Adorno's already correct transliteration from "Kabbalah" to "Cabbala."

[56] Scholem, NGLTK, 194 [my italics].

[57] Adorno, *QUF*, 2–3.

[58] Adorno, *QUF*, 4.

59 Adorno, *QUF*, 4.
60 Adorno, *QUF*, 5.
61 Regarding this linking of redemptive temporality to thinking, compare with Rosenzweig's innovative mapping in *Der Stern der Erlösung* of 1919, see Rosenzweig, *The Star of Redemption*, 442–443:

> There happens to the world indeed in its Creation the awakening to its own manifest consciousness of itself, namely to the consciousness of the creature, and in Redemption only is it really created, only there does it acquire that solid durability, that continual life instead of the ever new existence born of the moment. This inversion of the temporal sequence, where for the world, therefore, the awakening precedes being, establishes the life of the eternal people. Its eternal life, that is to say, constantly anticipates the end and makes it therefore into the beginning. In this reversal it denies time as resolutely as possible and places itself outside of it. To live in time means to live between beginning and end. . . . So it does not experience the between, although it naturally, really naturally, lives in it. It experiences precisely the reversal of the between, and so it disavows the omnipotence of the between and denies time in this way, and the same time is experienced on the eternal way.

62 Adorno, *QUF*, 297–298.
63 Adorno, *QUF*, 322.
64 Adorno, *ISW*, 148–149.
65 Adorno, *ISW*, 148–149.
66 Adorno, *ISW*, 149–150.
67 Adorno, *ISW*, 149.
68 Adorno, *ISW*, 151.
69 Adorno, *ISW*, 151.
70 Adorno, *ISW*, 156.
71 Adorno, *MAMP*, 141–142.
72 Adorno, *MAMP*, 145.
73 Adorno, *MAMP*, 145.
74 Adorno, *MAMP*, 146.
75 Adorno, *QUF*, "Sacred Fragment: Schoenberg's *Moses und Aron*," 248.
76 Adorno, *QUF*, 248.
77 Adorno, *QUF*, 225.
78 Adorno, *QUF*, 230.
79 Adorno, *QUF*, 243.
80 Adorno, *QUF*, 226.
81 Adorno, *QUF*, 226.
82 Adorno, *QUF*, 229.
83 Adorno, *QUF*, 232.
84 Adorno, *QUF*, 232.
85 Elliot R. Wolfson, "Erasing the Erasure/Gender and the Writing of God's Body in Kabbalistic Symbolism," *Circle in the Square: Studies in the Use of Gender in Kabbalistic Symbolism*, SUNY Press, New York, 1995, 49–79.
86 Adorno, *ND* (III: 10), 391/400.
87 A point of further exploration elicited in conversation with Wolfson is to determine the acoustic-ocular correlation in praxis of the community of contemplatives

in Jerusalem following the liturgy of Rabbi Shalom Sharabi. Their prayer book is replete with a complex system of imaging the divine by way of letters and vowels for their articulation. These extensive letter systems, which map out the godhead at a given moment in linguistic time, are then articulated in prayer. The question is whether the contemplative focus is primarily ocular with a silenced acoustic component or vice versa. I am indebted to Wolfson for elucidating the matter in the course of studying this *Siddur*. See Pinhas Giller, *Shalom Shar'abi and the Kabbalists of Beit El*, Oxford University Press, New York, 2008, 126–130.

[88]   Adorno, *MM*, 14/18.

[89]   Adorno, *MM*, 297/156.

[90]   This is by no means an exception, rather a recurrent, mimetic structure is evident also in *Negative Dialectics* as well as *Quasi Una Fantasia*. As Jameson has remarked, besides an overall indebtedness to Hegelian dialectics in general, the three transcendental Kantian ideas, in particular, may also be alluded to, namely, Immortality, Freedom, and God. See Jameson, *Late Marxism*, 74.

[91]   Walter Benjamin, "H. The Collector," *The Arcade Project*, trans. H. Eiland and K. McLaughlin, Belknap Press of Harvard University Press, Cambridge, 1999, [H4a, 1], 211 [henceforth, Benjamin, *AP*].

[92]   Benjamin, *AP* [H4a, 1], 211.

[93]   Benjamin, *AP* [H5, 1], 211.

[94]   Dallmayr, *LMC*, 59, esp. 70 n. 21.

[95]   In Jewish numerological interpretation, known as Gematria, 18 [*H"ai*] is the numerological equivalent of Life [*H"ai*]. Thus, only once the Roman numbering system of Life has reached its completion is there a possibility of shifting awareness within the same temporality to the linguistic alphabet.

[96]   Walter Benjamin, "Theses on the Philosophy of History," *Illuminations*, trans. H. Zubin, Schocken Books, New York, 1968 [henceforth, Benjamin, TPH]. For the shift from Roman Numerals to the Alpha Bet, see Benjamin, TPH, 263–264.

[97]   Benjamin, TPH, XVIII, 263.

[98]   I am grateful to Rebecca Comay for bringing this crucial linguistic matter to my attention during her Adorno/Benjamin Seminar (Fall 2000, University of Toronto). Much of Jephcott's translation seems to fall prey to such inaccuracies. My own dependence upon the parallels of what is translated as "Finale" [*Zum Ende*] to the redemptive vision of the "End of Days" is a case in point.

[99]   I am indebted to Tim Stock who shared this important observation during Comay's Adorno/Benjamin Seminar (Fall 2000, University of Toronto).

[100]   Adorno, *MM*, 141/80.

[101]   Adorno, *MM*, 144/81.

[102]   Adorno, *MM*, 143/80.

[103]   Adorno, *MM*, 141–142/80.

[104]   Adorno, *MM*, 144/81.

[105]   Adorno, *MM*, 144/81.

[106]   Moses Cordovero, *Pardes Rimonim*, Gate 6: chapter 8, Yerid ha'Sefarim Publications, Jerusalem, 1999, 77.

[107]   Heidegger, *CPFE*, 335.

[108]   Adorno, *MM*, 297/156.

[109]   Adorno, *MM*, 298/157.

110 Adorno, *MM*, 298/157.
111 Adorno, *MM*, 298/157.
112 Adorno, *MM*, 298/157.
113 Adorno, *MM*, 295/155.
114 Adorno, *ND*, 25/15.
115 Adorno, *ND*, 25/15.
116 Adorno, *ND*, 25/15.
117 Adorno, *MM*, 379/199.
118 Adorno, *MM*, 379/199.
119 Adorno, *MM*, 455/235. See Charles Baudelaire, "Le Voygage," *La Mort*, GF Flammarion, Paris, 1991, 186.
120 Adorno, *MM*, 456/235.
121 Adorno, *MM*, 457/236.
122 Adorno, *ISW*, 149–150.
123 Adorno, *MM*, 457/236.
124 Adorno, *MM*, 462–463/238.
125 Adorno, *MM*, 379/199.
126 Adorno, *MM*, 25/15.
127 Adorno, *MM*, 470/242 [my revision of the Jephcott translation].
128 Adorno, *MM*, 471/242.
129 Adorno, *ND* (III: 10), 391/400.
130 Adorno, *ND* (III: 10), 391–394.
131 Gershom Scholem, "*Shi'ur Komah:* The Mystical Shape of the Godhead," *On the Mystical Shape of the Godhead*, trans. J. Neugroschel and J. Chipman, Schocken Books, New York, 1991, 55, 281 n. 57 [henceforth, Scholem, *OMSG*]. Walter Benjamin, *Gesammelte Schriften*, vol. IV, Frankfurt am Main, Suhrkamp Verlag, 1955, 370.
132 Phil. 3:21. In its exoteric iteration, for instance, St. Paul addresses the community of saints in the Christ at Phillippi, whereby the Christ is the one: "who will transform our lowly body that it may be conformed to His glorious body, according to the working by which He is able even to subdue all things to Himself."
133 Scholem, *OMSG*, 28.
134 Adorno, *MM*, 25/15.
135 Adorno, *MM*, 379/199.
136 Benjamin, "Epistemo-Critical Prologue," 56.
137 Adorno, *MM*, 471/242.
138 Scholem, *OMSG*, 42.
139 I am indebted, as was Adorno, to the brilliant aphorism of Benjamin: "For the sake of the hopeless only are we given hope." Adorno, *ND*, 378.
140 Adorno, *MM*, 480/247.
141 Adorno, *MM*, 480/247.
142 Adorno, *MM*, 481/247.
143 Adorno, *ND*, 22/12.
144 Adorno, *MM*, 481/247. I am again indebted to Rebecca Comay in her revision of Jephcott's inaccurate translation of *Spiegelschrift* from "mirror-image" to a more exacting rendition of "mirror-writing."
145 *Genesis Rabbah* 34b.

[146] See b*Sanhedrin* 98a, where Elijah describes to Ben Levi the situation of the leper at the Gates of Rome who is the Messiah:

> Sitting amidst the beggars and the lepers; they are all unbinding and binding their wounds in one fell swoop, but he unbinds one and rebinds one, so he can then say: "If I am called then I should not be delayed."

[147] Adorno, *MM*, 12/17.
[148] Adorno, *ND* (II), 202–204.
[149] Adorno, *ND* (II), 202–204.
[150] Heidegger, *WHD*, 3.
[151] Adorno, *ND* (III: 12), 397 [my translation].
[152] Benjamin, TPH, 264 [my italics].
[153] Adorno, *ND* (III: 10), 400.
[154] Scholem, *OMSG*, 41–42.

Chapter 4

[1] Aharon Shabtai, "*Rosh HaShanah*," *J'accuse*, trans. Peter Cole, New Directions, New York, 2003, 15.
[2] Adonis (Ali Ahmen Said), "The Wanderer," *The Pages of Day and Night*, tr. Samuel Hazo, Northwestern University Press, Marlboro, 1994, 2.
[3] Gil Anidjar, "The Semitic Hypothesis (Religion's Last Word)," *Semites: Race, Religion, Literature*, Stanford University Press, Stanford, 2008, 33, esp. 28–38.
[4] "Government Announces National Hebrew Day," *Jerusalem Post*, January 27, 2010/12 *Shevat* 5770: Other figures yet to be sufficiently commemorated in the public mind for their contribution to the revival of Hebrew include laureate poet Hayyim Nahman Bialik, as well as David Yellin, Joseph Klausner, and Zeev Ben-Chaim.
[5] See www.handinhand12.org/index.cfm?content.display&pageID=175, for more on more on *Hand in Hand*.
[6] Anidjar, "The Semitic Hypothesis (Religion's Last Word)," 33.
[7] Gershom Scholem, "Confession on the Subject of Our Language" [*Bekenntnis uber usere Sprache*]: A Letter to Franz Rosenzweig, December 26, 1926, trans. Gil Anidjar, *Acts of Religion*, Routledge, New York, 2002, 237. For a more in depth history of Scholem's early pre-state conviction that bi-lingual cultural identity was part of the path to reconciliation within *Brit Shalom*, see Aharon Kaider, "The History of *Brit Shalom* in the years 1925–1928," *Research Chapters in the History of Zionism* [Hebrew], ed. Y. Bauer, M. David, I. Kulat, The Zionist Library, Jerusalem 1976, 229–30, 235–8, 254, 264–5. For more on Scholem's disenchantment with *Brit Shalom* by 1931 when he "expressed doubt about ever realizing his conception of Zionism as a 'religious-mystical quest for a regeneration of Judaism,'" see Gershom Scholem and Walter Benjamin, *The Correspondence of Walter Benjamin and Gershom Scholem, 1932–1940*, ed. G. Scholem, Schoken Books, New York, 1989, xxiv.
[8] Scholem, "Confession on the Subject of Our Language," 237.

9 Yehouda Shenhav, "Why Not 'The Occupation'" [Hebrew], *Theory and Criticism* 31, Winter 2007, 8–9.

10 A notable controversy emerges with the delay in publishing the 2007 fall edition of *Theory and Criticism* until the winter regarding the withdrawn articles of Eyal Weizman, "Walking through Walls," and Neve Gordon, "From Colonization to Separation." Weizman's important article uncovers the applications of socio-spatial theory in Gilles Deleuze and Felix Guattari to IDF military tactics used during *Operation Defensive Wall* in Jenin and Balata. While Weizman's article raises questions about ideology, epistemology and the migration of ideas, it does not separate theory from praxis. Rather using a conscious critical-political perspective, Weizman points out the responsibility of Brig. Gen. Dr. Shimon Naveh and Brig. Gen. Aviv Kohavi for application of these tactics that inflicted great harm on the civilian population. After Weizman's article was accepted for publication, editor Shenhav asked Naveh for a response which he never wrote. What ensued is a tragic story that included a legal threat from Kohavi's lawyer wrapped in the civil law of libel, militarism, and the occupation. What ensues throughout Shenhav's editorial introduction to the winter edition is the struggle *Theory and Criticism* continues to undergo in relation to the complex relations between free speech, the law of libel and what he sharply calls "the occupation within us." This crisis leads to further self-reflection and the reality that "an epistemological asymmetry exists between the ability to expose such evil acts in retrospect and the inability to prove them while they are happening, despite the vaunted ubiquity of the media." This crisis provided *Theory and Criticism* with its own "critical moment" to re-examine their critique of the occupation as well as self-critique. Despite the apparent loss of thinking through the occupation, a critical moment is recuperated and redemptive possibilities emerge in that unsaid (and unpublished) discourse. See Shenhav, "Why Not 'The Occupation'," *Theory and Criticism* 31, 11–13.

11 Zionism does not directly come up as a topic of any major focus in Adorno's work per se, unless one reads his reflections on Utopia as a model of Zionism in this vein. Notwithstanding, it is interesting to note that his friendship circle was permeated with ongoing reflections on Zionism, especially between Walter Benjamin and Gershom Scholem. Perusing Adorno's intellectual biography, for example, there are some references to Zionism, but only insofar as they relate to that circle, see Detlev Claussen, *Theodor W. Adorno: One Last Genius*, trans. R. Livingstone, Harvard University Press, Cambridge, 2008. Some of these Zionist friends of Adorno included: Leo Lowenthal (82, 238); Benjamin (100, 238, 279); Scholem (20, 100, 238); Kracauer (276, 279).

12 Hannan Hever, *Poets and Zealots: The Rise of Political Hebrew Poetry in Eretz-Yisrael* [Hebrew], Bialik Institute, Jerusalem, 1994; Hannan Hever, *Reading Poetry: Review, Essays and Articles about Hebrew Poetry* [Hebrew], Keshev Publication, Jerusalem, 2005; Hannan Hever, *From the Beginning: Three Essays on Nativist Hebrew Poetry* [Hebrew], Keshev Publication, Jerusalem, 2008.

13 Yitzhak Laor, *The Myth of Liberal Zionism*, Verso, New York, 2009, xiii. Compare with other essays on this theme, Yitzhak Laor, *Devarim sh'hashetikah (lo) yafe lahem: Massot*, Babel Publications, Tel Aviv, 2002, esp. the important essay that translates Adorno's thinking into Hebrew, called, "'Al Yahasiyut," 201–219, where Laor engages Adorno's discourse on post-Auschwitz thinking and praxis.

14 Anidjar, "The Semitic Hypothesis (Religion's Last Word)," 33. The recent *halakhic* review essay of Rabbi Yeshaya Dalsace is an attempt to redress the controversy surrounding the rental of apartments to Israeli Arabs in Israel (based on the responsa granting permissibility of such rentals by Rabbi David Golinkin). What is salient here is that after the *halakhic* discussions, Dalsace is ready to make "general conclusions" based on the need for critical thinking within the devotional sphere of *halakhah*. Notable is his insistence that the discourse of *halakhah* needs to transcend its medieval foundation and evolve, see www.masorti.com.

15 I am indebted here to Shenhav's expression of "the occupation within us", see above n. 10.

16 Amit Pinchevski and Efraim Torgovnik, "Signifiying Passages: The Signs of Change in Israeli Street Names," *Media, Culture & Society*, vol. 24, Sage Publications, London, 365–388.

17 Pinchevski and Torgovnik, "Signifiying Passages: The Signs of Change in Israeli Street Names," 366–367. Compare more recently with a struggle still taking place in France regarding street names, see Peter Hellman, "The Name of Pétain, Hero and Villain, Is Cleansed From the Streets of France: *Letter From Tremblois-lès-Carignan*," *The Forward*, New York, December 29, 2010.

18 Pinchevski and Torgovnik, "Signifiying Passages: The Signs of Change in Israeli Street Names," 368.

19 Darwish, "Mahmoud Darwish Bids Edward Said Farewell," 4.

20 Darwish, "Mahmoud Darwish Bids Edward Said Farewell," 4.

21 Darwish, "Mahmoud Darwish Bids Edward Said Farewell," 5.

22 David Shulman, *Dark Hope: Working for Peace in Israel and Palestine*, University of Chicago Press, Chicago, 2007, 1.

23 Shulman, *Dark Hope*, 1.

24 Shulman, *Dark Hope*, 1.

25 Shulman, *Dark Hope*, 2.

26 Shulman, *Dark Hope*, 4.

27 Shulman, *Dark Hope*, 2–3.

28 Shulman, *Dark Hope*, 3.

29 Shulman, *Dark Hope*, 213.

30 Darwish, "Mahmoud Darwish Bids Edward Said Farewell," 2.

31 There are a few notable exceptions within both Jerusalem and Tel Aviv. I have in mind the likes of the Van Leer Institute (Jerusalem), see: www.vanleer.org.il/eng/ especially noteworthy is their annual two-volume journal, *Theory and Criticism*, first published in 1989 as well as the monograph, *Theory and Criticism in Context*; also there is the Porter Institute for Poetics and Semiotics (Tel Aviv), see www.tau.ac.il/humanities/porter/.

32 I am referring to the sad state of affairs that would presumably have led to the necessity of inviting Rabbi Dr. Jonathan Sacks from England to Israel for a conference meant to be a local dialogue between secular and religious Zionisms, *Yisrael Halomot ve'Metzi'ut*, Bar Ilan University, May 24, 2001, see www.biu.ac.il/SOC/po/lainer/dreams.pdf.

33 Daniel Gordis, *Saving Israel: How the Jewish People Can Win a War That May Never End*, John Wiley and Sons, New Jersey, 2009.

34 Gordis, *Saving Israel*, 215.

35 Gordis, *Saving Israel*, 215.
36 Gordis, *Saving Israel*, 216.
37 Gordis, *Saving Israel*, 217.
38 Gordis, *Saving Israel*, 146.
39 www.shalem.org.il/page.php?cat=about&did=9.
40 www.nif.org/about/.
41 www.nif.org/about/.
42 Victor Ostrovsky, "Commission Report Leaks Make Strong Case for Complicity of Shabak Officers in Rabin Assassination," *Washington Report on Middle East Affairs*, January/February 1998, 30, 111–112, see www.washington-report.org/backissues/0198/9801030.htm.
43 http://imti.org.il/en/about_us.html.
44 It is not surprising to learn that "[d]onors to Im Tirtzu include the Christian American lobby CUFI—Christians United for Israel, headed by evangelist preacher John Hagee." See http://coteret.com/2010/02/01/breaking-hagee-and-cufi-fund-anti-nif-campaign-organizer/.
45 See n. 42 above.
46 Nahum Barnea, "How US Jewish Leaders Stepped in to Block the Knesset Anti-NIF Bill," *Yediot Ahronot*, Friday Political Supplement, February 5, 2010, see http://coteret.com/2010/02/05/nahum-barnea-how-us-jewish-leaders-stepped-in-to-block-the-knesset-anti-nif-bill/.
47 www.idi.org.il/sites/english/AboutIDI/Pages/MessagefromthePresident.aspx.
48 Axel Honneth, "Reification and Recognition," *Reification: A New Look at an Old Idea*, Oxford University Press, New York, 2008, 83.
49 Gordis, *Saving Israel*, 146.
50 Gordis, *Saving Israel*, 129.
51 Yitzhak Laor, *The Myth of Liberal Zionism*, Verso, New York, 2009, xiii. Compare with other essays on this theme, Yitzhak Laor, *Devarim sh'hashetikah (lo) yafe lahem: Massot*, Babel Publications, Tel Aviv, 2002, esp. the important essay that translates Adorno's thinking into Hebrew, called, "'Al Yahasiyut," 201–219, where Laor engages Adorno's discourse on post-Auschwitz thinking and praxis.
52 Gordis, *Saving Israel*, 8, 120–122.
53 Clearly this is an odd hybrid, especially considering Liebowitz was religious while Adorno was secular, but it remains a necessary one to exemplify what Adorno and his thinking might sound like if translated into Hebrew. It is worth noting Adorno's near lack of reception in the Israeli Academy seems to be slowly changing (due in no small part to the persistence of Laor's writing and activism in diverse media). One sign of this recognition taking place within Hebrew Culture is the unprecedented international conference, *Theodor W. Adorno: Philosopher of the Damaged Days*, [Hebrew] Tel Aviv University, November 16–18, 2003. Zukerman, "Was it a mistake to claim it impossible to write poetry after Auschwitz?" *Literature and Culture Supplement: Ha'aretz* (November 14, 2003) [Hebrew].
54 Gordis, *Saving Israel*, 118.
55 Gordis, *Saving Israel*, 117.
56 Avi Ravitsky, *Messianism, Zionism, and Jewish Religious Radicalism (Chicago Studies in the History of Judaism)*, trans. J. Chipman, University of Chicago Press, Chicago, 1996.
57 Nathaniel Berman, "Laws of War Apply, Irrespective of an Occupation's Legality," *Letters to the Editor, The Forward*, December 30, 2009.

58 Gordis, *Saving Israel*, 218.
59 To simply claim that H. N. Bialik's rereading of the *Mishnah* in his nursery rhyme called "SeeSaw" is a way of insisting that "the questions of yesteryear, and the warnings surrounding [the next generation of young Zionists] are better left ignored, even ridiculed" misses the point. But this poetic myopia and facile engagement with Bialik's deeply contemplative and mystical nursery rhyme misses much more than the struggle for a new spiritual lexicon in Israel, it reads a narrow agenda into a poetic masterpiece that eludes the secular and the sacred, see Gordis, *Saving Israel*, 171–172. By contrast see Glazer, *Contemporary Hebrew Mystical Poetry*, 263–264.
60 Gordis, *Saving Israel*, 177–178.
61 Laor, *The Myth of Liberal Zionism*, 126.
62 Daniel Boyarin, *Unheroic Conduct: The Rise of Heterosexuality and the Invention of the Jewish man*, University of California Press, Berkeley 1997, 28, 75–6, 79, 221–2, 231, 249, 259, 271–4, 276–9, 281–3, 286, 294–8, 300–11, 336, 346, esp. 301–2.
63 Honneth, "Reification and Recognition," 84.
64 Honneth, "Reification and Recognition," 84.
65 Axel Honneth, "Rejoinder," *Reification: A New Look at an Old Idea*, 148.
66 Honneth, "Rejoinder," 158.
67 See Laor, *The Myth of Liberal Zionism*, which can be compared with Laor's translation of Adorno's discourse on post-Auschwitz thinking and praxis into Hebrew, called " 'On relationality,' Matters for which silence is (not) becoming: Essays," 201–219.
68 Hever, *Poets and Zealots*; ibid, *Reading Poetry*; ibid, *From the Beginning*.
69 Shaul Magid, "The 'Jewish' Bible and the Construction of the (Anti) Rabbinic Hero: Abraham Isaac Ha-Kohen Kook, Rabbi Akiva, and the Song of Songs," *JQR* (forthcoming). I am grateful to Magid for sharing this draft prior to publication.
70 Magid, "The 'Jewish' Bible and the Construction of the (Anti) Rabbinic Hero," 6.
71 Magid, "The 'Jewish' Bible and the Construction of the (Anti) Rabbinic Hero," 6.
72 Magid, "The 'Jewish' Bible and the Construction of the (Anti) Rabbinic Hero," 13.
73 Magid, "The 'Jewish' Bible and the Construction of the (Anti) Rabbinic Hero," 20.
74 Pinchevski and Torgovnik, "Signifiying Passages: The Signs of Change in Israeli Street Names," 384.
75 Music, architecture, and literature are some of these other potent aesthetic modalities, see Jean Gebser, *The Ever-Present Origin* (1949), trans. Noel Barstad and Algis Mickunas, Ohio University Press, Athens, 1985, 454–545, esp. 454–527.
76 Magid, "The 'Jewish' Bible and the Construction of the (Anti) Rabbinic Hero," 20.
77 Magid, "The 'Jewish' Bible and the Construction of the (Anti) Rabbinic Hero," 21.
78 Magid, "The 'Jewish' Bible and the Construction of the (Anti) Rabbinic Hero," 22.
79 Beautifying the separation wall is one such example, see Philip Kleinfeld, "Where would Palestinian art be without politics? Palestinian street artists argue that the PLO rhetoric of putting Palestine before the Palestinian people has infused itself into local art," *Ha'Aretz*, 04.09.10, see http://www.haaretz.com/news/features/where-would-palestinian-art-be-without-politics-1.312153.
80 Shaul Magid, "Piety before Ecstasy," *Meditation from the Heart of Judaism: Today's Teachers Share Their Practices, Techniques and Faith*, Jewish Lights, Vermont, 1999, 201–208.

Chapter 5

1. Abraham Joshua Heschel, *Kotsk: In Gerangl far Emesdikeyt* [Yiddish], vol. 2, Tel Aviv, ha-Menorah, 1973, 523. Michael Rosen, *The Quest for Authenticity: The Thought of Reb Simhah Bunim*, Urim Publications, Jerusalem, 2008 [my italics].

2. Adorno, *JA*, 114–115 [my italics].

3. Honneth, *Pathologies of Reason*, 184 [my italics].

4. Honneth, *Pathologies of Reason*, 192.

5. Honneth, *Pathologies of Reason*, 185.

6. Honneth, *Pathologies of Reason*, 185.

7. Honneth, *Pathologies of Reason*, 184–185.

8. Adorno, *JA*, 115–116.

9. Adorno, *JA*, 116.

10. Adorno, *JA*, 116.

11. Adorno, *JA*, 3.

12. Adorno, *JA*, 3.

13. Adorno, *JA*, 4.

14. Gurt Ruppell, Peter Schreiner, eds. *Shared Learning in a Plural World: Ecumenical Approaches to Inter-Religious Education*, Lit Verlag Munster, London, 2003, 30.

15. Adorno, *JA*, ix.

16. Axel Honneth, *Reification: A New Look at an Old Idea*, The Berkeley Tanner Lectures, Oxford University Press, New York, 2008.

17. Adorno, *JA*, x.

18. Adorno, *JA*, xiii.

19. Adorno, *JA*, xiii.

20. Adorno, *JA*, xiii.

21. Adorno, *JA*, xiv.

22. Martin Buber, *I and Thou*, tr. Walter Kaufman, Scribners, New York, 1970.

23. Martin Buber, *Meetings: Autobiographical Fragments*, Routledge, New York, 2002, 54.

24. Buber, *Meetings: Autobiographical Fragments*, 54.

25. Buber, *Meetings: Autobiographical Fragments*, 54.

26. Buber, *Meetings: Autobiographical Fragments*, 55.

27. Heschel, *Kotsk: In Gerangl far Emesdikeyt*.

28. Compare Heschel, *Kotsk: In Gerangl far Emesdikeyt* with *A Passion for Truth*. Heschel once remarked that he wrote in Hebrew for Gershom Scholem, he wrote in Yiddish for his mother, and he wrote in English for Reinhold Neihbur, notwithstanding, each rendition of this theme is somewhat unique. I am grateful to Jack Riemer for sharing this oral communication from Heschel. However, the main concern remains what *Emesdikeyt* means to Heschel. In short, it is intrinsically tied to, and may even by synonymous with self-transcendence and the overcoming of "egocentricity." This is discussed at some length in the dissertation of Shai Held, "Reciprocity and Responsiveness: Self-Transcendence and The Dynamics of Covenant in the Theology and Spirituality of Abraham Joshua Heschel" (Ph.D. diss., Harvard University, 2010). Held was in the midst of completing this research, and as such I have not been able to review it extensively.

   Heschel's Yiddish perspective on Kotsk was not a systematic philosophical treatise by any means. Rather it was a retrospective, impressionistic, rambling discussion of Polish Hasidism. Heschel was not interested in a contemporary audience with the Yiddish book; rather *A Passion for Truth* filled that need. I am grateful to Morris Faierstein for this comment reflecting on his own unpublished translation of *Kotsk: In Gerangl far Emesdikeyt.*

Finally Prof. Jonathan Boyarin (UNC Chapel Hill) was in the process of translating the Yiddish version of Heschel's Kotsk book but was not available at the time of my research for further consultation.

29 Heschel, *A Passion for Truth,* xiv.
30 Heschel, *A Passion for Truth,* xv.
31 Heschel, *A Passion for Truth,* xv.
32 Heschel, *A Passion for Truth,* 123.
33 Heschel, *A Passion for Truth,* 127.
34 Heschel, *A Passion for Truth,* 127.
35 Heschel, *A Passion for Truth,* 132–135.
36 Heschel, *A Passion for Truth,* 144.
37 Heschel, *A Passion for Truth,* 144, 160.
38 Compare with Heschel, *A Passion for Truth,* 128.
39 Rosen, *The Quest for Authenticity.*
40 Rosen, *The Quest for Authenticity,* esp. 145–157, 157–160, 160–167.
41 Rosen, *The Quest for Authenticity,* 135–138.
42 Rosen, *The Quest for Authenticity,* 136 n. 2.
43 Rosen, *The Quest for Authenticity,* 138.
44 Heschel, *A Passion for Truth,* xiv.
45 Rosen, *The Quest for Authenticity,* 145.
46 Rosen, *The Quest for Authenticity,* 145.
47 Rosen, *The Quest for Authenticity,* 157.
48 Rosen, *The Quest for Authenticity,* 157.
49 Rosen, *The Quest for Authenticity,* 161.
50 Charles Taylor, *The Ethics of Authenticity,* Harvard University Press, Cambridge, 1991, 81–82.
51 Taylor, *The Ethics of Authenticity,* 81–82.
52 Martin Heidegger, s.v. *Eigentlichkeit, Being and Time: A Translation of Sein und Zeit,* trans. J. Stambaugh, SUNY Press, New York, 1996, 42–43: 40–41; 146: 137; 178: 166; 191: 178; 259–260: 239–240; 304: 281, 298–299: 325–326; 350: 321; 411: 377; 436–437: 396–397.
53 Heidegger, *Sein und Zeit,* 42–43: 40–41.
54 Heidegger, *Sein und Zeit,* 146: 137.
55 Heidegger, *Sein und Zeit,* 259–261: 239–241.
56 Heidegger, *Sein und Zeit,* 178: 166.
57 Heidegger, *Sein und Zeit,* 191: 178.
58 Adorno, *JA,* ii.
59 Adorno, *JA,* 112.
60 Adorno, *JA,* 114–115.
61 Adorno, *JA,* 115.
62 Adorno, *JA,* 116.
63 Adorno, *JA,* 116.
64 Adorno, *JA,* 117.
65 Adorno, *JA,* 18, 121.

66 Adorno, *JA*, 121.

67 Taylor, *The Ethics of Authenticity*, 83.

68 Taylor, *The Ethics of Authenticity*, 83.

69 Hölderlin, *Elucidations of Hölderlin's Poetry: Martin Heidegger*, "Homecoming/To Kindred Ones," 30–31.

70 Taylor, *The Ethics of Authenticity*, 83.

71 Taylor, *The Ethics of Authenticity*, 91.

72 Taylor, *The Ethics of Authenticity*, 91.

73 Taylor, *The Ethics of Authenticity*, 120.

74 Taylor, *The Ethics of Authenticity*, 121.

75 Taylor, *The Ethics of Authenticity*, 117–118.

76 Taylor, *The Ethics of Authenticity*, 118.

77 R. Asher Anshel Katz, *Shemen Rosh al Yamim haNoraim*, Brooklyn, 2005, 134.

78 Rosenzweig, *Franz Rosenzweig's "The New Thinking,"* 75.

79 Rosenzweig, *Franz Rosenzweig's "The New Thinking,"* 102.

Chapter 6

1 Adorno, *MM*, 113–114 [my italics].

2 Alain Finkelkraut, *Le Juif Imaginaire*, Les Éditions du Seuil, Paris, 1980, 30.

3 Harker claims that "[a]pparently, Adorno did nothing of a practical nature to oppose the Nazis, and he seems to have ignored Italian Fascism altogether." See Dave Harker, "In Perspective: Theodor Adorno," Humboldt Universität, Berlin, http://www2.hu-berlin.de/fpm/texte/harker3.htm Furthermore, Harker recounts how "[a]fter the distribution of a leaflet '*ADORNO ALS INSTITUTION IST TOT*' [as an institution, Adorno is dead], three young revolutionary females from the 'Basisgruppe Soziologie' circled around Professor Adorno, at first waving their bouquets of flowers, then kissing him, exposing their breasts, and confronting him with an erotic pantomime. Professor Adorno . . . tried to protect himself with his briefcase, and then left the lecture hall. He has since announced that his lectures and seminars on 'Dialectics' would be indefinitely postponed." See Harker, "In Perspective: Theodor Adorno"; see also, op. cit., Max Paddison, *Adorno's Aesthetics of Music*, Cambridge University Press, Cambridge, 1998, 289 n. 52.

5 While beyond the scope of the present investigation the political dimensions of Adorno's economic critique as developed by Jürgen Habermas and Oskar Negt are considered to have influenced the formation of the radicalized German Socialistic Student Organization (a.k.a. the S.D.S.). Adorno is said to have also been invited to address the S.D.S. at their meetings, see Brunkhorst, *Adorno and Critical Theory*, 56–57.

6 Yair Auron, *We are All German Jews: Jewish Radicals in France during the Sixties and Seventies* [Hebrew], Am Oved Publications, Tel Aviv, 1999, 27–30.

7 Many of *Havurat Shalom's* founding members include contemporary leaders in Jewish theory and praxis, including Arthur Green, Everett Gendler, Michael Fishbane, James Kugel, Michael Strassfeld, Arthur Waskow, and Zalman Schachter-Shalomi. See Riv-Ellen Prell, *Prayer & Community: The Havurah in American Judaism*, Wayne State University Press, Michigan, 1989. Compare with jonathan

Sarna, "'With-It' Judaism: The *Havurah* Movement and *The Jewish Catalog* Blended Judaism with the 1960s Counterculture," *American Judaism: A History*, Yale University Press, New Haven, 2004.

[8] Judith Friedlander, *Vilna on the Seine: Jewish Intellectuals in France Since 1968*, Yale University Press, New Haven, 1990, 2.

[9] Friedlander, *Vilna on the Seine*, 10.

[10] Friedlander, *Vilna on the Seine*, 10.

[11] Friedlander, *Vilna on the Seine*, 11.

[12] Friedlander, *Vilna on the Seine*, 11.

[13] Friedlander, *Vilna on the Seine*, 87.

[14] Marie-Anne Lescourret, *Emmanuel Lévinas*, Flammarion, Paris, 1994, 135, 152.

[15] Lescourret, *Emmanuel Lévinas*, 154.

[16] Lescourret, *Emmanuel Lévinas*, 155–156.

[17] Lescourret, *Emmanuel Lévinas*, 156.

[18] Lescourret, *Emmanuel Lévinas*, 158.

[19] Lescourret, *Emmanuel Lévinas*, 158.

[20] Martin Buber, *I and Thou*, tr. Walter Kaufman, Scribners, New York, 1970.

[20] Jacques Derrida, "Violence et métaphysique," *Écriture et différence*, Éditions du Seuil, Paris, 1967, 117–128.

[21] Martin Heidegger, *Being and Time: A Translation of Sein und Zeit*, trans. J. Stambaugh, section 44: *Da-sein, Disclosedness, and Truth*, SUNY Press, New York, 1996, 196–211.

[22] Heidegger, *Being and Time*, 44: 213:196–197.

[23] Heidegger, *Being and Time*, 204: 222.

[24] Emmanuel Lévinas, "*Vérité du dévoilement et vérité du témoignage*" (1972), "Truth of Disclosure and Truth of Testimony," *Emmanuel Lévinas: Basic Philosophical Writings*, ed. A. T. Peperzak, S. Critchley, and R. Bernasconi, Indiana University Press, Bloomington, 1996, 104.

[25] Heidegger, "What are Poets For?," *Poetry, Language, Thought*, trans. Albert Hofstadter, Perennial Library, New York, 1971, 129.

[26] Lévinas, "Truth of Disclosure and Truth of Testimony," 104.

[27] Lévinas, "Truth of Disclosure and Truth of Testimony," 104.

[28] Lévinas, "Truth of Disclosure and Truth of Testimony," 104.

[29] Lévinas, "Truth of Disclosure and Truth of Testimony," 105–106.

[30] Friedlander, *Vilna on the Seine*, 125 [my italics].

[31] Friedlander, *Vilna on the Seine*, 126–129.

[32] Friedlander, *Vilna on the Seine*, 126–129 [my italics].

[33] Friedlander, *Vilna on the Seine*, 135–139.

[34] Friedlander, *Vilna on the Seine*, 39–40.

[35] Friedlander, *Vilna on the Seine*, 40.

[36] Friedlander, *Vilna on the Seine*, 21.

[37] Friedlander, *Vilna on the Seine*, 148.

[38] Friedlander, *Vilna on the Seine*, 148–149.

[39] Friedlander, *Vilna on the Seine*, 140.

[40] Friedlander, *Vilna on the Seine*, 140.

[41] Friedlander, *Vilna on the Seine*, 140.

[42] Friedlander, *Vilna on the Seine*, 140.

[43] Friedlander, *Vilna on the Seine*, 141.

[44] Friedlander, *Vilna on the Seine*, 142.

⁴⁵ Friedlander, *Vilna on the Seine*, 44.

⁴⁶ Friedlander, *Vilna on the Seine*, 41.

⁴⁷ Lévinas, "*Éducation et Prière*" (1969), *Difficile Liberté*, Albin Michel, Paris, 1976, 348.

⁴⁸ Lévinas, "*Judaïsme et Révolution*," *Colloque des intellectuels juifs de langue française* (9e) ed. Jean Halpérin, Presses Universitaires de France, Paris, 1968, 66; ibid, "Judaism and Revolution," *Nine Talmudic Readings*, tr. A. Aronowicz, Indiana University Press, Bloomington, 1990, 103 [my italics].

⁴⁹ Lévinas, "Truth of Disclosure and Truth of Testimony," 106.

⁵⁰ Lévinas, "Truth of Disclosure and Truth of Testimony," 106.

⁵¹ Lévinas, "Truth of Disclosure and Truth of Testimony," 107.

⁵² Lévinas, "Truth of Disclosure and Truth of Testimony," 107.

⁵³ Lévinas, "Truth of Disclosure and Truth of Testimony," 107.

⁵⁴ Lévinas, "Truth of Disclosure and Truth of Testimony," 107.

⁵⁵ Lévinas, "Truth of Disclosure and Truth of Testimony," 107.

⁵⁶ Auron, *We are All German Jews*, 27–30.

⁵⁷ Yair Auron studied history and sociology at Tel Aviv University, while receiving his MA from Jerusalem's Hebrew University, and his Ph.D. from Université de la Sorbonne Nouvelle, Paris III, France, while teaching at Tel Aviv's Open University of Israel and the Kibbutz College of Education.

⁵⁸ Auron, *We are All German Jews*, 7–8.

⁵⁹ Auron, *We are All German Jews*, 8 [my italics].

⁶⁰ Auron, *We are All German Jews*, 227–229 [my italics].

⁶¹ Auron, *We are All German Jews*, 229.

⁶² For example, Halbertal understands the need to strike this balance between universal human rights and the particular existence of Jews in Israel, thus claiming it as "important, for this reason, that Israel respond to the U.N. report by clarifying the principles that it operated upon in Gaza, thus exposing the limits and the prejudices of the report. A mere denunciation of the report will not suffice. Israel must establish an independent investigation into the concrete allegations that the report makes. By clearing up these issues, by refuting what can be refuted, and by admitting wrongs when wrongs were done, Israel can establish the legitimacy of its self-defense in the next round, as well as honestly deal with its own failures." See Moshe Halbertal, "The Goldstone Illusion: What the U.N. report gets wrong about Gaza—and war," *The New Republic*, November 6, 2009, www.tnr.com/article/world/the-goldstone-illusion.

⁶³ Adorno, "Lyric Poetry and Society," *AR*, 211–229.

⁶⁴ Adorno, "Lyric Poetry and Society," *AR*, 221.

⁶⁵ Adorno, "Lyric Poetry and Society," *AR*, 221.

⁶⁶ Holderlin's, *Elucidations of Hölderlin;s Poetry: Martin Heidegger*, "Homecoming/ To Kindred Ones," 30–31.

⁶⁶ Adorno, "Lyric Poetry and Society," *AR*, 221.

⁶⁷ Adorno, "Lyric Poetry and Society," *AR*, 226 [my italics].

⁶⁸ Adorno, "Lyric Poetry and Society," *AR*, 227 [my italics].

⁶⁹ For example, Chalier imagines Lévinas as an ecstatic Hasid, while Ajzenstat yearns for Lévinas as the postmodern Kabbalist. See Catherine Chalier, *La Trace de l'Infini: Emmanuel Levinas et la Source Hebraique*, Editions CERF, Paris, 2002; Oona Ajzenstat, *Driven Back to the Text: The Premodern Sources of Levinas's Postmodernism*, Duquesne University Press, Pittsburgh, 2001. Compare with Michael

Fagenblat, *A Covenant of Creatures: Levinas's Philosophy of Judaism* (Cultural Memory in the Present), Stanford University Press, Stanford, 2010, 201 n. 4.

70 Lévinas, "Truth of Disclosure and Truth of Testimony," 107.

71 For example, there is the custom of supererogatory prostrations in prayer, see Paul Fenton, tr. *Deux traités de mystique juive: 'Obadya b. Abraham b. Moise Maimonide, Le Traité du puits, al-Maqala al-hawdiyya: David b. Josué, dernier des Maimonides: Le Guide du détachement, al-Mursid ila t-tafarrud*, Éditions du Verdier, Lagrasse, 1987. Further reflection is warranted on whether there is any influence of this research upon French Jewish communities, considering the fact that the pre-eminent scholar in this field, Paul Fenton, is a French Jew affiliated with the Jewish community. Also consider the recitation of Ibn Gabirol's *Keter Malkhut* each Sabbath as a supererogatory prayer (*i'tada al-tanafful bi-ha fi kull sabt*), see Y. Tzvi Langerman, "A Judeo-Arabic Paraphrase of Ibn Gabirol's *Ketter Malkhut*," *Zutot: Perspective on Jewish Culture*, vol. 3, Springer, Netherlands, 2005, 28–33.

72 Compare with more recent devotional study models, see Aubrey L. Glazer, "*Shir Yedidut*: A Pleasant Song of Companionship," *God's Voice from the Void: Old and New Studies in Bratslav Hasidism*, ed. Shaul Magid, SUNY Press, New York, 2002, 3–14.

73 R. Asher Anshel Katz, *Shemen Rosh al Yamim haNoraim*, Brooklyn, 2005, 134.

74 Most recently, Fagenblat makes an intriguing, albeit unverifiable speculation on this very issue, in that "Levinas was probably also familiar with Bahya ibn Pakuda's *Hovot HaLevavot, Duties of the Heart* . . . but Levinas did not cite de Leon or ibn Gabirol or ibn Pakuda . . . it is therefore a very different Maimonides— a Maimonides without the metaphysics of creation." Fagenblat, *A Covenant of Creatures*, 109, 110 (I am grateful to Elliot R. Wolfson for pointing me to this source in Fagenblat). For the original prayer in question, see Bahya ibn Paquda, *Hovot haLevavot*, ed. R. Kapach, Feldheim Publishers, New York 5755–5771, 1994, 319–324. Bahya ibn Paquda, "Appendix: *Tokheha* (Admonition)," *The Book of Direction to the Duties of the Heart* (from the original Arabic version *Al-Hidaya ila Fara'id Al-Qulub*), trans. and ed. Menahem Mansoor, Littman Library of Jewish Civilization, London, 1973, 448–452.

75 *Sifrei Deuteronomy* 346. This rabbinic rereading of Israel symbolizing witnesses (*ve'atem edai*, v. 8) to the divine realization of the prophetic word is remarkably radical, see Isaiah 44:6–8.

76 Eric L. Friedland, *"Were Our Mouths Filled with Song": Studies in Liberal Jewish Liturgy*, HUC Press, Cincinnati, 1997, 219.

77 Glazer, *Contemporary Hebrew Mystical Poetry*.

78 I am indebted to Rabbi Moshe Aaron Krassen for this ingenious reworking of the BeSH" Tian aphorism that to be a Jew is to be *Ois welt, in welt* (1 *Nissan*, 5770; March 16, 2010).

79 Glazer, *Contemporary Hebrew Mystical Poetry*, 241–242.

Chapter 7

1 Susan Buck-Morss, "The Aesthetic Model and Its Limits," *The Origin of Negative Dialectics: Theodore W. Adorno, Walter Benjamin, and the Frankfurt Institute*, The Free Press, New York, 1977, 133 [my italics].

2 Michel Camus, *Transpoétique: La main cachée entre poésie et science*, Trait d'Union, Montréal, 2002, 9 [my italics and translations henceforth].
3 Adorno, *MM*, 16 [my italics].
4 Adorno, *MM*, 16.
5 Adorno, *MM*, 16.
6 Buck-Morss, "The Aesthetic Model and Its Limits," 133.
7 Buck-Morss, "The Aesthetic Model and Its Limits," 133.
8 Buck-Morss, "The Aesthetic Model and Its Limits," 133.
9 Adorno, *MM*, 141/80. Compare with the reflections of Jewish theologians like Norbert Samuelson, Heidi Ravven, and Jacob E. Meskin at a recent panel, entitled, *Re-opening The Conversation Between Jewish Philosophy and Contemporary Science*, see especially, Jacob E. Meskin, "Searching for a Usable Past in the Judaism-Science Conversation: Contemporary Post-Empiricist Philosophy of Science as a Way of Retrieving the Work of R. Joseph Soloveitchik" (AJS, 42nd Annual Conference Boston, December 21, 2010). It is instructive to consider what this panel was working through guided by the following questions: (1) How well does Ian Barbour's typology of the general religion-science relationship— INDEPENDENCE, CONFLICT, DIALOGUE, and INTEGRATION—apply specifically to the Judaism-science relationship? What then are the epistemological and ontological consequences which follow from choosing any one of these rubrics to characterize the relationship? (2) How does modern science affect our thinking about the nature of basic assumptions, claims, and rituals in Judaism? Do certain scientific theories and findings require potentially transformative work in Jewish philosophy? (3) How might Judaism offer distinctive approaches to answering the complex and cutting-edge questions raised by bio-medical and neurobiological brain research? (4) How might the contemporary sciences—or even detailed reflection on them—inspire innovative work in Jewish philosophy? How does this approach compare to the more standard attempts to draw on literary studies, or on continental philosophers traditionally not deeply concerned with modern science, as dialogue partners for Jewish Thinking? See www.ajsnet.org/sched10.htm.
10 Camus, *Transpoétique*, 80.
11 Camus, *Transpoétique*, 9–10.
12 Camus, *Transpoétique*, 79.
13 Camus, *Transpoétique*, 53. Compare with the claim that implicit in Spinoza and explicit in Leibniz is the linkage of "the first buds of modern science with the kabbalistic, hermetic, and alchemical pre-science of the Renaissance." See Henri Atlan, *The Sparks of Randomness*, Vol. 1: Spermatic Knowledge, tr. L. J. Schramm, Standford University Press, Stanford, 2011, 268.
14 Camus, *Transpoétique*, 11.
15 Camus, *Transpoétique*, 18.
16 Camus, *Transpoétique*, 17.
17 Camus, *Transpoétique*, 18.
18 Camus, *Transpoétique*, 19.
19 There is a growing understanding of the impossibility in a physical sense of Infinity, but not necessarily in a poetic sense. This provides further appreciation as to why poetry is a necessary part of the transpoetic correlation with science.

Further consideration, however, should be given to the Aleph-Infinity of Cantor, see Glazer, *Living the Death of God*, 23 n. 58. A concerted attempt has already been made to disprove the eternity of space, time, and matter. According to Hedman: "Cantor claimed that he could use transfinite numbers to argue against the eternity of space, time, and matter, but apparently he never wrote the arguments down. It would be interesting to try to reconstruct them, along the lines of his arguments against infinitesimals. See Bruce A. Hedman, "Cantor's Concept of Infinity: Implications of Infinity for Contingence," *Perspectives on Science and Christian Faith* 46, March 1993, 8–16, www.asa3.org/ASA/PSCF/1993/PSCF3–93Hedman.html.

[20] Lisa Randall, *Warped Passages: Unraveling the Mysteries of the Universe's Hidden Dimensions*, Harper Perennial, New York, 2005.

[21] Green, *Radical Judaism*, Yale University Press, New Haven, 2010, 16.

[22] Green, *Radical Judaism*, 32.

[23] I am referring, for example, to Green's uncritical importation of the concept of Darwinian "evolution" into the spiritual realm. It really should be referred to as "*in*volution" to reflect the evolution of spiritual consciousness. For my response to an early draft of *Radical Judaism*, see Glazer, "*Durée, Devekuth*, & Re-Embracing the Godlover: *In*volution of *Unio Mystica* via Collocative HomosexuELity," *Vixens Disturbing Vineyards: The Embarrassment and Embracement of Scriptures—A Festschrift Honoring Harry Fox*, ed. T. Yoreh, A. Glazer, J. Lewis, and M. Segal, Academic Studies Press, Boston, 2010, 505 n. 1. In terms of the evolution of spiritual consciousness, my thinking remains deeply influenced by the work of Jean Gebser and his nuanced work, *The Ever-Present Origin*. The more recent review by Landes of *Radical Judaism* and the response by Green does little to deepen the discourse, see "God, Torah and Israel: An Exchange," *Jewish Review of Books*, Winter, 2011, 4. While in that exchange, Landes rightly notes that Green's presentation of evolutionary history is not sophisticated but sadly there is no suggestion made as to how to engage the challenge of spiritual *in*volution.

[24] Buck-Morss, "The Aesthetic Model and Its Limits," 133. The flaw is far reaching and has implications for Green's call for panentheism as contemporary theology, see Green, *Radical Judaism*.

[25] Randall, *Warped Passages*, 447–448.

[26] Randall, *Warped Passages*, 449–450.

[27] Randall, *Warped Passages*, 450–451.

[28] Randall, *Warped Passages*, 451–452.

[29] Randall, *Warped Passages*, 452–453.

[30] Randall, *Warped Passages*, 277–302.

[31] Randall, *Warped Passages*, 321–333.

[32] Reb Moshe Aaron Krassen has been engaged in this project for many years now throughout his oral teachings on neo-Lurianic Kabbalah, see www.rainofblessings. org. For a preliminary engagement with this discourse, see Karen Michelle Barad, *Meeting the Universe Halfway: Quantum Physics and the Entanglement of Matter and Meaning*, Duke University Press, Durham, 2007, esp. 247–353. There is much implied in the seventh chapter of this remarkable work of interdisciplinary scholarship by Barad and clearly much insight that is forthcoming. In terms of the scope of this present investigation relating to Jewish Thinking, what remains crucial are the implications of how quantum physics can reveal new pathways in

metaphysics or what she terms the "Experimental Metaphysics and the Nature of Nature." This is most salient after Adorno's legacy of doubt regarding the whole premise of metaphysics in a post-Auschwitz world.

[33] For a preliminary attempt at tracing this articulation of neo-Lurianic Kabbalah in contemporary Hebrew poetry and its convergence with Jewish Thinking, see Glazer, *Contemporary Hebrew Mystical Poetry*, esp. 291–309.

[34] Brunkhorst, *Adorno and Critical Theory*, 78.

Chapter 8

[1] Magid, "Piety before Ecstasy," 204 [my italics].

[2] Adorno, "Commitment," *AT*, 246 [my italics].

[3] Peter Brook, *The Open Door: Thoughts on Acting and Theatre*, Theatre Communications Group Inc., New York, 1995, 144 [my italics].

[4] Schachter-Shalomi and Siegel, *Integral Halachah*.

[5] Rabbi Daniel Nevins, "Walking the Walk," *Jewish Theology in Our Time: A New Generation Explores the Foundations & Future of Jewish Belief*, ed. Rabbi Elliot J. Cosgrove, Jewish Lights, Vermont, 2010, 143–148. Nevins makes the following attempt at reclaiming *halakhah* as the divine will as opposed to mind: "Given our inability to know the mind of God, *halakhah* offers us the next best thing. It attests to what millenia of Jews have discerned to be the divine will." Nevins, "Walking the Walk," 147.

[6] Green, *Radical Judaism*, 100–101.

[7] Green, *Radical Judaism*, 111–114.

[8] Emmanuel Lévinas, "*Liberté et Commandment*," *Revue de Metaphysique et de Morale* 58 (1953).

[9] It is unclear whether Nevins intends to keep immanence and transcendence in dialectical tension or whether the nuanced figure of the whole and its individual part lapses into a kind of identity-thinking: "Indeed, it is the imperfection of all formulations of Judaism—past, present and future—and the mechanisms for adjustment that keep the halakhic system vibrant and allow it to reflect the transcendent nature of God." See Nevins, "Walking the Walk," 148.

[10] Green, *Radical Judaism*, 102.

[11] I agree with Braiterman's astute study that suggests a clear distinction between art and aesthetics in relation to religion and revelation, see Zachary Braiterman, "Preface: Revelation and the Spiritual in Art," *The Shape of Revelation: Aesthetics and Modern Jewish Thought*, Stanford University Press, Stanford, 2007, xx–xxi [my italics]:

> I treat "aesthetic" and "art" here as two correlated terms, which both bear on religion. The former term refers to the intentional act that sustains contemplation of a sense impression, including art and the impromptu appearance of that which is not art. The more one looks to the sensual constitution of any object or group of objects . . . , and the longer that look endures, the more aesthetic the attention. "Art," on the other hand, is more limited in scope. It reflects the physical form of compressed sensation. . . . No matter how

large the object or fleeting its presence, it maintains a condensed character in relation to the cosmos at large and to history. Art works against the *ad hoc* and diffuse condition of everyday sensation, preserving a difference between art and life that radical practitioners of art seek to obliterate by means of new, unfamiliar modes of artifice. *Insofar as sustained attention to sensation enters into it, religion is aesthetic without being art; yet the more religion relies upon the intentional creation of specialized spatial environments, sonic patterns, and literary sign systems, the more it resembles art in its material makeup.*

¹² Rachel Adler, *Engendering Judaism: An Inclusive Theology and Ethics*, JPS, Philadelphia, 1998 (s.v. narrative, 25–26, 38, 40, 44, 48–51, 52; s.v. *halakhah*, 21–59). Compare with the work of Robert Cover, Alasdair MacIntyre, Stanley Hauerwas, and Michael Goldberg, see further references in Adler, *Engendering Judaism*, 227 n. 55.

¹³ Rabbi Edward Feld, "Genre and *Halakhah*," *Conservative Judaism*, Winter 2004; ibid, "A Divining Rod Has Two Branches," *Conservative Judaism*, Spring 2003.

¹⁴ Emblematic of a recent effort to reclaim that lost dialectic, see Nevins, "Walking the Walk," 143–148: "*Halakhah* is deeply exegetical, and aggadah is grounded in legal norms."

¹⁵ H. N. Bialik, "*Halachah* and *Aggadah*" (1916), trans. Leon Simon, *Revealment and Concealment*, Ibis Editions, Jerusalem, 2003, 45–89.

¹⁶ I am indebted to the provocative challenge of Scheindlin who makes the claim, "Judaism is my art form," but then goes on to admit "I have tried *halakhah* and strict observance, but came to realize that this is not my vehicle." See Raymond P. Scheindlin, "The Inner Art of Prayer," *The Unfolding Tradition: Jewish Law after Sinai*, ed. Elliot N. Dorff, Aviv Press, New York, 2005, 402. Part of the challenge being addressed here is applying Adorno's negative dialectical thinking to the equation so that *halakhah* can remain a vehicle as seen within the tension of a dialectic. Of course, one must be attentive to the possibility that this proposition of *halakhah* as art could lapse into identity-thinking, see Braiterman, *The Shape of Revelation: Aesthetics and Modern Jewish Thought*, xxiii:

> Art and religion are virtually identical in their appeal to the power of the imagination and to the creation of images. But the difference that remains between them resists easy proclivities to invest every human expression with spiritual significance or to see art in everything as art. Analytically, religion *is* not art and art is not religion, even as they indelibly stain each other in the historical culture of their production.

¹⁷ Magid, "Piety before Ecstasy," 204 [my italics].
¹⁸ Magid, "Piety before Ecstasy," 204 [my italics].
¹⁹ Adorno, *AT*, 246 [my italics].
²⁰ Adorno, *AT*, 246.
²¹ Adorno, *AT*, 247.
²² Buck-Morss, "The Aesthetic Model and Its Limits," 132.
²³ Adorno, *AT*, 246–247.
²⁴ Adorno, *AT*, 247.
²⁵ Adorno, *AT*, 247.

[26] For further preliminary reflections on aesthetics in Adorno's thinking, see Lescourret, *Introduction à l'esthèthique*, 14–16, 51, 95, 112, 137, 142, 150, 164, 186, 192–193.

[27] Magid, "Piety before Ecstasy."

[28] Adorno, *AT*, 49.

[29] Adorno, *AT*, 50.

[30] Adorno, *AT*, 49.

[31] Glazer, *Contemporary Hebrew Mystical Poetry*, 243–291, esp. 245–249, 255–268.

[32] Adorno, *AT*, 50.

[33] Harry Fox, "Poet*h*ics: How Every Poet is a Jew," *Contemporary Hebrew Mystical Poetry: How It Redeems Jewish Thinking*, ed. Aubrey L. Glazer, Edwin Mellen Press, New York, 2009, i–xxxiv.

[34] Compare with another rereading of Kantian aesthetics, see Braiterman, *The Shape of Revelation: Aesthetics and Modern Jewish Thought*, xxx:

> The give-and-take between image and word elides *a priori* philosophical and theological principles and privilege, pseudo-halakhic warrants and formalist aesthetics. Just as language in the picture-frame provides broader theoretical rubrics with which to interpret visual material, religion brings to art a dimension of linguistic content that is not restricted to optical experience. For their part, art and aesthetic form open religion further out into the world of sense and sensation, into the spatial and temporal orders shared with other people in what Kant called the "purposive purposelessness" of a system whose sole true purpose is nothing more than prolonged attention to the pleasure of its own shape. From this point of departure, the shape of revelation and its ethos ride upon the science of perception.

[35] Fox, "Poet*h*ics: How Every Poet is a Jew," v, n. 18, xi–xiv.

[36] Adorno, *AT*, 49.

[37] Fox, "Poet*h*ics: How Every Poet is a Jew," v, n. 18.

[39] Fox, "Poet*h*ics: How Every Poet is a Jew," xxxiii.

[40] Almut Sh. Bruckstein, "Textual Body Landscapes and the Artist's Geometry of Talmud: *Aetelier*-Work with the Materiality of Scripture," *New Directions in Jewish Philosophy*, ed. A. W. Hughes and E. R. Wolfson , Indiana University Press, Bloomington, 2010, 166.

[41] While I have articulated an initial call for this exploration over a decade ago in regards to the next steps of "transformance," much remains to be researched, see Glazer, *Living the Death of God*, 82–86. The need for a deity within this calculus remains, as some contemporary Continental philosophers have already noted. Some claim, for example, that there is a need for an event that can redefine the deity:

> [s]omething has to happen and the word 'God' designates this unheard of, incalculable event, alone able from now on to render thought to its original destination.

See Alain Badiou, *Manifesto for Philosophy*, tr. N. Madarasz, SUNY Press, New York, 1996, 114, esp. 103. Others claim the name of God needs to be redefined as a task of anarchic disruption that privileges the prophetic, messianic and eschato-logical, see John D. Caputo, "In Search of a Sacred Anarchy: An Experiment in Danish Deconstruction," *Calvin O. Schrag and the Task of Philosophy After Post-modernity*, ed. M. B. Matustik, and W. L. McBride, Northwestern University Press, Illinois, 2002, 226–250, esp. 247.

Addressing religion after God in Jewish thinking remains an ongoing concern, especially with regards to aesthetics, see Braiterman, *The Shape of Revelation: Aesthetics and Modern Jewish Thought*, xxii:

> At a second order of analysis, the relationship between aesthetic form and spiritual reality depends upon the presupposition of a god or God or spiritual presence is made manifest to human consciousness through sensual media, especially visual and aural form.

It is that very latent capacity for Immediate and Holy Theatre to revitalize the ritual rebirthing of the everdying name in religion that remains a matter worthy of further exploration. Peter Brook's work remains a touchstone in this regard, whereby this necessary negative dialect allows for a "constantly changing process . . . of growth," Peter Brook, *The Open Door: Thoughts on Acting and Theatre*, 144. Brook's most recent production of Shakespeare's sonnets as *Love is My Sin* (Duke Street Theatre, New York, 2010) is emblematic of the transformance taking place in theatre still awaiting its counterpart within religion. Further exploration into this correlation of *Judaism as Theatre-of-it-All*, building on Michal Govrin's pioneering work, is forthcoming. See Michal Govrin, "The Jewish Ritual as a Genre of Sacred Theatre," *Conservative Judaism* 36/3, Spring 1983; Michal Govrin, "*Body of Prayer*, with Jacques Derrida and David Shapiro," *Cooper Union School of Architecture*, New York, 2001.

Chapter 9

[1] Adorno, *MM*, no. 119: *Model of Virtue*, 187 [my italics].
[2] Rebecca Goldstein, *Incompleteness: The Proof and Paradox of Kurt Gödel*, Atlas Books, New York, 2005, 155–156 [my italics].
[3] Adorno, *MM*, no. 153: *Finale*, 247 [my italics].
[4] Wittgenstein, *Z*, no. 717, 124 [my italics]:

> *Gott kannst du nicht mit einem Andern reden hören,*
> *sondern nur, wenn du der Angeredete bist.*
> > —*Das ist eine grammatische Bemerkung.*

[5] Adorno, no. 119: *Model of Virtue*, *MM*, 187.
[6] Adorno, no. 151: *Theses against Occultism*, *MM*, 238–244.
[7] Wittgenstein, *PI*, x:

> I should not like my writing to spare other people the trouble of thinking. But, if possible, to stimulate someone to thoughts of his own.

Ich möchte nicht mit Schrift Andern das Denken ersparen.
Sondern, Wenn es möglich ware, jemand zu eigenen Gedanken anregen.

[8]   See Feld, "A Divining Rod Has Two Branches." In a May 2006 commencement speech, Chancellor Emeritus of JTS, Ismar Schorsch argued that the *Etz Hayyim Humash* was marked by an "ambivalence toward critical scholarship." The extent of Schorsch's critical thinking was evident in the dismissal of the forty one appended essays of modern commentary claiming most of them were spiritually inert: "Their rabbinic authors go through the paces without passion, making no effort to extract religious significance from the scholarship being mediated. While Conservative rabbis often chide the research-oriented faculty of JTS for allegedly doing just that in their classes, as transmitters of scholarship, the rabbis replicated what they condemn. Ironically, the rare spiritual voice to be heard in the end notes usually emanates from one or another of the academics in the roster." See "Anger over Schorsch Speech Fuels Questions about Seminary's Role," *The Forward*, June 9, 2006. The more particular problem with the logic of Schorsch's RA Address in Mexico City regarding Meta-*Halakhah* are addressed only through their rectification with the *Sprachspiel* below.

[9]   Brunkhorst, *Adorno and Critical Theory*, 97.

[10]   Brunkhorst, *Adorno and Critical Theory*, 104.

[11]   Ranjit Chatterjee, *Wittgenstein and Judaism: A Triumph of Concealment*, Peter Lang, New York, 2005, 228.

[12]   Wittgenstein, *TL-P*, 188–189: *"Wovon man nicht sprechen kann, darüber muss man schweigen."*

[13]   Adorno, *AT*, 205, 368 n. 3.

[14]   Adorno, *AT*, 205, 368 n. 3, n. 18; compare with 103.

[15]   Wittgenstein, *TL-P*, 186–187:

6.44 *Nicht wie die Welt is, ist das Mystiche, sondern dass sie ist.*

6.45 *Die Anschauung der Welt sub specie aeterni ist ihre Anschauung als—*
begrenztes—Ganzes.
Das Gefühl der Welt als begrenztes Ganzes ist das mystiche.

[16]   Adorno, *AT*, 371 n. 2.

[17]   Adorno, *AT*, 318, 371 n. 2.

[18]   See our previous discussion in Chapter 8 on artistic commitment in Adorno.

[19]   Adorno, *MM*, no. 153: *Finale*, 247.

[20]   Rabbi Edward Feld has already suggested a more valuable direction regarding the form of *halakhic* literature. Feld argues for *halakhah* to become galvanized as an essay that is open-ended (or what we have called, incomplete). This kind of *readerly-text* invites its community to feasibly author their own narrative conclusions as living applications, see Feld, "Genre and *Halakhah*.".

[21]   Goldstein, *Incompleteness*, 147.

[22]   Goldstein, *Incompleteness*, 159.

[23]   Rebecca Goldstein, *Betraying Spinoza*, Next Books, New York, 2006.

[24]   Wittgenstein's Judaism remains a concealed part of his philosophical legacy, perhaps due to his patrilineal descent or perhaps because of the history of conversion in his highly assimilated family. For an attempt at correlating his unique

thinking with Jewish thought, see Chatterjee, *Wittgenstein and Judaism*. Chatterjee's pioneering contribution to this project is beginning to influence other Jewish thinkers willingness to address Wittgenstein's impact on Jewish thought, dedicating sessions to explore this very theme, titled, *Wittgenstein and Judaism: Language, Psychology, and Prophecy* including: "Aspects of Wittgenstein: Duck-Rabbi?" Jay Geller (Vanderbilt University); "James, Wittgenstein, and Judaism: The Chatterjee Connection," Dennis Rohatyn (University of San Diego); "Revelation and Tradition: Wittgenstein and Language," Michael L. Morgan (Indiana University); and a response by Ranjit Chatterjee (Lado International College). 37th annual AJS conference, (AJS, Washington DC, December 19, 2005).

[25] *Sprachspiel* is a recurrent term in Wittgenstein's thinking, meant to give shape to those "philosophical problems [that] arise when language goes on holiday." See Wittgenstein, *PI*, no. 37: 15; no. 38: 16.

[26] Wittgenstein, *PI*, no. 37: 15.

[27] Wittgenstein, *PI*, no. 37: 15–16.

[28] Often Wittgenstein's thinking is divided into two distinct periods—the first up to *TL-P*, and the second afterwards. What unites Wittgenstein I [*WI*] and Wittgenstein II [*WII*] is a "preoccupation with language." *WI* sees our ordinary language as random and "attending to the hidden structure of language will enable us to solve puzzles." *WII* sees that "attending to the surface of language can solve puzzles and that our troubles arise when we try to burrow beneath this surface." What separates *WI* and *WII* is the reality of language as concealing or revealing. See D. Edmonds and J. Eidinow, *Wittgenstein's Poker: The Story of a Ten-Minute Argument between Two Great Philosophers*, HarperCollins, New York, 2001, 233. Another way of approaching Wittgenstein has recently challenged such divisions. Chatterjee argues that Wittgenstein's thinking cannot justly be divided into distinct periods but must be reconciled within itself: "The 'early' vs. 'later' division is really a part of the rhetoric justifying this piecemeal extrapolation. If each phase constituted a whole philosophy, it could more legitimately be "applied" without regard to the lifelong, overriding concerns of the writer. Such a fate is usual even for the philosopher who is trying to establish a controlled and predictable 'school.' Realizing that he would not escape it either, Wittgenstein, investing no energy in building a 'school,' wrote for the pleasure of the one reader who already understood." Chatterjee, *Wittgenstein and Judaism*, 21.

[29] Edmonds and Eidinow, *Wittgenstein's Poker*, 22.

[30] See above n. 24.

[31] Chatterjee, *Wittgenstein and Judaism*, 175–179.

[32] Chatterjee, *Wittgenstein and Judaism*, 2.

[33] Chatterjee, *Wittgenstein and Judaism*, 228.

[34] Wittgenstein, *TL-P*, 188–189: "*Wovon man nicht sprechen kann, darüber muss man schweigen.*"

[35] Edmonds and Eidinow, *Wittgenstein's Poker*, 228.

[36] Edmonds and Eidinow, *Wittgenstein's Poker*, 168.

[37] F. Rosenzweig, *Der Stern der Erlösung* (1921), Bibliothek Suhrkamp, Frankfurt, 1988; Rosenzweig, *The Star of Redemption*.

[38] P. Hadot, *Wittgenstein et les limites du langage*, Éditions J. Vrin, Paris, 2005, 45.

[39] Edmonds and Eidinow, *Wittgenstein's Poker*, 159.

40 Wittgenstein, *PI*, 22: 9; 96: 38.
41 Wittgenstein, *PI*, 230.
42 Edmonds and Eidinow, *Wittgenstein's Poker*, 159.
43 Wittgenstein, TL-P, no's 6.44–6.45, p. 000.
44 Hadot, *Wittgenstein et les limites du langage*, 45.
45 Wittgenstein, *TL-P*, no. 6.522: 187. We have modified Anscombe's translation of *Unaussprechliches* from "inexpressible" to "ineffable" for more precision: "*Es gibt allerdings Unaussprechliches. Dies zeigt sich, es ist das Mystiche.*"
46 Wittgenstein, *TL-P*, no. 4.1212: 78: "*Was gezeigt werden kann, kann nicht gesagt werden*" [my italics].
47 Goldstein, *Incompleteness*, 113–120.
48 Wittgenstein, *PI*, no. 38: 16 [my italics].
49 Wittgenstein, *PI*, no. 39: 17.
50 Menahem Mendel of Kotsk, *Amud ha'Emeth*, s.v. *Dibbur*, ed. M. B. Altar, Pe'er Publications, Jerusalem, 2000, 190.
51 b*Berakhot* 17a, b*Megilla* 15b. Compare with Wolfson, *Through a Speculum That Shines*, 361–368.
52 This prooftext of Exodus 15:2 for the primacy of aesthetics as a religious experience is redolent in rabbinic literature, see, for example, b*Shabbat* 133b, *ad. loc. Rashi*, where it becomes a possible to forge connection with the Law through aesthetics.
53 Isaiah Horowitz, *Sefer haShlah haQadosh, Toldot Adam Remazai Otiyot leHatimat haHaqdamah* 16.
54 m*Baba Metzia* 1: 1.
55 b*Baba Metzia* 7b–8a.
56 b*Baba Metzia* 7b–8a, *Rosh ad. loc.*
57 b*Baba Metzia* 2a, *Ritva ad. loc.*
58 Natan Sternharz of Nemirov, *Liqqutai Halakhot, Hilkhot toen ve'nit'an* 4, 74.
59 Natan Sternharz of Nemirov, *Liqqutai Halakhot, Hilkhot hezqat metaltelun* 5: 7, 278.
60 Wittgenstein, *Z*, no. 717: 124.
61 Wittgenstein, *PI*, x.

Chapter 10

1 Adorno, *AT*, 135–136 [my italics].
2 Henri Corbin, "The *Imago Templi* in Confrontation with Secular Norms" (1974), *Temple and Contemplation*, trans. P. Sherrard, KPI, London, 1986, 264 [my italics].
3 Adorno, *AT*, 135–136 [my italics].
4 Brunkhorst, *Adorno and Critical Theory*, 114 [my italics].
5 Adorno, *NM*, "Painting and Music Today," 421.
6 Brunkhorst, *Adorno and Critical Theory*, 115.
7 Adorno, *AT*, 121.
8 Adorno, *ND*, 13/3 [my italics].
9 Adorno, "Sociological and Empirical Research" (1957), *AR*, 84.
10 Adorno, "Sociological and Empirical Research," *AR*, 190.
11 It is worth noting that feminist Marsha Aileen Hewitt prefaces her own Critical Theory of religion which draws on the Frankfurt School as well as with contemporary

feminist thinkers on religion with a similar intention: "Rather than reject religion altogether, this book arises out of the conviction that religion, with the aid of critical social theory, may once again emerge as an emancipatory force within history." See Marsha Aileen Hewitt, *Critical Theory of Religion: A Feminist Analysis,* Fortress Press, Minneapolis, 1995, ix. This quotation is attributed to Adorno but not referenced as such [my italics].

12 See Scholem, TUMI, 35.

13 Adorno, "Music and Language: A Fragment," *QUF,* 6.

14 Adorno, "Lyric Poetry and Society," *AR,* 218.

15 Adorno, *QUF,* 2.

16 Jameson, *LM,* 118.

17 Jameson, *LM,* 118.

18 Dufrenne, *L'Oeil et L'Oreille,* 92: "*Il y a plus: je suis moi-même un être sonore . . .*" [my translation].

19 Dufrenne, *L'Oeil et L'Oreille,* 91: "*. . . je résonne en lui comme il résonne en moi, je vibre.*"

20 Adorno, *QUF,* "Music and Language: A Fragment," 1 [my italics].

21 Adorno, *QUF,* "Vers une musique informelle," 303 [I have slightly modified this translation] [my italics].

22 Adorno, *VM,* 322.

23 Adorno, *MM,* 156/297.

24 Benjamin, "Epistemo-Critical Prologue," 36.

25 Jameson challenges such a postmodern reading as espoused by Richard Rorty. What concerns the present investigation, however, is that both thinkers are turning to Adorno's reflections on music as the pathmarks of a different type of thinking. Jameson, *LM,* 247.

26 Adorno, *MLF,* 2.

27 Adorno, *BTPM,* n. 244, 305.

28 Adorno, *MLF,* 4.

29 Adorno, *MLF,* 4.

30 Adorno, *MLF,* 5.

31 Adorno, *MLF,* 297–298.

32 Adorno, *VMI,* 322.

33 Adorno's reflections on musical thinking are so prolific that delimitation was required for the sake of the present investigation on redemption. However, a similar study could be constructed according a tetrahedral structure as follows: Paul Hindemith and Hans Eisler; Kurt Weil; Igor Stravinsky; Arnold Schoenberg. The present investigation focuses on the Triadic structure of Wagner, Mahler, and Schoenberg, given that entire book-length studies were already completed by Adorno, facilitating a sustained analysis of his musical thinking.

34 Gebser, *The Ever-Present Origin,* 455.

35 Gebser, *The Ever-Present Origin,* 455.

36 Gebser, *The Ever-Present Origin,* 456.

37 Gebser, *The Ever-Present Origin,* 456. See Hermann Scherchen, *Vom Wesen Der Musik,* Mondial, Zurich, 1946, 149.

38 Gebser, *The Ever-Present Origin,* 456.

39 Gebser, *The Ever-Present Origin,* 456.

40 Gebser, *The Ever-Present Origin,* 456.

41 Adorno, *SF*, 123–145, 145–197.
42 Gebser, *The Ever-Present Origin*, 456.
43 Gebser, *The Ever-Present Origin*, 456.
44 Gebser, *The Ever-Present Origin*, 457.
45 Gebser, *The Ever-Present Origin*, 463.
46 Gebser, *The Ever-Present Origin*, 463.
47 Adorno, *QUF*, "Stravinsky: A Dialectical Portrait," 145–175.
48 Adorno, *QUF*, 145–146.
49 This is the recurrent reading by Bernstein of Adorno on Stravinsky throughout his final two lectures in the Norton series, see Leonard Bernstein, *The Unanswered Question: Six Talks at Harvard*, Harvard University Press, Cambridge, 1976, 329, 389.
50 Bernstein, *The Unanswered Question: Six*, 389.
51 Bernstein, *The Unanswered Question: Six*, 331.
52 Bernstein, *The Unanswered Question: Six*, 345.
53 Bernstein, *The Unanswered Question: Six*, 351.
54 Bernstein, *The Unanswered Question: Six*, 378.
55 Gebser, *The Ever-Present Origin*, 463. See Igor Stravinsky, *Poetics of Music*, Harvard University Press, Cambridge, 1947, 27.
56 Gebser, *The Ever-Present Origin*, 463.
57 Gebser, *The Ever-Present Origin*, 463.
58 Adorno, *QUF*, 151 n. 7.
59 Adorno, *QUF*, 151 n. 7.
60 Adorno, *QUF*, 166–167; Richard Leppert, "Composition, Composers and Works: Commentary," *Essays on Music: Theodor W. Adorno*, University of California Press, Berkeley, 2002, 555.
61 Adorno, *QUF*, 174.
62 Adorno, *QUF*, 174.
63 Adorno, *SF*, 131.
64 Adorno, *AR*, 179.
65 Adorno, *AR*, 183.
66 Adorno, *SF*, 132.
67 Adorno, *AR*, 187, 188.
68 See our reflections on attunement, both in the opening Prelude, (11–13) as well as in the second chapter, (35, 37, 43).
69 Adorno, *SF*, 1.
70 Adorno, *SF*, 1.
71 Adorno, *SF*, 1 [my italics].
72 Adorno, *SF*, 2.
73 Adorno, *SF*, 2.
74 Adorno, *SF*, 2.
75 Adorno, *SF*, 4.
76 Adorno, *SF*, 4.
77 Adorno, *SF*, 8.
78 Adorno, *SF*, 9.
79 Adorno, *SF*, 9.
80 Adorno, *SF*, 9.
81 Adorno, *BPM*, 32.
82 Adorno, *MM*, 10.

[83] Adorno, *MM*, 11.

[84] Adorno, *BPM*, 31.

[85] Adorno, *BPM*, 31.

[86] Adorno, *BPM*, 32. The implication is that God is the ultimate point of silence rather than being deaf to the world (even though the Sages already decried this their perception of reality in their exegesis of liturgy, shifting from the question "Who is like You among the gods?" to "Who is like You among the deaf?" see *Mekhilta of Rabbi Ishmael*, Exodus 15:11).

[87] Adorno, *BPM*, 39.

[88] Adorno, *MM*, 456/235.

[89] Adorno, *MM*, 457/236.

[90] Adorno, *MM*, 457/236.

[91] Adorno, *MM*, 462–463/238.

[92] Adorno, *MM*, 462–463/238.

[93] Adorno, *MM*, 378–379/197–199.

[94] Adorno, *MM*, 25/15.

[95] Sarah Lyall, "Making Squid the Meat of a Story," July 23, 2010, *New York Times* [my italics].

[96] Adorno, "Difficulties," *EM*, 658 [my italics].

[97] Alain Badiou, "Dance as a Metaphor for Thought," *Handbook of Inaesthetics*, tr. A. Toscano, Stanford University Press, Standford 2005, 57–71.

[98] I am indebted to Hullot-Kentor's critique of Adorno's thinking still resonating: "The process of barbarization itself has consumed the capacity for its own differentiation and jettisoned the idea when it was done with it." Robert Hullot-Kentor, "The Exact Sense in Which the Culture Industry No Longer Exists," *Cultural Critique* 70, Fall 2008, 147, esp. 137–157.

[99] Adorno, "Painting and Music Today," *NM*, 425.

Afterword

[1] Rosenzweig, *The Star of Redemption*, 113, 116.

[2] Franz Rosenzweig, "The New Thinking," *Philosophical and Theological Writings*, trans and ed, with notes and commentary, by Paul W. Franks and Michael L. Morgan, Hackett Publishing Company, Indianapolis, 2000, 131.

[3] Wolfson, *Venturing Beyond*, 241–261. The material here is a reworking of that analysis.

[4] Rainer M. Rilke, *Duino Elegies and the Sonnets to Orpheus*, trans. A. Poulin, Jr., Houghton Mifflin, Boston, 1975, 92–93.

[5] Charles H. Kahn, *The Art and Thought of Heraclitus: An Edition of the Fragments with Translation and Commentary*, Cambridge University Press, Cambridge, 1979, 195.

[6] Rilke, *Duino Elegies*, 94–95.

[7] Ernst Bloch, *The Principle of Hope*, trans. Neville Plaice, Stephen Plaice, and Paul Knight, MIT Press, Cambridge, 1986, 1056.

[8] Bloch, *The Principle of Hope*, 1057.

[9] Bloch, *The Principle of Hope*, 1062.

10 *Genesis Rabbah* 78:1; Babylonian Talmud, Ḥagigah 14a, Ḥullin 91b; Louis Ginzberg, *The Legends of the Jews,* Jewish Publication Society of America, Philadelphia, 1968, 5: 21 n. 62, 24 n. 69. See also *Exodus Rabbah* 15:6, where the angels who perish after having fulfilled their liturgical obligation are said to be resurrected on the next day, a theme that is meant to give hope to Israel (compared to angelic beings) who will be forgiven in spite of their transgressions. The rabbinic legend is cited as well by Benjamin in his 1931 essay on Karl Kraus. See Walter Benjamin, *Reflections: Essays, Aphorisms, Autobiographical Writings,* trans. Edmund Jephcott, Schocken Books, New York, 1986, 273, and discussion in Susan Handelman, *Fragments of Redemption: Jewish Thought and Literary Theory in Benjamin, Scholem, and Levinas,* Indiana University Press, Bloomington, 1991, 17.

11 Some of the rabbinic sources that served as the basis for this tradition are listed in the previous note. Adorno's rendering of the mythical idea, especially the description of the angels being made out of grass and being consumed in sacred fire, reflects the reworking of this aggadic motif in *Zohar* 1:19a; hence his reference to "Jewish mysticism" as the origin of the idea. He learnt of this passage from reading the translation included in Scholem's *Die Geheimnisse der Tora.* The precise words of the zoharic passage relate to the four forms (*diyoqnin*), that is, the angelic images of the chariot, that emerge from the divine realm as translucent lights. These lights produce seed in the world and thus they are denoted by the biblical locution "seed-bearing plants," *esev mazri'a zera* (Genesis 1:11). Evidently, the word *esev* has been rendered literally as "grass," and thus the celestial beings are identified as "grass angels."

12 Adorno, *BTPM,* 176–177.

13 Adorno, *QUF,* 229.

14 Adorno, *QUF,* 2–3. For an alternate rendering, see Adorno, *EM,* 114.

15 Adorno, *EM,* 4.

Bibliography

Primary Sources

Adorno, Theodor W. *Minima Moralia: Reflexionen aus dem beschädigten Leben*, Suhrkamp, Frankfurt, 1951.
— *Quasi Una Fantasia: Essays on Modern Music*, trans. R. Livingstone, Verso, London, 1963.
— *Negative Dialektik*, Suhrkamp, Frankfurt, 1966.
— *Jargon of Authenticity*, trans. Knut Tarnowksi and Frederic Will, Northwestern University Press; Chicago, 1973.
— *Negative Dialectics*, trans. E. B. Ashton, Continuum, New York, 1973.
— *Minima Moralia: Reflections from Damaged Life*, trans. E. F. N. Jephcott, Verso, London, 1974.
— *In Search of Wagner*, trans. R. Livingstone, NLB, Great Britain, 1981.
— "Trying to Understand *Endgame*," *Notes to Literature*, vol. 1, trans. S. W. Nicholsen, Columbia University Press, New York, 1991.
— *Mahler: A Musical Physiognomy*, trans. E. Jephcott, University of Chicago Press, Chicago, 1992.
— *Aesthetic Theory* [1970], trans. R. Hullot-Kentor, University of Minnesota, Minneapolis, 1997.
— *Beethoven: The Philosophy of Music*, ed. R. Tiedemann, trans. E. Jephcott, Stanford University Press, Stanford, 1998.
— *Sound Figures*, trans. R. Livingstone, Stanford University Press, California, 1999.
— "Lyric Poetry and Society," *The Adorno Reader*, ed. Brian O'Connor, Blackwell Publishers, Oxford, 2000.
— "Sociological and Empirical Research" (1957), *The Adorno Reader*, ed. Brian O'Connor, Blackwell Publishers, London, 2000.
— *Negative Dialectics*, trans. Dennis Redmond, 2001, www.efn.org/~dredmond/ndtrans.html.
— *Essays on Music: Theodor W. Adorno*, trans. S. H. Gillespie, comm. R. Leppert, University of California Press, Berkeley, 2002.
— *Night Music: Essays on Music 1928–1962*, trans. W. Hoban, ed. R. Tiedemann, Seagull Books, London, 2009.

Secondary Sources

Adler, Rachel. *Engendering Judaism: An Inclusive Theology and Ethics*, JPS, Philadelphia, 1998.

Ajzenstat, Oona. *Driven Back to the Text: The Premodern Sources of Levinas's Postmodernism*, Duquesne University Press, Pittsburgh, 2001.

Altmann, Alexander. "Judaism and World Philosophy," ed. L. Finkelstein, *The Jews: Their History, Culture and Religion* 2, 1949, 954.

Anidjar, Gil. "The Semitic Hypothesis (Religion's Last Word)," *Semites: Race, Religion, Literature*, Stanford University Press, Stanford, 2008.

Auron, Yair. *We are All German Jews: Jewish Radicals in France during the Sixties and Seventies* [Hebrew], Am Oved Publications, Tel Aviv, 1999.

Bal, Mieke. "*Réfléchir la réflexion*," *Femmes Imaginaires: L'Ancien Testament au risque d'une narratologie critique*, Brèches, Québec, 1985.

Barad, Karen Michelle. *Meeting the Universe Halfway: Quantum Physics and the Entanglement of Matter and Meaning*, Duke University Press, Durham, 2007.

Baudelaire, Charles. "Le Voygage," *La Mort*, GF Flammarion, Paris, 1991, 186.

Benjamin, Walter. *Gesammelte Schriften*, vol. IV, Suhrkamp Verlag, Frankfurt am Main, 1955.

— "Theses on the Philosophy of History," *Illuminations*, trans. H. Zubin, Schocken Books, New York, 1968.

— *Reflections: Essays, Aphorisms, Autobiographical Writings*, trans. Edmund Jephcott, ed. Peter Demetz, Schocken Books, New York, 1986.

— "Epistemo-Critical Prologue," *The Origin of German Tragic Drama*, trans. J. Osborne, Verso, London, 1998.

— "H. The Collector," *The Arcade Project*, trans. H. Eiland and K. McLaughlin, Belknap Press of Harvard University Press, Cambridge, 1999.

Berger, Peter. *In Praise of Doubt: How to Have Convictions without Becoming a Fanatic*, Harper Collins, New York, 2009.

Berkovits, Eliezer. "What is Jewish Philosophy?" *Tradition* 3, 1961.

Bernstein, Leonard. *The Unanswered Question: Six Talks at Harvard*, Harvard University Press, Cambridge.

Bialik, Hayyim Nahman. *Revealment and Concealment: Five Essays*, Ibis Editions, Jerusalem, 2003.

Bloch, Ernst. *The Principle of Hope*, trans. Neville Plaice, Stephen Plaice, and Paul Knight, MIT Press, Cambridge, MA, 1986.

Boericke, W. *Pocket Manual of Homeopathic Materia Medica and Repertory*, B. Jain Publishing, India, 1927.

Braiterman, Zachary. *The Shape of Revelation: Aesthetics and Modern Jewish Thought*, Stanford University Press, Stanford, 2007.

Brook, Peter. *The Open Door: Thoughts on Acting and Theatre*, Theatre Communications Group Inc., New York, 1995.

Bruckstein, Almut Sh. "Textual Body Landscapes and the Artist's Geometry of Talmud: *Aetelier*-Work with the Materiality of Scripture," *New Directions in Jewish Philosophy*, ed. A. W. Hughes and E. R. Wolfson, Indiana University Press, Bloomington, 2010.

Brunkhorst, Hauke. *Adorno and Critical Theory*, University of Wales Press, Cardiff, 1999.

Buber, Martin. *Meetings: Autobiographical Fragments*, Routledge, New York, 2002.

Buck-Morss, Susan. "The Aesthetic Model and Its Limits," *The Origin of Negative Dialectics: Theodore W. Adorno, Walter Benjamin, and the Frankfurt Institute*, The Free Press, New York, 1977.

Camus, Michel. *Transpoétique: La main cachée entre poésie et science*, Trait d'Union, Montréal, 2002.

Castoriadis, Cornelius. *World in Fragments: Writings on Politics, Society, Psychoanalysis and the Imagination*, Stanford University Press, Stanford, 1997.

Celan, Paul. *Der Meridian*, Suhrkamp Verlag, Darmstadt, 1999.

— "Todtnauberg," *Selected Poems and Prose of Paul Celan*, trans. J. Felstiner, W. W. Norton, New York, 2001.

Chalier, Catherine. *La Trace de l'Infini: Emmanuel Levinas et la Source Hebraique*, Editions CERF, Paris, 2002.

Chatterjee, Ranjit. *Wittgenstein and Judaism: A Triumph of Concealment*, Peter Lang, New York, 2005.

Claussen, Detlev. *Theodor W. Adorno: One Last Genius*, trans. R. Livingstone, Harvard University Press, Cambridge, 2008.

Corbin, Henri. "The *Imago Templi* in Confrontation with Secular Norms" (1974), *Temple and Contemplation*, trans. P. Sherrard, KPI, London, 1986.

Cordovero, Moses. *Pardes Rimonim*, Gate 6: chapter 8, *Yerid ha'Sefarim* Publications, Jerusalem, 1999.

Cosgrove, Rabbi Elliot J. ed. "A Quest-Driven Faith," *Jewish Theology in Our Time: A New Generation Explores the Foundations & Future of Jewish Belief*, Jewish Lights, Vermont, 2010.

Dallmayr, Fred. "Adorno and Heidegger," *Life-World, Modernity and Critique: Paths between Heidegger and the Frankfurt School*, Polity Press, Cambridge, 1991.

Darwish, Mahmoud. "Mahmoud Darwish Bids Edward Said Farewell," trans. Mona Anis, www.mahmouddarwish.com, 2010.

Derrida, Jacques. "Violence et métaphysique," *Écriture et différence*, Éditions du Seuil, Paris, 1967.

DiCenso, James J. "Splitting Religion: Heteronomy, Autonomy, and Reflection," *Journal for Cultural and Religious Theory* 1/3, 2000.

Dufrenne, Mikel. *L'Oeil et L'Oreille*, L'Hexagone, Montréal, 1987.

Edmonds, D., and J. Eidinow. *Wittgenstein's Poker: The Story of a Ten-Minute Argument between Two Great Philosophers*, HarperCollins, New York, 2001.

Emad, P., and K. Maly. "Translator's Foreword," *Contributions to Philosophy (From Enowning)*, Indiana University Press, Bloomington, 1999.

Fackenheim, Emile. "The 614th Commandment," *The Jewish Thought of Emile Fackenheim: A Reader*, ed. Michael L. Morgan, Wayne State University Press, Detroit, 1987.

Fagenblat, Michael. *A Covenant of Creatures: Levinas's Philosophy of Judaism* (Cultural Memory in the Present), Stanford University Press, Stanford, 2010.

Feld, Rabbi Edward. "A Divining Rod Has Two Branches," *Conservative Judaism*, Spring 2003.

— "Genre and *Halakhah*," *Conservative Judaism*, Winter 2004.

Fenton, Paul, trans. *Deux traités de mystique juive: 'Obadya b. Abraham b. Moise Maimonide, Le Traité du puits, al-Maqala al-hawdiyya: David b. Josué, dernier des Maimonides: Le Guide du détachement, al-Mursid ila t-tafarrud*, Éditions du Verdier, Lagrasse, 1987.

Finkeilkraut, Alain. *Le Juif Imaginaire*, Les Éditions du Seuil, Paris, 1980.

Fishbane, Michael. *Sacred Attunement: A Jewish Theology*, University of Chicago Press, Chicago, 2008.

Fox, Harry. "Poet*h*ics: How Every Poet is a Jew," *Contemporary Hebrew Mystical Poetry: How It Redeems Jewish Thinking*, ed. Aubrey L. Glazer, Edwin Mellen Press, New York, 2009.

Friedland, Eric L. *"Were Our Mouths Filled with Song": Studies in Liberal Jewish Liturgy*, HUC Press, Cincinnati, 1997.

Friedlander, Judith. *Vilna on the Seine: Jewish Intellectuals in France Since 1968*, Yale University Press, New Haven, 1990.

Gadamer, H. G. "Under the Shadow of Nihilism," *Hans-Georg Gadamer on Education, Poetry, and History: Applied Hermeneutics*, ed. D. Misgeld and G. Nicholson; trans. L. Schmidt and M. Reuss, SUNY Press, New York, 1992.

Gebser, Jean. *The Ever-Present Origin: Part One: Foundations of the Aperspectival World*, trans. Noel Barstad and Algis Mickunas, Ohio University Press, Ohio, 1985.

Gersonides. *The Wars of the Lord*, 2 vols., trans. Seymour Feldman, JPS, Pennsylvania, 1984.

Gibbs, Robert. "Seven Rubrics for Jewish Philosophy," *Correlations in Emanuel Lévinas and Rosenzweig*, Princeton University Press, New Jersey, 1992.

Gillman, Neil. *Doing Jewish Theology: God, Torah & Israel in Modern Judaism*, Jewish Lights, Vermont, 2008.

Ginzberg, Louis. *The Legends of the Jews*, Jewish Publication Society of America, Philadelphia, 1968.

Glazer, Aubrey L. "*Shir Yedidut*: A Pleasant Song of Companionship," *God's Voice from the Void: Old and New Studies in Bratslav Hasidism*, ed. Shaul Magid, SUNY Press, New York, 2002.

— "Rebirthing Redemption: Hermeneutics of *gilgul* from *Beit Lehem Yehudah* into Haviva Pedaya's Poetry," *Kabbalah: A Journal for the Study of Jewish Mystical Texts* 11 (2004), ed. D. Abrams, A. Elqayam, Cherub Press, Los Angeles, 49–83.

— "*Tikkun* in Fackenheim's *Leben-Denken* as a Trace of Lurianic Kabbalah," *Emil L. Fackenheim: Philosopher, Theologian, Jew*. Supplements to the *Journal of Jewish Thought and Philosophy*, vol. 5, ed. S. Portnoff, J. A. Diamond, and M. D. Yaffe, Brill, Leiden, 2008.

— *Contemporary Hebrew Mystical Poetry: How It Redeems Jewish Thinking*, Edwin Mellen Press, New York, 2009.

— "*Durée, Devekuth*, & Re-Embracing the Godlover: *In*volution of *Unio Mystica* via Collocative Homosexu*EL*ity," *Vixens Disturbing Vineyards: The Embarrassment and Embracement of Scriptures—A Festschrift Honoring Harry Fox*, ed. T. Yoreh, A. Glazer, J. Lewis, and M. Segal, Academic Studies Press, Boston, 2010.

— *Living the Death of God: Delimiting the Limitless in Edmond Jabès*, Lambert Academic Publisher, Germany, 2010.

Goldstein, Rebecca. *Betraying Spinoza*, Next Books, New York, 2005.

— *Incompleteness: The Proof and Paradox of Kurt Gödel*, Atlas Books, New York, 2005.

Gordis, Daniel. *Saving Israel: How the Jewish People Can Win a War That May Never End*, John Wiley and Sons, New Jersey, 2009.

Gordon, Rabbi Jeremy. "More *Theos*, Less *Ology*," *Jewish Theology in Our Time: A New Generation Explores the Foundations & Future of Jewish Belief*, ed. Rabbi Elliot J. Cosgrove, Jewish Lights, Vermont, 2010.

Govrin, Michal. "The Jewish Ritual as a Genre of Sacred Theatre," *Conservative Judaism* 36/3, Spring 1983.

— "*Body of Prayer,* with Jacques Derrida and David Shapiro," *Cooper Union School of Architecture,* New York, 2001.

Green, Arthur. *Eheyeh: A Kabbalah for Tomorrow,* Jewish Lights, Vermont, 2003.

— *Radical Judaism: Rethinking God and Tradition,* The Franz Rosenzweig Lecture Series, Yale University Press, New Haven, 2010.

Guttman, Julius. *Philosophies of Judaism,* Rinehart and Winston, New York, 1964.

Habermas, Jürgen. "Der deutsche Idealismus der jüdischen Philosophen," *Philosophisch-politische Profile,* Suhrkamp Verlag, Frankfurt, 1971.

Hadot, Pierre. *Wittgenstein et les limites du langage,* Éditions J. Vrin, Paris, 2005.

Halbertal, Moshe. "The Limits of Prayer: Two Talmudic Discussions," *Jewish Review of Books* 2, Summer 2010.

Handelman, Susan. *Fragments of Redemption: Jewish Thought and Literary Theory in Benjamin, Scholem, and Levinas,* Indiana University Press, Bloomington, 1991.

Harker, Dave. "In Perspective: Theodor Adorno," Humboldt Universität, Berlin, www2.hu-berlin.de/fpm/texte/harker3.htm.

Hedman, Bruce A. "Cantor's Concept of Infinity: Implications of Infinity for Contingence," *Perspectives on Science and Christian Faith* 46, March 1993, 8–16, www.asa3.org/ASA/PSCF/1993/PSCF3–93Hedman.html.

Heidegger, Martin. *Aus der Erfahrung des Denkens,* Pfullingen, Neske, 1947.

— *What is Called Thinking?,* trans. J. Glenn Gray, Perennial Library, New York, 1968.

— *Poetry, Language, Thought,* trans. A. Hofstadter, Perennial Library, New York, 1971.

— *Was Heisst Denken?,* Max Niemeyer Verlag Tübingen, Germany, 1971.

— "*Einleitung in die Phänomenologie des Religiösen* (lectures 1920–21)," *Gesamtausgabe,* vol. 60: *Phänomenologie des Religiösen Lebens,* ed. Jung, trans. Graeme Nicholson, Regehly and Strube, Frankfurt A. M Klostermann, Verlag, 1995.

— *Being and Time:A Translation of* Sein und Zeit, trans. J. Stambaugh, SUNY Press, New York, 1996.

— "Phenomenology and Theology (1927)," *Pathmarks,* ed. W. McNeill, Cambridge University Press, United Kingdom, 1998.

— *Contributions to Philosophy (From Enowning),* trans. P. Emad and K. Maly, Indiana University Press, Indianapolis, 1999.

— *Elucidations of Hölderlin's Poetry,* trans. K. Hoeller, Humanity Books, New York, 2000.

Held, Shai. "Reciprocity and Responsiveness: Self-Transcendence and The Dynamics of Covenant in the Theology and Spirituality of Abraham Joshua Heschel" (Ph.D. diss., Harvard University, 2010).

Heschel, Abraham Joshua. *Kotsk: In Gerangl far Emesdikeyt* [Yiddish], 2 vols. (694 pp.) Tel Aviv, ha-Menorah, 1973.

— *A Passion for Truth,* Jewish Lights, Vermont, 1995.

Hever, Hannan. *Poets and Zealots: The Rise of Political Hebrew Poetry in Eretz-Yisrael* [Hebrew], Bialik Institute, Jerusalem, 1994.

— *Reading Poetry: Review, Essays and Articles about Hebrew Poetry* [Hebrew], Keshev Publication, Jerusalem, 2005.

— *From the Beginning: Three Essays on Nativist Hebrew Poetry* [Hebrew], Keshev Publication, Jerusalem, 2008.

Hewitt, Marsha Aileen. *Critical Theory of Religion: A Feminist Analysis,.* Fortress Press, Minneapolis, 1995.

Honneth, Axel. *Reification: A New Look at an Old Idea*, Oxford University Press, New York, 2008.

— *Pathologies of Reason: On the Legacy of Critical Theory*, trans. James Ingram, Columbia University Press, New York, 2009.

Hughes, Aaron W., and Elliot R. Wolfson. "Charting an Alternative Course for the Study of Jewish Philosophy," *New Directions in Jewish Philosophy*, Indiana University Press, Bloomington, 2010.

Hullot-Kentor, Robert. "The Exact Sense in Which the Culture Industry No Longer Exists," *Cultural Critique* 70, Fall 2008.

Idel, Moshe. "Music and Prophetic Kabbalah," *Yuval* 4, 1982.

— "Music in sixteenth-century Kabbalah in Northern Africa," *Yuval* 7, 2002.

Jameson, Fredric. "Baleful Enchantments of the Concept," *Late Marxism: Adorno, or, the Persistence of the Dialectic*, Verso, London, 1990.

Jay, Martin. *The Dialectical Imagination: A History of the Frankfurt School and the Institute of Social Research, 1923–1950*, University of California Press, Berkeley, 1996.

Kahn, Charles H. *The Art and Thought of Heraclitus: An Edition of the Fragments with Translation and Commentary*, Cambridge University Press, Cambridge, 1979.

Kant, Immanuel. *Critique of Pure Reason*, trans. Norman Kemp Smith, St. Martin's Press, New York, 1929.

Kaploun, Yonadav. *You are Still Writing* [Hebrew], Keter, Jerusalem, 2004.

Kellner, Menahem. *Must a Jew Believe Anything*, Littman Library of Jewish Civilization, London, 2006.

Kraus, Hans-Joachim. "Psalm 29: The Powerful Appearance of Yahweh in a Thunderstorm," *Psalms 1–59*, Fortress Press, New York, 1993.

Langerman, Y. Tzvi. "A Judeo-Arabic Paraphrase of Ibn Gabirol's *Ketter Malkhut*," *Zutot: Perspective on Jewish Culture*, vol. 3, Springer, Netherlands, 2005.

Laor, Yitzhak. "'On relationality," Matters for Which Silence is (Not) Becoming: Essays [Hebrew], Babel Publications, Tel Aviv, 2002.

—, *The Myth of Liberal Zionism*, Verso, New York, 2009.

Leppert, Richard. "Composition, Composers and Works: Commentary," *Essays on Music: Theodor W. Adorno*, University of California Press, Berkeley, 2002.

Lescourret, Marie-Anne. *Emmanuel Lévinas*, Flammarion, Paris, 1994.

—, *Introduction à l'esthèthique*, Champs Université/Flammarion, Paris, 2002.

Lévinas, Emmanuel. "Les Dommages Causés par le Feu," *Lectures Talmudiques*, Éditions de Minuit, Paris, 1977.

— "Envers L'Autre," *Lectures Talmudiques*, Éditions de Minuit, Paris, 1977.

— "Towards the Other," *Talmudic Readings*, trans. A. Aronowicz, Indiana University Press, Indianapolis, 1994.

— "*Vérité du dévoilement et vérité du témoignage*" (1972), "Truth of Disclosure and Truth of Testimony," *Emmanuel Lévinas: Basic Philosophical Writings*, ed. A. T. Peperzak, S. Critchley, and R. Bernasconi, Indiana University Press, Bloomington, 1996.

Magid, Shaul. "Piety before Ecstasy," *Meditation from the Heart of Judaism: Today's Teachers Share Their Practices, Techniques and Faith*, Jewish Lights, Vermont, 1999.

— "Jewish Renewal, American Spirituality, and Post-Monotheistic Theology," *Tikkun* May/June 2006.

— "Is 'Radical Theology' Radical?" *Tikkun*, March/April 2010.

— "The 'Jewish' Bible and the Construction of the (Anti) Rabbinic Hero: Abraham Isaac Ha-Kohen Kook, Rabbi Akiva, and the Song of Songs," *JQR* (forthcoming).

— *Jews and Judaism in Post-Ethnic America: New Particularism, Ethnic Identity, and the Struggle to Become an American Religion*, Indiana University Press, Indiana (forthcoming).

Matt, Daniel C. "The Old Man and the Ravishing Maiden," *The Essential Kabbalah: The Heart of Jewish Mysticism*, HarperCollins, New York, 1995.

Menahem Mendel of Kotsk. *Amud ha'Emeth*, ed. M. B. Altar, *Pe'er* Publications, Jerusalem, 2000.

Mörchen, Hermann. *Adorno und Heidegger: Untersuchung einer philosophischen Kommunikationsverweigerun*, Klett-Cotta, Stuttgart, 1981.

Nevins, Rabbi Daniel. "Walking the Walk," *Jewish Theology in Our Time: A New Generation Explores the Foundations & Future of Jewish Belief*, ed. Rabbi Elliot J. Cosgrove, Jewish Lights, Vermont, 2010.

Nietzsche, Friedrich. "*Der tolle Mensche* [*The Madman*]," Book III: no. 125 of *Die Fröhliche Wissenschaft* [*The Gay Science*] in *The Portable Nietzsche*, ed. Walter Kaufmann, Viking Press, New York, 1954.

Novak, David. *The Election of Israel: The Idea of the Chosen People*, Cambridge University Press, Cambridge, 2007.

— *Natural Law in Judaism*, Cambridge University Press, Cambridge, 2008.

Paddison, Max. *Adorno's Aesthetics of Music*, Cambridge University Press, Cambridge, 1998.

Paquda, Bahya ibn. "Appendix: *Tokheha* (Admonition)," *The Book of Direction to the Duties of the Heart*, trans. and ed. Menahem Mansoor, Littman Library of Jewish Civilization, London, 1973.

— *Hovot haLevavot*, ed. R. Kapach, Feldheim Publishers, New York, 1994.

Pinchevski, Amit, and Efraim Torgovnik. "Signifiying Passages: The Signs of Change in Israeli Street Names," *Media, Culture & Society*, vol. 24, Sage Publications, London.

Prell, Riv-Ellen. *Prayer & Community: The Havurah in American Judaism*, Wayne State University Press, Michigan, 1989.

Randall, Lisa. *Warped Passages: Unraveling the Mysteries of the Universe's Hidden Dimensions*, Harper Perennial, New York, 2005.

Ravitsky, Avi. *Messianism, Zionism, and Jewish Religious Radicalism (Chicago Studies in the History of Judaism)*, trans. J. Chipman, University of Chicago Press, Chicago, 1996.

Rey, Alain. *Le Robert Dictionnaire Historique de la Langue Française*, Tome 1, Paris, 1992.

Ricoeur, Paul. *The Symbolism of Evil*, Beacon Press, Boston, 1967.

Rilke, Rainer M. *Duino Elegies and the Sonnets to Orpheus*, trans. A. Poulin, Jr., Houghton Mifflin, Boston, 1975.

Rose, Rabbi Or N. "Spiritual Mappings: A Jewish Understanding of Religious Diversity," *Jewish Theology in Our Time: A New Generation Explores the Foundations & Future of Jewish Belief*, ed. Rabbi Elliot J. Cosgrove, Jewish Lights, Vermont, 2010.

Rosen, Michael. *The Quest for Authenticity: The Thought of Reb Simhah Bunim*, Urim Publications, Jerusalem, 2008.

Rosenzweig, Franz. *Der Stern der Erlösung* (1921), Bibliothek Suhrkamp, Frankfurt, 1988.

— *Franz Rosenzweig's "The New Thinking,"* ed. and trans. A. Udoff and B. E. Galli, Syracuse University Press, Syracuse, 1999.

— "The New Thinking," *Philosophical and Theological Writings*, trans. and ed. Paul W. Franks and Michael L. Morgan, Hackett Publishing Company, Indianapolis, 2000.

— *The Star of Redemption*, trans. Barbara E. Galli, University of Wisconsin Press, Wisconsin, 2005.

Sarna, Jonathan. "'With-It' Judaism: The *Havurah* Movement and *The Jewish Catalog* Blended Judaism with the 1960s Counterculture," *American Judaism: A History*, Yale University Press, New Haven, 2004.

Schachter-Shalomi, Rabbi Zalman, and Rabbi Daniel Siegel. *Integral Halachah: Transcending and Including*, Trafford Publishing, New York, 2007.

Scheindlin, Raymond P. "The Inner Art of Prayer," *The Unfolding Tradition: Jewish Law after Sinai*, ed. Elliot N. Dorff, Aviv Press, New York, 2005.

Scherchen, Hermann. *Vom Wesen Der Musik*, Mondial, Zurich, 1946.

Scholem, Gershom. "The Name of God and the Linguistic Theory of the Kabbalah," trans. S. Pleasance, *Diogenes* 80, 1971.

— "Towards an Understanding of the Messianic Idea," *The Messianic Idea in Judaism*, trans. M. E. Meyer, Schocken Books, New York, 1971.

— "*Shi'ur Komah:* The Mystical Shape of the Godhead," *On the Mystical Shape of the Godhead*, trans. J. Neugroschel and J. Chipman, Schocken Books, New York, 1991.

— "Confession on the Subject of Our Language" [*Bekenntnis uber usere Sprache*]: A Letter to Franz Rosenzweig, December 26, 1926, trans. Gil Anidjar, *Acts of Religion*, Routledge, New York, 2002.

Schwarzschild, Steven. *The Pursuit of an Ideal: Jewish Writings of Steven Schwarzschild*, SUNY Press, New York, 1990.

Shabtai, Aharon. "*Rosh HaShanah*," *J'accuse*, trans. Peter Cole, New Directions, New York, 2003.

Sharabi, Shalom R. *Siddur ha'RaShaSh, Yeshivat ha'Hayyim v'ha-Shalom*, n.p., Jerusalem, 1990.

Shenhav, Yehouda. "Why Not 'The Occupation'" [Hebrew], *Theory and Criticism* 31, Winter 2007.

Shulman, David. *Dark Hope: Working for Peace in Israel and Palestine*, University of Chicago Press, Chicago, 2007.

Sirat, Colette. *A History of Jewish Philosophy in the Middle Ages*, Cambridge University Press, Cambridge, 1990.

Smith, Norman Kemp. *A Commentary to Kant's "Critique of Pure Reason,"* second edition, Humanities Press International, Inc., New Jersey, 1992.

Smith, R., and K. Woodward. s.v. "meridian" *Derby & District Astronomical Society*, England, 2002, www.derbyastronomy.org/.

Stravinsky, Igor. *Poetics of Music*, Harvard University Press, Cambridge, 1947.

Taylor, Charles. *The Ethics of Authenticity*, Harvard University Press, Cambridge, 1991.

Vital, Hayyim. *Sha'ar ha-Haqdamot, Qol Qitvai ha-Ari*, n.p., Jerusalem, 1988.

— *Sha'ar ha-Kavvanot, Qol Qitvai ha-Ari*, n.p., Jerusalem, 1988.

— *Sha'ar Ma'amarai Rash"Bi, Qol Qitvai ha-Ari*, n.p., Jerusalem, 1988.

Vries, Hent de. *Minimal Theologies: Critiques of Secular Reason in Adorno and Levinas*, trans. G. Hale, Johns Hopkins University Press, Baltimore, 2005.

Wittgenstein, Ludwig. *Philosophical Investigations* (1945), trans. G. E. M. Anscombe, Basil Blackwell, Oxford, 1953.

— *Tractatus Logico-Philosophicus* (1922), ed. G. E. M. Anscombe and G. H. von Wright, Basil Blackwell, Oxford, 1967.

— *Zettel*, ed. G. E. M. Anscombe and G. H. von Wright, Basil Blackwell, Oxford, 1967.

Wolf, Rabbi Daniel. "*Machshevet Yisrael*—Survival or Endurance?" *ATID*, 2008.

Wolfson, Elliot R. *Through a Speculum That Shines*, Princeton University Press, New Jersey, 1994.

— "Erasing the Erasure/Gender and the Writing of God's Body in Kabbalistic Symbolism," *Circle in the Square: Studies in the Use of Gender in Kabbalistic Symbolism*, SUNY Press, New York, 1995.

— *Language, Eros, Being: Kabbalistic Hermeneutics and Poetic Imagination*, Fordham University Press, New York, 2004.

— *Alef, Mem, Tau: Kabbalistic Musings on Time, Truth, and Death*, University of California Press, Berkeley, 2006.

— *Venturing Beyond: Law and Morality in Kabbalistic Mysticism*, Oxford University Press, New York, 2006.

— "Light Does Not Talk but Shines: Apophasis and Vision in Rosenzweig's Theopoetic Temporality," *New Directions in Jewish Philosophy*, ed. A. W. Hughes and E. R. Wolfson, Indiana University Press, Bloomington, 2010.

Wolpe, David. *Why Faith Matters*, HarperOne, New York, 2009.

Yovel, Yirmiyahu. *The Other Within: Split Identity and Emerging Modernity*, Princeton University Press, New Jersey, 2009.

Index